The Space in Between

A STORY ABOUT NINA

Also by Diane Eklund-Āboliņš

On the Circle
Glänsande vitt på blått

The Space in Between

A STORY ABOUT NINA

Diane Eklund-Āboliņš

Published by AoE Publishing 2012

Copyright © Diane Eklund-Āboliņš
All rights reserved

The moral right of the author has been asserted

This work is copyright. Apart from any use as permitted under *Copyright Act 1968*, no part may be reproduced, copied, scanned, stored in a retrieval system, recorded, or transmitted, in any form or by any means, without prior written permission of the publisher.

Excerpt from *The Three Sisters* by Anton Chekhov, translated by G.R.Ledger © 1998, reprinted by permission of G.R.Ledger
Excerpt from F.Dostoevsky's letter to his brother 22nd December 1849, in R.Pevear's introduction to *The Brothers Karamozov* by Fyodor Dostoyevsky, translated by R.Pevear & L.Volokhonsky, Everyman's Library, 1992, © 1990 R.Pevear & L.Volokhonsky. Reproduced by kind permission of the translators

This work is a mixture of fact and fiction, and, although all care has been taken, it cannot pertain to have presented all factual events or characters – personal and/or historical – with complete accuracy; also, many of these events and characters have been filtered through the perceptions of characters in the book and, as a result, do not necessarily reflect the opinions of the author. The author is, therefore, not to be held responsible or liable for any content deemed inaccurate, incomplete or contrary to general, accepted and/or private opinion. Most of the main characters have retained their correct names; however, a few names have been changed, and some characters and names are completely fictitious

First published in Australia in 2012 by
AoE Publishing
Sydney, Australia

ISBN:978-0-9873473-0-5

Typeset in Times New Roman
Maps by AA
Printed and bound by LSI

The time will come when we will be gone forever, we will be forgotten, our faces, our voices, and even how many of us there were. But our suffering will be transformed into happiness for those who live after us, peace and contentment will cover the earth, and they will remember and bless with kind words all those who live now.

Anton Chekhov (1860–1904), *The Three Sisters*, Finale, Act IV

One

I

He parks the car close to the kerb and pockets his keys, the late Swedish summer of 1986 pressing upon the many ordered blocks of flats with a soft laziness. Sounds of children's voices and the coarse cries of seagulls break through the inertia, but the sounds do not seem to reach him. Enclosed within his own thoughts, he walks quickly up the short pathway from the street to the door of the cement-rendered building. He passes some dark-green rhododendron bushes, the remaining few blooms faded and already whispering about autumn. Then he climbs the three flights of cold grey stone stairs, his steps ringing sharply behind him. The drabness around him contrasts with the light he has left outside, making him only more aware of the anxiety which, octopus-like, is coiling against the sides of his stomach.

He does not need to ring the doorbell as he has his own key, and he knows that she does not like him to ring.

'They would always come at night,' she had told him when he was small and also when he was older. 'We would sit, holding our breath, listening to the heavy footsteps on the stairs and then the sharp, impatient knocking on doors and the shouting. We would remain in the darkness and pray that they would not come to our door, that they would not see it, that they would suddenly remember other things that they had to do and that they would quickly leave in their black cars and trucks.'

But this time he rings anyway, and the sudden sound echoes off into the distance behind the brown timber door with the small round peep-hole at eye level. He rings a second time and waits, *the sound once more breaking into the silence. Then, he takes his key from his pocket, puts it into the lock and turns it. He almost knows what he is about to find, and he knows that there is no path backwards from the present to the past. In that instant of turning the key, the future becomes both the present and the past before he even has time to open the door. As he crosses the threshold, he crosses from his own past to his future.*

A silence has filled the rooms of the small flat and is apparent in drawn curtains and in newspapers and letters scattered near the door. It has mingled with the half-darkness and it wraps itself tightly around him, forcing him from the hall to her room. It sweeps him, reluctantly, through that in-between space to the end.

II

The blue-black entry halfway down the page of the parish register recalled the barely audible scratch of a pen on the almost-white paper: Nikolina Edvīna Kindahle, 26th March 1906, female. Parents: Zacharias Kindahls, foreman, forty-three and Rozalija Kindahle, housewife, thirty-two, both from Rīga. Siblings: Hermanis, male, twelve. Hugo Maksimiljāns, male, ten. Jānis Edvards, male, eight. The parish clerk would have then put down his pen and blotted the page. And closed the book.

The entry was concise. It did not mention that Hermanis was usually called Ermonis, that Hugo was known as Maksis or that Jānis was often called Jāncis. Nor was there any mention of Nika or Nina, Nikolina's other names.

Had there been sufficient space, the clerk could have added that Zacharias was short and compact, with large square hands and a similarly shaped head. His brown hair, already turning grey, was nearly always hidden beneath a black bowler hat – the bowler, along with white starched collars, appearing several years ago when he was made foreman. His promotion had been the pinnacle; now he was on the plateau. Eventually, he would reach the edge, and finally he hoped to meet his God. He had always been a religious man. Life for him was about fearing his God, respecting the German baron and loving Tsar Nicholas II. He could not understand those who wanted a free, autonomous Latvia, and he did not understand what difference the word *free* would make to anyone. He had only ever known the German estate: the fields, the workshops, the sawmill, the dairy and the big house. He had begun life on an estate in Estonia before eventually moving to the estate where he now worked. He had no complaints. His wife ran the household, and the baron and the Tsar ran the country.

Rozalija had not wanted to marry Zacharias. They were two very different planets orbiting the sun with a ten-year gap between them. But, in 1892, Rozalija's mother, Ieva, with four daughters to marry off, had already made up her mind.

"You have to marry him, Roza!"

"And if I don't?" Rozalija had asked, curling the end of her dark-brown hair around her finger, passing it between moistened lips. "If I refuse to marry him?" She was thinking of Mihails, who worked at the timber mill. Mihails with the very dark eyes and the little moustache.

Barely eighteen, Rozalija was of average height with thick brown hair, which she usually wore gathered up loosely on the top of her head. Her eyes were green-grey and her skin olive. When her mother told her that she was going to marry Zacharias, she was in the front room, standing near a window, while her mother was sitting in front of her on the dull-red sofa, sewing. Behind her mother there was a large gold-framed mirror, and the mirror reflected both Rozalija and the window.

"And, if I don't marry him?" she repeated, looking past her mother at the mirror and at the window in the mirror. Thinking hard-to-define thoughts about openings and exits. Still thinking of Mihails.

Ieva, distantly connected on her father's side to Polish nobility, had looked at her daughter for a moment, not wanting to recognize the hesitant defiance behind the words.

"Why must you make things so difficult for me, Roza? Can't you imagine how trying it is to find husbands for all of you? First Matilda and now you and Paulina." Ieva sighed and looked at the sewing lying in her lap. "Anyway, I have already spoken with his family. It is all but agreed." She looked up at Rozalija. "You cannot refuse. It is completely impossible. Imagine the talk!" She put her sewing to one side and stood up, almost blocking out the window in the mirror. "Give *some* thought to your mother, child! If you don't marry him, it will be my death. I can assure you of that."

Rozalija wondered if things might have been different had her father, Fridrichs Kupč, involved himself, at least a little, in his wife's matchmaking, but she knew that he had not the slightest interest in such things. She sighed audibly while she thought of her father's large black moustache and twinkling eyes and how he preferred to let Ieva run everything at home while he ran the family business.

Standing in the sitting room, trying unsuccessfully to locate the entire window behind the ample form of her mother, Rozalija knew that there were no exits. There was nothing more to say. She may have wanted something else, but she did not want to be the cause of her mother's premature death. So she did as she was told. Perhaps, she argued with herself, it really did not make that much difference whom she married.

As time went on, she discovered that she was wrong and that there was a difference. She thought about Mihails and about how things might have been, and she was never completely happy in her marriage. But that, she decided, was life. She took care of Zacharias and was kind to him, but she never really learnt to love him.

At eighteen, when she rescued her mother from certain death, she was considered beautiful; fourteen years later, her beauty, like the meadow flowers she had picked in her youth and then pressed between the pages of heavy books, had already begun to fade. She knew that Zacharias loved her in his own silent, uncommunicative manner, but, when she thought of Mihails, she knew that there should have been something else. She became a little aloof and somewhat severe. Behind the wall that she placed between herself and the world, she was disciplined and efficient. By 1906, she had almost forgotten what the meadow was like.

Zacharias's mother, Anu Kindahle, was Estonian, and she had grown up on a German estate in Veru, in the southern part of Estonia, where all her grandparents had worked as serfs.

"They were beaten!" Grandmother Kindahle had once told Nina, shaking her head, still somewhat in disbelief, even after all the years that had passed.

Sitting by the small window in the kitchen, holding a book in her hand, Nina had tried very hard to imagine these people, all of them long since dead. She was wondering why anyone would have wanted to beat them.

Anu, chopping cabbage into long thin strips, said, "And it wasn't just work that the baron expected." She was thinking of their daughters.

Nina thought of the long-dead beaten serfs and the barons expecting more than work. She wondered what else might have been expected, but her grandmother was talking about serfs who tried to escape.

"They were nearly always caught and brought back to the estate, often with their ears cut off. And, sometimes, their noses as well!" She dropped the almost-green cabbage into the heavy black pot, in which pieces of pork were already swimming in a shallow pool of salted water, and then returned the pot noisily to the stove.

Nina found the image of chopped ears and noses very disconcerting. For some time afterwards, she could not look at people without imagining them minus ears and noses. She closed her book and put it on the window-sill.

Anu, unaware of the pictures filling her granddaughter's head, continued, "Though some did manage to reach the towns, where they were able to hide."

In Nina's mind the images were quickly changing to undernourished serfs in cellars and large wardrobes. Somewhere on the edge, she could still glimpse a number of shadowy forms without ears and noses.

"Until people just forgot about them." Anu paused, thinking about those few who escaped while still retaining all their facial features. She was also thinking about others who chose a more definite kind of escape.

"All my grandparents were freed before they died." Anu carefully pushed some wood into the stove, slamming the metal door with a sharp bang. "But, by then, the estates owned all the land." She shrugged, looking at her granddaughter, thinking of words like *land* and *independence* and *liberty*.

"And without land, there's no freedom." She put the lid on the pot simmering on the stove. "When I was no older than you, I remember hearing about land at the Black Sea."

Nina was wondering where the Black Sea was and why it was black.

"All we had to do was to leave the Lutheran god and join the Russian church." Anu sat down on her chair in the corner, next to Nina.

"But you know, it had nothing to do with land or freedom; it was all about converts." She leant back in the chair while she thought of the rivalry between the Orthodox Russians and the Lutherans. She was also thinking of the years of drought when crops had consistently failed and people had starved. "People would have done anything, gone anywhere, for land. It didn't much matter that it was the Black Sea. I don't think that they..."

Rozalija had come into the room, holding the wicker egg basket. She handed it to Nina, who stood up, still looking at her grandmother.

Standing near the table, her fingers tracing the coarse, open weave of the basket, Nina asked, "And what happened afterwards? After everyone moved to the Black Sea?

Anu shook her head. "But, child, there wasn't any land at the Black Sea. There wasn't any land anywhere."

Rozalija was also listening although she had heard Anu tell the story many times before.

"The barons saw that it could all end in disaster and not just for the Russians. They didn't want a revolution; they needed their workers. So they let them buy the houses and the land." Anu ran her hand over her apron. "And most of the converts returned to the German church."

As Nina left the kitchen, the basket firmly in her hand, she thought of the crowds of people leaving the Russian church and of the German vicar welcoming them all back. Opening the door to the barn, she could see herself in the small Lutheran church, sitting in a polished brown pew. She was holding her grandmother's hand tightly while she watched the vicar in his black clothes and strange white collar, his loud, deep voice echoing through the church, filling all the spaces while pushing outwards towards the stone walls of the building. She wondered if it was so very different in the Russian church.

Anu returned to the stove. She was also thinking about the converts returning to the Lutheran fold, remembering how, when she was still a child, everyone on the estate attended the German church. It was there she learnt about sin and suffering and the rewards she could expect in the next life. Then, when she was sixteen, a tall, quietly spoken Swede appeared on the estate looking for work, and she found herself daring to hope that the rewards might actually be redeemable already in this life.

Jan Kindal was given work in the stables, and Anu would often take a detour on her way between the big house and the dairy. Walking slowly past the wide, black-painted doors of the stables, she would attempt to catch the eye of the Swede while she smiled shyly and lingered just a few extra moments before hurrying away. Anu was not at all unattractive, and Jan was eventually forced to admit that he enjoyed her attentions. Before the end of the year, they were promised to each other, and, by the time Zacharias was born in the spring of 1862, Anu was quite certain that rewards were not necessarily limited to the afterlife.

They remained in Veru for some years before moving south to another estate, on the outskirts of Rīga. Here they bought the small timber house on Kalnciema iela with its four windows at the front: two downstairs and two upstairs. Soon they had a cow and some chickens in the barn. In the fields, they sowed rye and potatoes. Close to the house, Anu planted flowers and herbs. Carts and carriages and, later, trams rattled along the wide dirt road that ran past their house. The years passed by; Zacharias grew up and married, and life turned a corner into a new century. Then Jan became ill.

Anu moved the heavy pot on to the table, remembering her husband's incessant coughing and the weeks of fever and how he had gradually became weaker until, finally, she had to accept that nothing she could do was likely to make him better. After the funeral, she packed together her many herbs and potions, sadly acknowledging the futility of fighting against that which had already been predestined. But, while she may have understood the pointlessness of pitting herself against something that was much stronger than herself, she was quite sure that Jan had not completely left her. She knew that when she talked to him – as she did quite often – he was still able to hear her.

Although she would have preferred that he had remained with her in the cottage on Kalnciema iela, she knew something about flow and hidden currents and the debris that sometimes floated on the surface. She knew that life was a force against which no one was able to compete; it was just a matter of hanging on while trying to avoid all the refuse and the currents. She placed some dishes on the table, thinking that, in spite of all the things she would never be able to change, there had been at least one thing in her life for which she would always be extremely thankful.

III

It was the eve of midsummer, the twenty-third of June 1913. It was also the year before the world span completely out of control, like some small cork bobbing in a stream about to rush down a precipice, and before the people clinging to that cork-world lost their grip and fell in all directions, without any time to reflect on what was happening.

But, in June 1913, as people prepared to celebrate the shortest night of the year, I do not believe that they knew anything about the precipice. The sun-kissed stream was still meandering across flat ground, and the world had no reason to worry. We had no reason to worry; there were so many things we could celebrate: life, summer, *Jāņi* night.

I was already seven, and I was standing at the back of the house, listening to Ermonis playing his violin. The music was somehow wrapping itself around me like hundreds of long coloured ribbons. When I closed my eyes, I felt that the ribbons were lifting me above the green grass between the house and the barn. I was almost sure that if I reached out, I would be able to touch the chestnut tree in front of the barn.

I do not think that my brother could see the ribbons. He stood there, the violin pushed up against his chin, smiling at me. He would have been about nineteen, slight and not particularly tall, with the same dark-brown hair and grey-green eyes as Mother. Everything in my life had always revolved around him; I loved my other two brothers, but Ermonis was very special. There was no one else quite like Ermonis.

I smiled back. As a child, I had no need to identify the many different emotions rushing through me; they were simply part of the flood that joined me to my brother. It was only much later that all the separate feelings of security and admiration and love unravelled from that one initial, overpowering emotion, creating images and memories. While Mother's love for me did not allow for any demonstration of affection, my eldest brother's love was an intrinsic part of everything he did and everything he was.

I became aware that the music had stopped, and I saw that Ermonis was helping Maksis and Jānis with the bonfire. I also saw that Grandmother Kindahle, with her tired, grey-white plaits wound around her head and her steel-framed glasses on her long, thin nose, was sitting on a chair near the back door.

I sat down on the soft grass near my grandmother's feet as she settled herself back in her chair, one of her hands resting on my shoulder. I smiled up at her, aware of the bonfire writhing and dancing: red and orange with small purple and white star-like sparks shooting up into the sky. Everything within its radius had been pulled into a wonderful cocoon of warmth and light.

Behind the fire, I could see Jānis wearing the crown of oak leaves Mother had plaited earlier in the day. It was already falling over one eye, and he was laughing, as he held on to it with one hand, while he threw more wood on to the fire with the other. He was tall, yet slightly built, with blue eyes and fair hair that he wore combed back from his forehead. Jānis was the only one in the family with blue eyes; everyone else had grey eyes like mine. Father said that they were Swedish eyes, the same as his father's.

Maksis was helping Mother place food on the wooden table, now standing on the grass, all the while joking with Ermonis, who was once again holding the violin in his hand.

Jāņu nakts. We were all so happy then. Even Father took part, his bowler hat on the back of his head, the fire painting his face with shadows. I can still see him standing there, clapping out the rhythm while Ermonis played. Later, Jānis and I ran through the fields. He was holding my hand, and I remember that we were laughing, the soft night dew caressing our bare feet and the hem of my skirt while we picked daisies and small pink flowers and cornflowers and green stems covered with a dust of tiny white blossoms. Then I was running ahead, my hands filled with so much wonderful colour, dropping the occasional flower in my haste, before turning back to look at my brother, the oak-crown askew on his head, a bunch of ill-assorted flowers in his hand, and I remember feeling completely happy.

But Nina's few fragile wild-flowers could not help stop forces that had already been set in motion, like waters pressing against a broken dam wall or an avalanche of snow no longer resisting gravity. Treaties and the alliances, drawn up in cold, austere rooms by men unacquainted with wild-flowers, were supposed to have held the water and stopped the avalanche. August 1914 demanded that the alliances should be honoured while the dam wall broke and the avalanche buried everything that was in its path, including the wild-flowers. It was a game that everyone said would not last longer than a month or two, long enough for the French to win back territory from the Germans, for Germany to show off her military strength and for the English conservatives to rein in the trade unions. After the game, everyone expected to be able to pack up and go home, satisfied with what they had managed to achieve. But, as the waters surged through the dam wall and thundered along new courses, it was realized, all too late, that the force which had been unleashed could not be stopped.

When the war broke out in August 1914, the Imperial Army became like a huge whale, sucking into itself thousands upon thousands of plankton-like conscripts. Hermanis was one of these conscripts. He was already twenty, but men were being conscripted from the age of eighteen. He did not believe in fighting, nor did he believe in a war that was focussed on turning men into plankton to keep Imperial interests alive. He thought of Russia and Germany and Britain, thinking how similar they all were; each with an own agenda that had nothing to do with all the men being issued with uniforms and rifles. The men killed on the battlefields were no longer men, they were not even plankton; they were numbers and statistics, and, once they were depersonalized, they could be subtracted so much more easily. The faceless people moving the pieces across the chessboard were completely focussed on winning; they were not interested in men who now were only numbers.

Hermanis was interested only in his studies at the Rīga Polytechnic Institute and his violin; he did not want to kill anyone. But Russia and Britain and France were warning of a German invasion should the Germans win the war. No one wanted the Germans to win, and hate was suddenly quite acceptable and fashionable, even encouraged. Hermanis did not hate anyone. He had heard people say that the war would not last long, and he hoped that he would soon be home again with his studies, his violin and his family.

There had been much whispered talk around me, somewhat like long trails of mist breathing across the river on early summer mornings before slowly disappearing. The words had been deftly caught behind lifted hands, punctuated by raised eyebrows and then dissected behind barn-doors and even over shop counters. I was only eight and I did not understand very much, but I had heard about a war, and I tried to imagine what it might be like. The most frightening thing I could imagine was Mr Kalmanis's very large black bull, though I suspected that even five such bulls all charging at me at once would not be as terrifying as war. My friend Ugis had heard his father talking about people being killed and houses being burnt. At night, I lay in bed, watching shadows – dark and light, large and small – move across walls while I thought about war and wondered if there was any chance that we would be able to outrun it. Then, while I was grappling with all the hazy, abstract images of war and ways of escaping it, Hermanis told us that he had been conscripted.

Hermanis in a grey-brown uniform with a rifle. It did not

make sense, but nothing made sense any more. Not the war, not all the men in uniforms, not the nightmare of five bulls charging all at once. I remembered what Ugis had said about the killing and the burning.

"You mustn't!" I cried, standing in the middle of the room, my small hands clenched tightly, my eyes burning. "You can't leave me, Ermonis!" I could not imagine him not being there; he had always been the most important part of my life.

He knelt down and hugged me very tightly. I could feel the stiff coarse material of his coat against my skin, and I closed my eyes, wanting the moment to continue for ever. I feared that something was coming to an end and that there was nothing I could do to stop it happening. It was as though an enormous brick wall had begun to appear, bricks still being thrown into place, cutting me off from my brother. As the wall sped closer and closer, I slipped my thin arms around his neck. I was desperate to keep him close, knowing that life could never be the same without him. He had always been there: he had taken care of me, read to me, played music for me. Listened to me. The wall was coming closer.

"Please stay," I begged. Tears now overflowing.

He shook his head slowly, his hand gently touching my face. "Everything will be all right, Nika." he said as he stood up. "I'll be back home with you very soon." He smiled at me, buttoning his coat. "You won't forget me, will you?"

The wall had reached the place where we had been standing; now he was walking towards the door. Soon he would be gone. From the middle of the room, I could hear the wall continuing past the door, intent on cutting us off from each other.

I ran to the open door as he lifted his hand to wave goodbye. He stopped for a moment, his hand half-raised, and I wanted to run after him, but Mother caught hold of me and held me back.

She kept her hand on my arm until he disappeared around a bend in the road, and then we went back inside the house and closed the door. I knew that even my life had now turned a bend and that nothing could ever be the same again. My body was completely filled with the memory of my brother looking back at me, and I concentrated on hiding that memory somewhere where no one else would ever be able to find it.

IV

December 1914. Winter. A scream, sharp and cold like thin tapered slivers of ice, excruciatingly painful against the skin. The scream hung tenuously in the air, seemingly for ever, followed then by a second of no sound, a vacuum when nothing at all was heard and nothing happened. Then, after the silence, came an avalanche of new screams, plaintive and high-pitched, cutting through the space, exploding everyone into a film where the images and the sound did not completely correspond.

The engine had stopped, its first carriage barely level with the station, the other carriages far behind, ostracized and locked out of the screams. The engineer stepped down. He was trembling. He could see that there was blood on the tracks and on the snow. He could also see what was lying on the tracks, and he knew that there should not have been anything on the tracks.

The engineer sat on the wrought iron step leading up to the cabin of the engine. The metal was very cold, but the man did not seem to notice. He ran his large hand nervously across his face, smudging the soot and leaving streaks of blackened perspiration behind. The screaming had changed into an eerie low moan. Somewhere, there were people shouting while his mind was trying to isolate what was actually important. A young woman was being led into the station house. He could hear the snow crunching under her feet and under everyone's feet. He noted that the door to the station house was reddish-brown; above the door, there was a sign saying *Tukums*, the name of the station. Through the window of the station house, he could see that the woman was now sitting. She had on a half-long grey dress of some kind of shiny material with lace around the neck and wrists. Partially covering the dress was a plain black woollen coat, while her short fair hair was all but hidden under a neat black cloche hat. Her eyes were open but they were empty. He found it remarkable that he could register so many unnecessary details when everything had stopped.

The station master, a large man with a full black beard, was now standing in front of him, asking him something. The engineer was not quite sure what he was asking. Something about the train and the man on the tracks. Did he run? Was he pushed? The engineer shook his head. How could he possibly know? All he saw was the scream, the cold, icy scream, and, afterwards, the silence.

Two station-hands had arrived with a stretcher and a coarse grey blanket. They went about their work silently, occasionally blowing on their fingers, their breath-clouds moving in low, cold banners before being absorbed into the sparkling, ice-tinged air.

Some soldiers, with rifles slung over their shoulders, were keeping people away from the track. The people in the carriages tried to lean out of the windows and the doors to see what had happened. To see what was happening. Why was the train standing still? They needed to know.

More Russian soldiers, those who had been in charge of the Germans waiting at the station, were now moving along the length of the train – the snow speaking harshly beneath the soles of their heavy boots – shouting orders, opening doors, closing doors. The new passengers were being helped on board, firmly and efficiently. Without emotion. But, from his seat on the step, the engineer saw that several of the soldiers were visibly distraught. No one had expected the man to run in front of the train. Not the soldiers, not the other Germans and not the engineer.

The man's wife would not be travelling on the train. She was still sitting in the station house, bathed in a circle of yellow light, her coat open, her head resting on her hand. A woman was sitting next to her, an arm around her shoulder. A young soldier came with a glass of dark-red tea, unsure of himself, conscious only of his largeness compared with the smallness of the woman on the seat. The woman suddenly without a husband.

The war was barely a few months old, and Russia had already begun to move many of the Baltic Germans, suspicion and anxiety spreading quickly like autumn cobwebs across fields. These people spoke German and acted like Germans, but they were also Russian citizens and should have been fighting for the Tsar. The centuries-long understanding between the barons and the Russian aristocracy was obviously disintegrating. After the revolution of 1905, when Latvian peasants burnt many of the German estates, the Germans had brought in thousands of German farmers. Did these Germans have the same understanding with the Russians? No one could be completely certain. The mistrust and suspicion stirred up by war has no grey tones, only the black and white of perceived realities. All Baltic Germans were removed from administrative posts, and many were sent to the inner parts of the Russian Empire.

Some of the Germans had recognized the smell of fear on the wind blowing from the east, and they had already packed up and left before the Russian soldiers came. They left on trains and in carriages, taking with them their families and a few possessions, leaving behind them empty houses with furniture under dust-covers, and gardens entrusted to the care of selected estate workers, expecting to return as soon as Germany won the war. Many stayed in northern Poland; others travelled further south and west into Germany. There they discovered that, after having pulled themselves out of the maelstrom of several centuries, they were no longer completely German, nor were they Russian or Baltic. They were an elite minority. They were Baltic Germans, and the Baltic was their home. They could not understand why they should be exiled from their homeland.

Others were forcibly exiled. When their questions received inadequate answers, they became pompous, angry and afraid. Wives and children were also afraid as they stood quietly next to husbands, sons and brothers. The Russians had not intended to move the women and children – women and children did not carry arms – but, in the end, they had no choice.

The men, with their wives and children, were moved by train into inland Russia while some, like the man at Tukums, never arrived. Families were decimated by cold and hunger, and those who survived wondered about the meaning of life, without finding any answer.

Then, after the Baltic Germans had left, the Russians looked around for a new reason for their anxiety, and they noticed the Jews.

It was not until 1917 that Nina heard about the Jews. By then, she was already in Petrograd with Maksis, and it felt as though several lifetimes had slipped by, each of them losing itself somewhere in all the formless greys of the past.

It was a summer afternoon and the trees, cutting out irregular shapes from the powder-blue sky, were painting the ground with soft, cool shadows. After following the Neva for some distance through the city, Nina and her brother stopped and sat on the grass, not far from the Hermitage.

Maksis had been talking about 1915, after the Baltic Germans had been sent east. He was telling Nina how the Germans had pushed north into Lithuania and Latvia. He was also talking about an incompetent Russian defence.

She remembered 1915: that was when they left Latvia. She looked around her, thinking of all that had happened since then. She knew that the Tsar and his family were now imprisoned somewhere, and that no one seemed to know what was likely to happen next.

At eleven, Nina's world no longer had any signposts, but no one had signposts any longer. She freed her feet from her very worn brown boots, thinking that at least she had Maksis. She looked at him quickly while she placed the boots neatly together on the grass like two squat animals looking out over the river. He had stretched his length on the grass, his head resting on his jacket, which he had removed and rolled into a pillow.

In front of them, there were a few boats making their way up and down the wide river, and Nina sat for a long while, her arms clasped around her knees, thinking about the boats and wondering how far they would have to travel before they reached the sea. She was also trying to imagine what the sea looked like. Before she was able to ask her brother about the sea, Maksis was once again talking about the invading Germans and the retreating Russians.

He sat up and looked across at Nina. "But you probably don't remember?"

She shrugged slightly, thinking of shadows and black bulls, and Hermanis going away. She was still trying to imagine the sea.

He continued, "The Russians decided to blame the Jews." Maksis picked at the grass near his hand, breaking each strand into smaller and smaller pieces. "They said that the Jews had been spying for the Germans. I don't think many people believed them, but it didn't much matter whether we believed them or not." He sprinkled a little pile of green grass-cuttings over his sister's stockinged feet.

"Thousands of Latvian Jews were expelled to Russia."

"There were many Jews in Orsha," Nina said, watching her brother light a cigarette, watching some ducks drifting down the river.

Maksis nodded, exhaling softly, the cigarette between his fingers. "Some had family or friends in Russia and Belorussia..." He drew on his cigarette and looked at his sister. "For others, it was not so easy."

He was silent for a moment while Nina thought that it was not easy for anyone: not for the Jews, not for the Baltic Germans and not for themselves.

Nina saw that two small grey ducks, with green and brown markings, had left the water and were walking clumsily across the grass. She looked at them, envying them not knowing anything about war and being able to continue living their lives, as they always had, on the banks of the Neva.

The sun disappeared behind a cloud and a sudden chill settled over the grass as the long afternoon shadows joined together, painting patches of dark-green and black.

Maksis looked up the sky, snubbed out his cigarette and picked up his jacket.

"We'd best be getting back," he said.

As Nina brushed the grass off her feet and pulled on her boots, she thought: *Back* – what a strange word! How far *back* should they go?

V

Many of the carriages used to transport all these people east were only ever intended for freight or animal transport, but there was no freight to be moved and most animals were being bartered or eaten. As 1915 hurtled towards summer, and distinctions between class became blurred, passenger carriages, with six- or eight-person compartments, panelled walls and water jars in polished timber holders, took more and more passengers. People were pushed into the spaces, which were then compressed until there was no space left, and the water in the glass jars became less and then disappeared altogether.

The long journey east very rarely followed a direct route. Carriages were sometimes shunted on to sidings while the engines disappeared to pull other carriages filled with troops, the wounded, the dying and even the dead. In mist-filled mornings, the abandoned carriages could sometimes resemble Dorés illustrations of *The Divine Comedy*. Had they already reached Hell or was this only Purgatory? No one seemed to know. Eventually, the engine might return and the carriages would be shunted back on to the main track, or another engine might arrive and the journey would continue. It was all about delay and discomfort. In the winter and the spring, there was also the freezing cold and the snow and trains that gave up completely and refused to move.

The third and final wave of people surged eastwards in the late spring of 1915. By then, Liepaja and all of Courland in the West were in German hands, and Latvians, having nowhere else to run, fled into Russia. Even Russians in Latvia were moving, dismantling industries and sending them and the workers across the border.

"I'm being moved!" It was the end of May and Maksis stood at the kitchen door, his bag slung over his shoulder. "To Orsha, in Belorussia."

When he began working as a signalman, the world had been at peace and now it was at war. He had expected to be conscripted, but then he was told that he was needed where he was. He was still not sure that he would not be conscripted: no one could be sure of anything any longer.

They needed an extra signalman in Orsha and they were asking him. Maksis doubted that he had a choice. People in charge did not ask; they simply said what they wanted. They gave the orders, and others obeyed. He knew for certain that a refusal would have meant a change of uniform.

He had heard that Orsha was a busy railway hub where lines from all directions converged. Trains from Poland and Russia passed through Orsha on lines connecting Warsaw, Moscow, Petrograd and Rīga. With the Germans moving closer to Rīga, Russia was concentrating on other centres. Orsha was one of these.

The man in the dark-blue uniform, standing at the door of the control room, had finished talking. He looked around the small room before looking back at Maksis.

Maksis did not particularly like the alternative; he nodded.

"We'll have you on a train as soon as possible." There may have even been a look of relief on the man's face as he flicked through the papers in his hand. "Your family..." He glanced at Maksis and then continued shuffling his papers. "They can go with you if you like; no one seems to know what will happen here. It's chaotic..." Then he stopped looking through his papers, and studied Maksis for a moment, without saying anything.

Maksis wondered briefly if the man in the blue jacket expected him to have an answer to the chaos.

"Call into the office tomorrow," the man said, his hand already on the metal door handle.

Maksis listened to the sound of boots disappearing down the iron steps while he remained standing near the window, his eyes following the patterns of tracks below.

The other signalman looked across at him. "Better there than here, Hugo. They're already outside Jelgava." He removed his glasses and rubbed his eyes. Then he replaced his glasses and checked the chart on the wall before pulling down two of the levers. He looked as though he was about to say something more, but then the train approached, a phone rang and what he was about to say disappeared completely in billowing clouds of white smoke.

Rozaljia looked at her son still standing in the doorway. She wondered, "Moving? Orsha?"

She was churning butter, perspiration glistening in small round beads on her forehead. In her imagination, she had been somewhere far beyond the house on Kalnciema iela. It was a place that she did not recognize; it was made up of images floating in and out of each other. Woven through the images, she was sure that she could hear the sound of guns. She was also sure that Hermanis was somewhere there, but she could not see him. She had not heard from him for weeks, and she thought about him constantly.

The smoke from fires in the West had not yet reached Rīga, but anxious frightened words had run ahead, painting worrying, discordant images of the Germans moving closer and of the Russians moving eastwards.

"Yes, to Orsha." Maksis looked at his mother and was then silent for a moment. "All of us."

Taller and more heavily built than his older brother but with the same dark colouring, Maksis moved away from the door and walked across the room to the table. He was thinking only about possibilities, not frustrating turns and brick walls, still unaware of a future that would eventually teach him to trust only his own ingenuity and optimism.

He pulled out a chair, dropping his bag on the floor, and sat down. "You will, won't you?"

Rozalija was back in the house in Rīga; the images still taunting her. A chance to escape? A chance to leave Rīga? She tested the butter and stopped churning.

She heard the latch click on the front gate – a short, metallic sound – then familiar voices and heavy footsteps along the side of the house. She could also hear some irritated coughing. The coughing stopped as Zacharias and Jānis opened the back door and entered the kitchen. Jānis nodded at his mother, throwing his cap on to the table before sitting down on one of the chairs. He leant back, looking around the room, and then pulled out a small tin box from his coat pocket. Zacharias had already hung his hat on the peg inside the door, and he poured himself some tea from the samovar before sitting down next to his youngest son.

"It doesn't necessarily mean that we'll be safe." Maksis was thinking of Orsha's position, more south than east, closer to Poland. "But it may be safer than here. At least, for a while."

Rozalija had already decided. The Germans would soon be in Rīga, and then their only option would be to join the thousands of people already spread out between Latvia and the other side of Russia.

She looked hurriedly at her husband while Maksis repeated what he had already told his mother.

Jānis lit a cigarette. Zacharias drank his tea, his eyes on his older son.

"Of course, you must leave," he said as soon as Maksis had finished talking. "All of you. But I will remain here." He moved the empty glass, and it made a soft sliding sound on the timber surface of the table. "They've always been good to me; they've treated me well. They need me."

Rozalija's thoughts were filled with the German baron and the estate where her husband had always worked, and she wondered if this was simply what her husband wanted to believe.

"But they're Germans!" said Maksis, speculating on abstracts like loyalty and obedience. He was even thinking about passivity and compliance. Then he reflected that these people were not really Germans, not like the ones pushing in from the West.

"They'd understand..." he began.

His father shook his head. "It's got nothing to do with understanding."

Rozalija knew that he had already made up his mind. He would not be coming with them. A decision that seemed so easy and obvious a moment ago had suddenly become difficult and complicated. She looked at her husband and then looked away. She closed her eyes. She knew that she could manage most things, but to leave her husband on his own was daunting, even for her. The choice was between her husband and her children. She looked down at the butter in the churn: creamy-coloured and almost smooth. She did not want to leave her husband alone in Rīga, but she had to try to protect her children. She knew that whatever she did or did not do, she would be unfairly judged. By herself and by others. She sighed and walked towards the door. There were things to be done.

"I must talk to Nika," she said and left the room.

VI

There was an enormous snake that everyone feared. It was grotesquely fat and so long that it was impossible to see both the head and the tail at the same time. Its skin glistened green and black, constantly rippling as it moved. Few dared touch it, and those who did said that it was rough and cold and that the coldness ran into their veins where it remained. The people were the snake's prisoners: the reptile having coiled itself firmly around the country. Finally, tiring of imprisonment, the people chose three of their strongest men, who then sharpened their axes and chopped off the snake's head.

With the head now lying on the ground, the people rejoiced because they were now free, and they no longer had any cause for fear. But, while they were celebrating, the tail of the headless snake whipped around them, clasping them all in an iron grip. The few who survived understood, too late, that the tail, not the head, was the most dangerous part of the snake.

Rozalija's dream woke her one night before they all left for Orsha. She knew that the dream was trying to tell her something, but she did not know what, and a sense of danger remained with her long after she had woken. Pressed down by the dream, she pulled the bedclothes closer around her while she imagined reptiles in the shadows and heard voices beyond the wardrobe, behind the dresser and outside the window.

Eventually, she woke Zacharias and told him about the dream. He tried to tell her that it was just a dream; knowing Rozalija, he also knew that it was not an ordinary dream.

VII

I was nine and it was late spring. Looking back, I can see my almost round, fairly plain, face and my somewhat serious mouth, grey eyes and blonde pigtails. When I ran, the pigtails bobbed loosely against my shoulders, and I remember liking the feeling. My shoulders were thin and the pigtails were firm like short pieces of rope.

I was running. I enjoyed running, the wind hitting my face, taking away my breath. Before the world began to fall apart, I used to run with my friends Ausma and Ugis, and we would chase each other, jumping over the paving stones. Sometimes in the autumn and the spring, we would have to side-step rivulets of water charging across those same stones or gouging micro-rivers in streets where there were no stones.

Now there was no water, but there were many people in the streets. Most of them were not actually running, but they were all hurrying as though they had to be somewhere very soon, and it seemed as though everyone around me was moving in the same direction. I found myself in a world of trouser legs and black woollen skirts. There were no faces. Then, while I was still thinking about the pigtails on my back, my brother bent down and lifted me up on to his shoulders.

I closed my eyes for a few seconds, trying to locate a feeling of normality. As I opened them, I drew in a large breath and looked around me.

Normal is often an elusive word, and it changes meaning as a chameleon changes its colour. Perhaps, when I was very young, it may have implied the absence of fear. When there was no fear, it would have been normal to see people working in the fields, horses pulling ploughs, children chasing balls down cobbled roads. It would have also been normal for people to laugh and sing while they worked, just as it was normal for Mr Kalniņš, the grocer, to let me choose just one large, round, sticky, brightly-coloured boiled sweet from the tall glass jar he always had on the counter. But now there was no time for singing or for laughing, not even for boiled sweets, because everyone was on the move. They were all going somewhere and *somewhere*, I had heard, was east. East was where the sun rose, so it should be a happy, beautiful place, I thought, but I was not sure.

I knew that life was no longer normal. It had not been normal for almost a year, not since Ermonis had gone away.

"You are so kind, Maksis." I breathed in his familiar smell, mixed with the smell of tobacco and the summer outdoors and pine trees, as I lifted one hand from his neck and slid it over his cheek and up into his thick dark-brown hair.

While Nina's thoughts were still swirling around balls and sweet, sticky lollies, Maksis stopped for a moment, putting down the heavy brown case he was carrying. He lit a cigarette while he looked at the people around him, with their cases and bags and handcarts representing some small part of the past. He knew that the future was uncertain. He drew on the cigarette, wondering which was more uncertain – staying or leaving.

Everyone was trying to get away before it was too late, but Maksis knew there were not enough places on the trains and that people were always left behind. With the cigarette between his lips, he turned his head and smiled up at Nina as she hung on to him tightly. Then, bending his knees, he picked up the suitcase. It was not far now; they had already crossed the Daugava.

For a moment, Nina wondered where her mother and Jānis were, then she looked down at the cobbled ground, imagining that she was on a boat on the sea and that the cobbles were the water. As she and her brother moved further and further from the shore, she thought of Grandfather Kindahls. She wondered what it had been like, crossing from Sweden to Estonia, but she could not ask him because he was dead. Then she remembered that Grandmother Anu was also dead.

When Anu Kindahle's life suddenly came to an end in the late autumn of 1913, bunches of dried herbs and flowers remained hanging from the ceiling while different-sized bottles, filled with dark, strange-smelling liquids, seemed to retreat further into the murkiness of the kitchen cupboard. Her prophecies and superstitions had already collected in the spaces within the house, and now the dusty, brittle leaves and the dark bottles merged into the gloominess of the cupboard and the blackness of the ceiling. The cats, sensing Anu's presence, took it in turns to sleep curled up in her chair while her stories and her memories continued to push against the walls and the tired, unopened windows.

Nina had often heard how Anu had met the tall, blue-eyed Swede, Jan Kindal, in 1860 when she was only sixteen. Anu had told Nina that he had stowed away, some years earlier, on a small cargo ship going east. Other Swedes were moving westwards, but Jan crossed the Baltic Sea to Tallinn. Anu was not sure why he had left Sweden; he never told her, and she never thought to ask him.

But he did tell her that he had worked on the wharves in Tallinn where timber hulls and tall masts spoke in creaking, discordant voices while noisy white gulls screeched overhead. Where water lapped the sides of ships, uneasily at rest. Where men moved along rough planks, carrying cargo and cursing heavy loads. Where the loud and jarring sounds of machinery and sharp voices and heavy boots were woven into the sounds of birds and masts and water. Occasionally, he thought of returning home – ships were crossing the Baltic all the time – but he could not decide and time rushed past. Then, having learnt the language, he left Tallinn and the ships and the sea, and he moved south. In Veru, he found work in the stables; he met Anu, they married, and their only child, Zacharias, was born.

Nina's thoughts stopped at her father. Now that his parents

were both dead, he was an orphan. It was strange to think of him as an orphan; he was almost fifty-three. She thought of the black bowler hat and the white starched collars he always wore and of his own special language, which was a mixture of both Latvian and Estonian. On the estate, she knew that he spoke German, and everywhere else he spoke only Russian.

Nina looked around her as they entered the railway station. There were crowds of people and lots of luggage everywhere, and, wrapped around everything, there was the noise. She put her hands over her ears, screwing up her eyes as Maksis lowered her on to the stone floor.

Beyond the concourse, the enormous black engine was softly growling like some tethered animal fretting to be free. Nina could hear the hissing jets of white steam, and she could almost see the red flames and the man shovelling the coal. Then Maksis pulled her further along the platform to where people were already disappearing into the long line of brown carriages.

Later, when she looked back on that day, she was not sure what she remembered most: the multitude of pictures moving like acrobats before her eyes or the smells – the incense-like smell of smoke, the earthy smell of the engine, the smell of oil on warm metal. The smells of people and luggage and food. Smells that became a backdrop to the many images that rushed past her, pirouetting before making a hasty exit for yet another lot of images, sometimes darting back for an encore, sometimes lingering a moment in the wings. Properly dressed people and less properly dressed people, women with long skirts wrapping around boots, new and old, some with buttons, some with laces. Men with coats of serge or wool or cotton, new coats and not-so-new coats flapping open as the wearers hurried through the station, or else held stiffly in place by rows of buttons or leather belts. Faces framed by hats and scarves and shawls, and marked by apprehension, worry and even fear. People walking or running in all directions. Children filling in the lower level – Nina's level – seen against a mother's skirt or a father's trouser leg, competing with the bags and baskets, sometimes crying, often looking lost and afraid, with one hand clenched tightly in the grasp of a mother, father or a sibling.

VIII

Two months earlier, when summer was beckoning winter-weary souls to forget the trials of a northerly climate, she had asked him to take her to the island of Gotland, the closest point of connection with her homeland and the point where she was to have made contact with Sweden, all those years ago.

Not understanding time's urgency, he said he would take her, and he continued to do lots of other things while she sorted and labelled and threw things away. For him, time was still infinite, but she now knew that life had both a beginning and an end. She also knew that she would never see her homeland again.

She asked him several times. He had always intended to take her. Later. Next spring. Next summer. Next year. He had really wanted to take her. Sometime.

IX

Maksis took my hand, and we pushed our way along the very crowded, narrow corridor where people were looking for compartments or simply for an unoccupied corner. It was quite noisy. Several times I was sure that I would lose Maksis as we wove our way past the crush of people, clambering awkwardly around assorted pieces of luggage.

When we finally reached our compartment, Maksis pushed me gently inside and closed the door behind us. I could see that Mother and Jānis were already there, and I noticed the look of relief on Mother's face as we came through the door.

"Thank God!" she said, looking at Maksis.

Maksis did not say anything, but he smiled at Mother and lifted the case up on to the luggage rack. Then we looked around for somewhere to sit.

The carriage already seemed full. Besides Mother and Jānis, there were three Russian soldiers in brown-grey uniforms, as well as an elderly man and two women – one quite young and one about the same age as Mother. We hesitated briefly before squeezing ourselves on to the seat between two of the soldiers and the younger woman. It was a compartment meant for eight people, and we were ten. From what I had seen, I guessed that there were many more people in other compartments.

There was still a lot of commotion in the corridor when the conductor – an elderly, white-haired man in a dark-blue uniform – called out that the train to Orsha and Warsaw was about to leave. I heard doors being closed loudly, then I understood that the conductor must have waved his flag, because the engineer sounded the whistle, the wheels began to turn, and the train moved out of the station, slowly gathering speed.

Through the window, which broke the vertical line of the brown timber wall, I could see Rīga receding beneath clouds of grey-white smoke. My feet did not quite reach the floor, and I was still holding on to Maksis. Though there were no other children in our compartment, I knew that there were children on the train; I had seen them at the station, and I understood that they must have disappeared into other carriages and other compartments. I wondered vaguely if they knew anything at all about the sun, then I closed my eyes and listened to the monotonous sound of the wheels. All I knew was that I was travelling southeast to Belorussia and that I was leaving Father behind. There was also the possibility that I might see where the sun came from. How long we would be away from home was a question to which there did not seem to be an answer.

Nina's maternal grandparents, Ieva and Fridrichs Kupč, lived in a narrow two-storey house in the central part of Rīga, not far from the river. Before Orsha, Rozalija and Nina would often visit them, taking the tram that ran down Kalnciema iela and across the river. In the large front room, Nina would sit quietly on a small red upholstered stool next to her mother and grandmother, mentally absorbing the unusual, but friendly, smells of soft armchairs and sofas while she ran imaginary fingers down long, heavy curtains. When she tired of smells and curtains, she would sometimes lean outwards from her stool in different directions, attempting to gaze at a small part of her reflection in the large, heavily framed mirrors. Very occasionally, Grandfather Fridrichs would also be present, a smile often bubbling beneath his heavy moustache as he drank his tea and watched both his granddaughter and her reflection.

Grandmother Ieva had an older brother, Jānis, and two half-sisters, Karlina and Anna. Nikolina had never really known her two great-aunts as they had both been much older than her grandmother. For a while, at family reunions like funerals and christenings, they could be glimpsed, in their black dresses and high lace collars, against a backdrop of glass ornaments, mirrors, embroidered cloths and highly polished floors. Eventually, they must have died, because, without anyone really noticing, there was a space in the room beyond the small tables clustered with pieces of glass and in front of the mirrors that reflected everyone else, but not them. For Nikolina, they merely faded away, and life continued without them.

While her two great-aunts disappeared silently into the past, Great-Uncle Jānis became an important part of Nina's childhood, filling out the spaces with his bulk and his unpredictable and boisterous laugh. He and his wife – who died when Nina was still very small – had several children. For Nina, the only one of importance was Aunt Auguste.

At the end of the nineteenth century, Auguste, already thirty, married a gardener, Ernests Āboliņš, and their only child – also called Ernests – was born a month before Nina. As the cousins, Auguste and Rozalija, had always been close friends, their children spent much of their early years together until, when she was nine, Nina left Rīga and moved to Orsha.

Maksis leant back in his seat and looked at the countryside rushing past the train window. He was hoping that everything would soon revert to some semblance of normality while, at the same time, his thoughts circled around the idea of responsibility: responsibility for those on the train with him and also for his father back in Rīga. He decided that things were always somehow tied up with predestination, but he was not sure if predestination completely cancelled the responsibility.

He closed his eyes, listening to the wheels of the train on the track and the soft sounds of people talking around him. Latvia was being moved east across the border. Would Latvia still be Latvia, Maksis wondered, when all the people had gone? Was Latvia only the fields and lakes and forests and buildings, a place where people lived and died, or was it also all those people and all those things that were disappearing eastwards?

He continued to think of all the people on the move, no one wanting to stay if Latvia was to become German. He recalled how, only a year ago, when the world was still standing on the threshold of war, Latvia had dared anticipate her freedom. Then there had been many who had argued that a victory for Russia would cancel Germany's claims on Latvia, the Baltic Germans would be toppled, and Latvia would belong to the Latvians. But, amid all the pro-Russia feeling, no one seemed to have considered what Russia might do if she won the war. Maksis did not believe that Latvia, caught between the interests of Russia and Germany, as she had been for so many centuries, would be given complete autonomy.

Latvia as an autonomous country was incomprehensible to both the Germans and the Russians: the Germans alluding to Latvia as Germany's northern province and Russia regarding the Baltic as her western border. It was indisputable that one of these two powers would finally subdue the other and would then assume the right to pursue an own agenda in the Baltic, but the likelihood of this being Russia was becoming more and more remote.

While Maksis' thoughts were shifting somewhat erratically between responsibility and autonomy, Nina was thinking of Hermanis and her father. She had definitely not wanted to leave her father on his own in Rīga; all she had wanted was for her brother to come home and for everyone to be together again. She watched the shadows moving across the fields, beneath the clouds of smoke, thinking about that midsummer before Grandmother Anu died and before Hermanis went away, trying to understand why life had suddenly become so grey and sad and complicated.

The soldiers smoked and talked. When one of them took out a pack of cards from his pocket, he nodded towards Jānis, who changed places with the person next to him and joined the game.

Nikolina continued looking out the window, wondering about

the distance to Orsha and whether the sun would actually make any difference after all. When the train passed through small villages, she read the names above the station houses, and she knew that they were still in Latvia, even though the names were all in Russian. She was used to everything being Russian on the outside; that is all she had ever known.

Much later, when it was night, with his sister resting her head in his lap, Maksis looked out into the darkness, seeing nothing and still thinking about choice and predestination.

X

During the night, I dreamt that the train had unexpectedly stopped. Although it was almost summer, it was unusually dark, possibly because of a heavy mist. In my dream, Maksis walked out into the corridor and pushed open a window, the carriage immediately filling with a rush of cold night air. He said that he thought that we may have been in Latgalia, but I could see no station, just dark fields.

I saw some of the passengers climb off the train to stand in the ditch near the rails, talking quietly while peering across the fields. Most of them seemed cold and only half awake. Even in my dream, I thought it strange that they did not stay on the train.

Then I saw that I was also standing outside the train, and I could see that the engineer was in conversation with two Russian officers. I had not seen them arrive, and I did not know from where they had come; they simply appeared. I expected that the Russians may have wanted to commandeer the train. Maksis had once told me that such things happened, with so few trains and so many people and troops that had to be moved. I do not think that the officers could see me; it was my dream, not theirs. I stood and watched them. I could see Maksis framed by a window of the train. He was saying something, but I could not hear him.

The officers did not seem to be very interested in the engineer waving his hands. They said something to each other and stood looking at the train. Then the thinner of the two peered at the passengers standing along the tracks. There were so many of them, many more now than would ever find place on the train. I wondered where they had all come from. The officer looked at all these people and ran his hand over the buttons of his double-breasted jacket and then touched the shiny visor of his cap. His companion was round and short, but his face was not very clear. In my dream, he kept fading away until I could almost see right through him. Before he faded completely, I could see that he had a large bushy moustache. He said something to the engineer, and then both officers saluted and left, gradually becoming part of the mist before disappearing altogether.

The people who had disembarked from the train remained standing where they were on the tracks, and, to one side, I could see Father and Ermonis. They were both looking at me, but they did not say anything. I tried to move from where I was standing. I wanted to run towards them, but, for some reason, my legs would not work properly. All the time, Father and Ermonis continued to look at me without seeing me.

Then, about fifty metres from the train, I saw some indistinct, blurred shapes gradually take on the appearance of men, and the men were walking, almost floating, towards the train. In front of them I could see the two officers. The mist was parting and letting them all pass while the engineer and the guard were making sure that there was no one left on the train.

I could see Jānis standing near the train, but I could not see Maksis, and I did not know where Mother was. Then, while I was wondering about her, she was suddenly there, standing next to me with a basket of freshly baked bread, and she was telling me that I should eat. I did not feel like eating; I was still wondering why Father and Ermonis could not see me.

People were moving around, changing places, appearing and then disappearing. No one was talking. Mother was now handing out bread to everyone. The Russian officers had begun to direct men on to the train. There were lots and lots of men: all of them soldiers. They kept coming, even after I thought that the train would have to be full. Then the rounder of the two officers thanked us for helping the Mother Homeland, the guard closed all the doors, and the engineer, somewhat unwillingly, climbed back up on to the engine. All the while, the crowds of people along the tracks stood very still, not making a sound.

As the train began to move, I saw a face at one of the windows: it was Ermonis. I cried out to him, but he was not looking at me. I found that I could move my legs again, and I ran along the side of the train, screaming. People moved back to let me pass, but the train was already gathering speed. Then it disappeared altogether.

"Nika! What is it?" exclaimed Maksis, holding me tightly. "You were screaming."

I was awake now, and the dream was receding even faster than the train.

"I saw Ermonis," I said. "He was on a train, this train, but the train was disappearing, and I couldn't talk to him." As things around me began to became more real, I said, "Father was also there, but I only saw him for a moment."

Maksis pulled the coat closer around me and told me to go back to sleep. He said that it was just a dream and that Hermanis, wherever he was, was quite all right.

They crossed the border into Belorussia the following day, the train stopping briefly at a small country station to take on coal and water. It was raining and there were no longer any sharp lines; colours had merged making everything appear grey. A few people left the train while some new people climbed on board.

Jānis swung himself down from the carriage on to the track, pleased to be off the train and away from all the people. He stretched, breathing in the damp, fresh air. Outside the station house, he stood under the eaves, smoking a badly rolled cigarette while trying to avoid the rain. There were a few other people walking along the tracks, talking and smoking. He looked at them, thankful for the space between them and himself.

He was only seventeen, too young to fight. Next year, if Germany and Russia were still at war, he would have no choice, but he did not want to fight for Imperial interests. If he was going to fight, he wanted to fight for Latvia, and that was not a possibility. He thought about it while he watched the smoke from his cigarette mix with the misty rain. He knew that Latvia was not Russia. His father disagreed with him, but Jānis also knew that, no matter what his father thought, things were going to change.

Jānis had been working with his father on the estate when the war started, but he wanted to do something else with his life; he was just not sure what. Everything around him was disintegrating; he would have to wait and see if there was anything left after all the fighting.

The rain became less heavy until it finally stopped, the sun pushing its way through grey clouds, painting them white while bringing back all the sharp lines and the colours. In patches, he could even see blue sky. He ground the cigarette butt into the dirt with his boot and moved further down the track to where the engine stood. It was still connected by a long, tired-looking pipe to the large water tank balanced on a wooden stand. The fireman was carefully watching the water pouring into the boiler, ready to close off the spout once the tank was full. While Jānis had been standing under the eaves of the station house, the man had shovelled black, wet-glistening coal into the tender from a mountain of coal near the water platform. Now Jānis watched, breathing in the sharp, dusty smell. The man nodded to him, closed the spout and then swung the pipe back towards the tank away from the train.

"Almost ready," he called, wiping his hands on his overalls.

Jānis quickly moved back along the track, looking for his carriage. A burst of noisy, white steam shot up into the air as the engineer pulled on the whistle, and people clambered back on board. When all the doors were closed, the engineer waved to the fireman, pulling once more on the whistle handle. He released the brakes and opened the throttle slowly, moving the lever back and forwards until the engine was up in speed, and they were again moving south.

They arrived in Orsha the following day. The station, enormous and white, filled a large island of space between countless tracks, a space that was soon dotted with grey-black people flowing erratically from the train. Part of that grey stream, Nina held Jānis's hand tightly, occasionally taking small running steps to keep pace, breathing in the sharp, unrefined smell of engines and smoke and railway platforms.

Maksis left his family near the main entrance and returned into the station area to look for the station master. Nina sat on one of the cases, and Jānis lit a cigarette. For a while, Rozalija stood watching all the people who were being sucked into the mouth of the station only to be regurgitated seconds later as new people. The idea of transformation was beginning to run ahead of her, leading her down strange paths she had not seen before. For a moment, she wondered if life might be easier if she was something else: a rabbit, a bird or even a fish, and she wondered what it would be like to be transformed into something that only needed to concentrate on existing and nothing else.

She left the entrance to the station and walked towards the end of the station precinct before turning and looking back at the station. It had obviously been built quite recently, for she could see that it had still not quite managed to merge with everything around it. She felt as though she was witnessing a process of transformation in slow motion, and, thinking again of herself, she was uncertain whether she would be able to merge with all the new things around her, or whether she would simply remain somewhere on the periphery, obvious and only partly transformed.

After Maksis returned and they left the station precinct, they immediately turned right and walked along a dirt road running parallel to the tracks. Several black cars passed them, sending clouds of grey-white dust into the air. Then, a horse, pulling a cart laden with turnips, walked past slowly, the lazy creaking of the cart quickly disappearing into the sounds of tools and machinery and men's voices coming from the rail yard where railway lines drew long repetitive patterns, broken only by low-lying sheds and tall water towers and piles of black, dusty coal.

As they turned left, away from the railway, Jānis took the suitcase that Maksis was carrying, as well as his own, and Maksis hoisted his little sister up on to his shoulders. She was still aware of the noise from the railway, but now she could see the large brick buildings of the town, and rows of small grey cottages. Further away, she could see a tall white church safely surrounded by a wall of the same colour. Beyond the buildings, there were fields and the dark uneven lines of a forest.

She was still wondering about the forest when she realized that they were on a bridge. Looking down, she could see wide ribbons of blue-green water drawing hurried patterns around large black rocks. Nina liked the look of the rocks with their ever-changing film of white foam, and she would have been happy to have remained on the bridge, but Maksis did not stop. He left the bridge and the stream and turned on to a short road lined on one side with box-like stone buildings.

Maksis set his sister down in front of one of the houses and lifted the gate-latch. There was no one around. He knocked on the door while everyone else, wearily deflated now that their journey was at an end, waited at the gate. The two cases stood nearby on the path, looking somewhat insignificant and almost vulnerable. He was about to knock a second time when the door opened halfway, and a short, somewhat round, woman appeared in the opening.

Maria Elsky, wearing a grey headscarf, a brown knitted cardigan, a maroon skirt and short black boots, looked at Maksis and then, beyond him, at the people near the gate. She had been expecting him. As he introduced himself, indicating his family with a short sweep of his hand, she opened the door further and invited them into the house.

Maria's husband, Valentin, worked at the railway, and when he heard about the man being sent down from Rīga, he said that the top floor of his house was empty and that the man could stay there for a few kopeks a week. When Valentin's parents were still alive, he and Maria and the children had lived upstairs, but then the parents died, and Valentin and his family had moved into the rooms downstairs. Later, his two older boys had moved back upstairs, but the war came and the boys were conscripted, and the top part of the house was once again empty.

A narrow stone staircase, opposite the door leading to the rooms downstairs, ascended from the cramped entry hall, and Maksis and Rozalija followed Maria while Jānis and Nina remained outside with the bags. Upstairs, to the left of the stairway, there was a door leading into what had probably once been an attic; Rozalija, standing on the outside looking in, noted the sloped ceilings and the dark, heavy beams, the whitewashed walls and the small windows. She saw the couches and the lamps, the handwoven mats, the heavy table and the mismatched chairs, the two cupboards and, against the centre wall, the black stove with the tall bricked chimney disappearing into the ceiling. As they crossed the threshold and walked into the space, she saw the two small sleeping alcoves with beds and wash-tables and, in the corner, the different sized boxes piled on top of each other while sheltering a few, disparate pieces of furniture, creating some shrunken version of the attic that once may have been. To the left of the boxes, some old coats, still hanging on the wall, had most probably been long forgotten.

Maria then left them, saying that she would be downstairs if they needed anything. Rozalija undid her coat and removed her hat, placing it carefully on the table. She noted a small window, at the front of the room, looking out towards the town, while a couple of windows at the back looked over the fields.

Unusual smells and shadows falling across the unfamiliar furniture made the rooms strangely alien, and both Maksis and Rozalija felt as though they were on the outside of something, looking in. They were uncertain about the feeling, and neither of them said anything, the sensation of alienation still clinging to Maksis, even as he returned downstairs to fetch his brother and sister and the two bags. While he was gone, Rozalija removed her coat and opened the windows, hoping to let the early summer air sweep through the house to replace all the strangeness with something familiar. Soon she had the fire alight in the stove, the water was boiling, and smells of soap and burning wood were mixing with the smells of cold air and furniture and dust and wet floors.

While her mother moved around the space, making it her own, Nina climbed up on to a bench under the window in what was the living area. She looked out at the apple trees at the side of the house; most of the pale pink and white flowers had fallen to the ground, and the grey-green leaves had already filled out, creating strangely shaped patches of shade under the tree. She saw a small black cat scratching its claws on one of the tree trunks, and she thought of going downstairs to play with it, but she felt too tired. She slid further down on the bench. The afternoon sun was reaching in through the window in one long band of light. Then the room, the last few days, the train, her father, Ermonis and the noises from outside began to swirl around her in a cloud. She was lying on the bench, but she could feel her body rushing away from her, joining everyone and everything that was spinning around her. She was in the centre of a haze that was filling the room, then the cloud sank swiftly though layers and layers of nothingness until she was no longer aware of anything.

The days slipped by and that which may have at first felt unusual soon became normal. The small flat quickly filled with all the familiar sounds and images and even smells of the people from Rīga, and, gradually, the strangeness that had met them on that first day almost completely disappeared.

They met Valentin – short like his wife, with heavy eyebrows and dark eyes and with wispy grey tufts of thinning hair hidden under a flat brown cloth cap – and the youngest son, Viktor. Crippled in an accident with a runaway horse when still a child, Viktor had been rejected by the Imperial Army, and Maria made no secret of the gratitude she felt to both God and the Russians. But with Valentin at the railway and her two older sons gone,

Maria had only Viktor to help her with the farm. When Rozalija and Jānis offered their help in place of rent, Maria's gratitude increased exponentially.

Further down the road from the Elskys' house was an ugly grey cement building: the sauna. It had a small entrance-room, with benches for clothing, as well as two larger rooms. The first of these was empty except for a bench pushed up against one wall and a few zinc buckets that could be filled from a pump outside the building. Behind this room was the sauna itself where three-tiered timber benches ran along two opposite walls, and a large black stove stood in the middle of the floor. The sauna was heated up only twice a week: on Fridays for women and on Saturdays for men.

Behind the houses and the sauna were the fields with a rough track bisecting them, joining the houses to the forest. The track was sandy with small grey-brown stones littering its surface. Mixed up with the sand and the stones, there were patches of green grass or random indentations and long furrows made by horseshoes and cart-wheels – depressions that quickly turned into Lilliputian rivers and ponds when it rained. In the summer, wild strawberries grew along the edges of the track, decorating all the green with small dots of red.

If Nikolina had been a bird, she would have been able to fly high above Orsha and its surrounds, and she would have seen lakes and rivers and forests filling the space between herself and the horizon. She would have looked down on all the tiny grey and white houses and ant-like people working in the fields. Her eyes might have followed silver rail-lines cutting across the fields, and long snake-like trains behind engines blowing clouds of smoke. In the centre of all the green and blue and brown, she would have seen the buildings of the town, all huddled together.

But she remained on the ground, and life wove new patterns around both her and her family. While the present attempted to fuse with the past, becoming a little of each, she held on tightly to memories of her father and Hermanis, trying to pretend that they were still with her. In her imagination, everything was the way it used to be, and everyone was still together. She often wondered why things had had to change.

Nina may have looked to the past for answers to the present, but Jānis was only focussed on the future; soon he would be eighteen, and there was still no sign of the war ending. He began to despair of being able to make the decision he wanted to make; he knew that unless there was a change very soon, his future had already been decided and there was absolutely nothing he could do about it.

In the late summer, Nina started at the nearby school: a two-storey timber and brick building that stood not far from the bridge, and from where it was possible to see across to the rail yard and the station while listening to the sounds of clanking and shunting, whistles blowing and wheels turning.

Close to the school, looking out over a small town square, was the library. It was not large and had timber-panelled walls on the inside and two elongated windows, one on each side of the heavy door that led out on to the cobbled street. The librarian, an elderly man with sparse white hair and a limp, spent much of his time in a back room, drinking tea. On both sides of the library, and filling most of the space in the middle of the room, there were dark-brown shelves reaching almost as high as the ceiling – all of them packed with books. Against the back wall, near the door leading to that small back room, was the highly-polished librarian's desk with pens and a white marble inkwell and sheets of blotting paper and, at one side, a small table lamp with a shade made of coloured glass, depicting blue and orange birds in flight.

Nina would walk along the lines of shelves, breathing in the sensuous smells of paper and leather bindings, reading titles, occasionally taking down a book, holding it in her hand, turning the pages. Sometimes, the librarian would fetch his ladder and, leaning it carefully against the shelves, would climb up. Lifting down a book from one of the shelves closer to the ceiling, he would hand it to Nina as he gingerly climbed back down to the ground. Other times, she would find a book on one of the lower shelves and would then glance quickly into the back room.

"So you're here again, Maksimovna!" the elderly man would call out between noisy sips of tea. "Just one moment and I'll be with you."

Eventually, he would shamble out of the back room into the library space, straightening his glasses as he came. He would then sit down at his desk while rearranging the blotting paper and his pen. Taking the book Nina had found on the shelf, he would carefully write her name and the date on its card and then place the card with all the others in a wooden box on his desk.

"Dostoyevsky." He slid his finger over the front cover as he began to push the book back towards Nina, shaking his head. "Poor Raskolnikov!"

For a moment, he looked uncertain as to whether or not he would say anything more, but then, as the moment passed, he asked, almost without expecting an answer, "Can a crime ever not be a crime?"

She looked back at him slightly confused.

"Is it possible to do bad things for a good reason? Or, for that matter, good things for a bad reason?" He paused, his hand still lying across the book. "And if someone does do something bad for a good reason, should he then be punished?" He sighed as he removed his hand from the book. "A far too difficult question, Maksimovna."

Nina never knew how to answer such questions, but she would nod and curtsy, and she would then leave the library, the little bells ringing sharply as the door closed behind her.

Out on the street, she would hold the book tightly while she ran back home, side-stepping people and horses and carriages, thinking only about the book and all the other books she hoped to read. Though, as she ran along the dirt road, she may have also thought briefly of the librarian's question but realized that she had no answer.

XI

We wrote many letters: words on paper to paint pictures in the minds of those far away. It was the only connection we had between that which was and that which had been. Every week, I wrote to Father; sometimes, I wrote to Aunt Auguste.

Before the war, Aunt Auguste, Uncle Ernests and cousin Ernests lived in a small grey house near St Peter's Church in the centre of Rīga. I have very little memory of Uncle Ernests, but Aunt Auguste was quite tall, with thick fair hair, pulled back from a slightly elongated face, and blue eyes that always seemed to be smiling. In many ways, she was like Ermonis.

"My dear, dear Nika!" she would say, hustling Mother and me into the tiny living room. "I am so happy to see you!" Then, as I sat next to her on the sofa, she would hold my hand in hers, the warmth making me believe that I was somehow special, and that, of all my aunts, Aunt Auguste was my favourite.

But, almost a year before we left Rīga and only a few days after the declaration of war and the mobilization of soldiers, Uncle Ernests suddenly died. He was only forty-four. Perhaps, from the small flat in that grey-timbered house in the shadow of the church, he could already see the destruction and the devastation into which the world was about to fall, and he did not want to be part of it. That was understandable, but his death did not help Aunt Auguste, who dressed in black and attempted to reconcile herself to her sudden loss. She also did her best to comfort her son who, with his straight black hair and round-rimmed glasses, knew that his father would not be coming back. In some strange, unspecified way, he also knew that his position in the family had suddenly changed.

The following year, both Ernests and I turned nine, and then I left Rīga and moved to Orsha.

XII

In October 1915, Auguste wrote: 'My dearest Roza, Maksis, Jāncis and Nika,

'We had a worrying time here in August when the Germans attacked some Russian ships in the Gulf. We thought everything was lost, especially when one of the Russian ships was damaged and withdrew. But some British submarines turned up, and the Germans retreated, so God must have been watching after all.

'Did you know that we now have an all-Latvian Division in the Imperial Army: the Latvian Rifles? It was after Jelgava, and the Tsar really had no choice. You heard about what happened in Jelgava? The Home Guard held off the Germans there after the Russians had already given up and were retreating. The Latvian Rifle Divisions are only for Latvians, and so many men have already volunteered – none of them had to be conscripted.

'I have not heard anything about Ermonis, possibly because I have not seen Zacharias for several weeks. I know that our dear Paulina visits him when she can, and she may know something. I believe that the Polytechnic is now closed, and that it has been moved to Moscow or Petrograd.

'There are so many people in Rīga now, and nowhere near enough food. We can only pray to God that all this madness will soon end and that everything will return to normal.

'Your Auguste'

In the tall, narrow school with its two classrooms and its mixture of children from the town and much further afield, there was a girl called Audra. Fair-haired and blue-eyed, she had fled from Courland in Latvia's west.

She said: "Suddenly, the Germans were everywhere, and the Russians were nowhere; they had simply disappeared."

The mid-morning sun was feebly trying to push its way through a layer of white clouds, the warmth not quite reaching the low brick wall at the back of the school building where Audra, Nikolina and a couple of other girls were sitting. Their teacher, an elderly Russian woman, was still in the classroom drinking tea, her feet resting comfortably on a small, colourfully embroidered footstool. She was reading, but every few minutes her eyes wandered to the clock on the wall. Soon she would have to resume class. She took another sip of tea and turned the page.

"My sister, Rasma, and I were too terrified to sleep. We hid under the table with our hands over our ears, trying to block out all the noise. That was before the Russians disappeared, and then the Germans pulled down all the street signs and put up signs in German. There were so many soldiers and horses everywhere. The Germans even moved into the town hall..."

At the far end of the wall, there were still some sunflowers standing upright: the flowers now completely withered, the seeds already bird-picked.

Looking at the sunflowers, thinking about the Germans, Audra said, "Though some of them actually seemed to be kind; they gave us food, and they told us that they were saving us from the Russians. But Father did not believe them: he was really very angry, and he told us not to listen to them. I know that he and Mother argued a lot about the German soldiers. I think that Mother also felt that they were trying to be kind, but Father would not listen to Mother. Then, one day, he got into a fight with a German officer, and they took him away, and that was the last time we saw him."

Nina felt her chest tighten as virtual steel bars snapped into place. Her thoughts were filled with her own father: could he also be taken away? She did not want to hear any more, but she still had to listen. She was looking for some kind of reassurance. She needed to hear someone, anyone, say that such a thing would not happen to Father.

Audra was talking again. "... and Mother said we would have to leave. I don't think that there were any trains, because we walked. Sometimes we were able to ride, but there weren't many people with horses and carts..." She was thinking of the road always stretching out in front of them without an end, and the thick, sticky, brown mud, after the rains came. She was also thinking of the ditches, full of prickly grasses and water, where they hid when the shooting was close by.

"I don't know how long it took, but we finally reached Rīga." She stopped talking while her mind sorted through a multitude of images, pushing aside those of Rasma drifting beyond the nightmares to some other place, her mother holding her and pleading with her to stay.

She shrugged, trying to ignore the memories. "Eventually, we managed to get on to a train..."

Just then the teacher, having finished her tea, closed her book and pushed the footstool under her chair before walking to the door. She clapped her hands and the children sitting on the wall slipped down to the ground, their eyes still on Audra, their minds still filled with a myriad of half-formed, grey images. As Nina followed them to the classroom, she was unable to stop thinking about her father.

When Nikolina was not at school or the library, she would often join her mother in the fields. When there was little to be done, she and the other children would play on a row of uneven ridges between the end of the field and the forest, a place where many imaginary worlds easily fused with one another and where yesterday's world could always be replaced with something different and more exciting.

In the autumn, she would watch while the women bound sheaves of harvested wheat, or while they threshed the cream-coloured oats on the floor of the barn. Often she would sit quietly in some corner, reading. If she was inside and it was summer, she would look out of open windows, feeling part of the green and the blue and the sleepy warmth while, in the winter, she would listen to the rush of snowflakes on the other side of closed, frosty windows. Sometimes she and the other children would run races along the unpaved street where indentations made by carts formed long shallow gutters waiting to trip them up. Other times, they would create small dolls from bits of straw and cast-off pieces of fabric, and they would then try to convince both themselves and the dolls that everything was once again wonderful and that there was no longer anything to fear. Later, tiring of make-believe, they would leave their offspring lying on the grass and, forgetting their responsibilities, would run to their houses or to the fields, while the dolls would be left on the grass in the sun, questioning all the ideas of wonder and fear.

XIII

In April 1916, Zacharias wrote: 'Ermonis has been home on leave. He had hoped that you would have been here, but he has also written...'

Nina was devastated. She thought: But we should have been there!

She wondered how long Ermonis had been in Rīga, and if he was still there. She closed her eyes, fighting back tears.

Her mother was still reading: "'... They have begun conscription again. So many men volunteered for the Rifles last year, but not now...'"

Rozalija stopped reading and looked up from the letter, straightening her glasses as she did so. She had been wearing glasses for several years, round with steel frames.

She looked at Maksis. "I wonder why?" she asked.

Jānis said nothing. He could imagine the chaos within the Imperial Army. Repetitive wrong moves followed by so many unnecessary deaths. He was still waiting for the people to demand change, and he was hoping that the change would mean a free Latvia.

His mother was reading again; he had already missed a few lines.

"'... many people have left. The German has asked after you several times.'"

Jānis knew that the German was the baron. He was deeply moved to think that he would have asked after them or even thought about them. After all, he *was* German, and they had left Latvia to escape the Germans. He shook his head, thinking how senseless it all was. People were the same everywhere; it was not a question of nationality, it was a question of politics.

He had missed too much of the letter. He got up and left the room. He would read it later. He went down the stairs and sat on the steps at the front of the house, smoking a cigarette, looking out over the town. There would have to be a change soon. He watched the smoke from the cigarette hang in the air and then slowly disappear. When the change came, he wanted to be part of it.

Later, Jānis sat on his bed and read his father's letter, and then he read the few lines from his brother. Hermanis had written that he was disappointed not to find them at home, even though he could understand why they were not there. He wrote nothing about where he had been or what it was like. It was as though all of that was not happening and had never happened. He did write that he had transferred to the Rifles and that he was now with Latvians fighting for Latvia.

Jānis thought about what his brother had written about fighting for Latvia; he wondered how true it really was. It had to be true, because that is what he was clinging to: the possibility of a free, independent Latvia.

Hermanis had also written that his father's cough was worse, but he had then added that it was probably nothing to worry about. Jānis knew that his mother would have begun to worry anyway.

Rozalija wrote to her husband: 'I am concerned about you, and I no longer know where I am needed most. Please write and let me know how you really are, and tell me if I should return home.'

XIV

"There was a very large tree growing in the middle of a field. The trunk was so thick that four big men, pressed up against the tree, were not able to join hands. Branches grew out in all directions from the trunk, and from each main branch there grew smaller branches. All the branches were completely covered with dark-green leaves. Standing under the tree and looking upwards, it was almost impossible to see the sky through all the green and brown.

"The people feared the tree, which had never been harvested, its fruit growing only on the uppermost branches, and they often looked at it, wondering what use it was. So they decided to chop it down. They could then enjoy one big harvest, and the tree would no longer be able to frighten them.

"It took two men all day to cut through the trunk, and, towards evening, the huge tree toppled and fell across the field. Then the people came with their baskets to collect the fruit, but the fruit was not ripe, even though autumn was almost finished, and all other fruits had already been harvested.

"Disappointed, they went away and left the tree with its unripe fruit, and the fruit sank into the earth and poisoned it, and nothing ever grew again in that field."

"Your dream – what does it mean?" Nikolina asked her mother. "Why was the fruit not ripe?"

Looking at her daughter, Rozalija sighed deeply and said, "I think it means that someone will want to push something upon us; something that we will not want and for which we will not be ready."

XV

It was a Friday not long after we had arrived in Orsha, and Maria, Mother and I were sitting in the sauna with the other women. The fire in the black iron stove was both white and red, and the little room, already filled with heat and steam, was breathlessly warm. A large pot of water, boiling on the stove, was waiting to be mixed with cold water from the buckets in the outside room. I sat on one of the lower benches, watching flames dancing behind the grilled door of the stove and listening to the women talking. I liked the feeling of warmth spreading through my body and rising to a crescendo, which would eventually force me out of the heat and into the other room.

Then Mother took the pot of boiled water as we made our way out of the room. At the doorway, I stopped, my hand still holding on to the door. In spite of the warmth all around me, I froze: the floor in front of me was actually moving, and, like a small, naked statue, I stood there, unable to do anything. I was neither in the sauna nor out of it. All I could do was stare at the floor in front of me. A lamp hanging on the wall above the bench cast a strange, yellow light over the mass, which spread out beyond the light's rays in all directions and into the darkness beyond.

Mother, who had reached the middle of the room, stopped suddenly and screamed, "Oh, my God! Cockroaches!"

She may have also wanted to turn into a statue, but, instead, she threw the boiling water in a wide, hot, wet arc over the entire mat of shiny, black insects crowded on the floor.

Several of the women from inside the sauna cried out at the

same time, jumping up from their benches and pushing past me where I was still standing, paralysed, in the doorway. I looked at the wet floor with all the dead and dying creatures, knowing that many had survived the deluge, scuttling under benches and into holes where we could no longer see them. While I was trying to make some sense of everything in front of me, more women had pushed their way out of the sauna and were looking accusingly at Mother.

"God's church and all His saints!" An older woman who lived several doors down from the Elskys stepped forward. "What have you done, woman?" She stood, in her nakedness, looking at Mother.

Mother was standing on the wet floor, still with the empty pot in her hand. She was completely confused. "But they're cockroaches!" She shivered slightly; if she was not thinking about statues, she may have been hoping for a large hole to engulf her.

I could see that the women were very angry and their anger frightened me. I wanted to pull on my clothes and go home. Everything had suddenly become cold and dank and grey, in spite of the heat.

"Yes, cockroaches." The older woman was still glaring at Mother. "How could you?" Somewhere behind the words, there may have been a scream threatening. "My God! What could you have been thinking? They're God's holy creatures..."

I put my hands to my ears. All the white, naked flesh, the wet, black floor and the noise was wrapping around me; I felt that I was suffocating. I looked at Mother, thinking about cockroaches and cleanliness and God, and all I wanted was to be able to close my eyes and wake up somewhere else, far beyond that room with all the wailing women.

Many years later, I was actually able to laugh when Mother mentioned holy cockroaches, but, while it was all happening, I was definitely not laughing. The strange superstition, conceived somewhere among these women's Orthodox beliefs, had leapt into life, filling the entire room like some angry genie breaking out of a bottle.

Then, while I was still vainly trying to either turn invisible or to disappear, Maria pushed her way out of the sauna, stepping carefully over the small carcasses spread across the floor. She took the pot from Mother as she turned to face the other women.

"Stop!" There was a sound of exasperation in her voice. "Cockroaches!" She looked around the room, the empty pot in her hand. "The place is crawling with them. God help us! Filthy, disgusting insects!" She bent down and filled the pot with water from one of the buckets on the floor, and then she looked back at the women. "Holy creatures! What stupidity!"

Her voice filled the room, taking charge of the space, pushing the superstition into the darkest corner of the room while the noise around us changed to quiet mutterings, and the women slowly returned to their places in the sauna. Maria followed, setting down the pot on the stove with a loud bang.

"I'd say that God has too many other things to worry about at the moment." She sat down on one of the lower benches. "I don't think he'll miss a few cockroaches, dead or alive."

There was a long silence; no one said anything. Then the elderly woman lent over and touched Mother on her shoulder. A reconciliation? An apology? I was not sure, but the tension had gone, and I was able to breathe again.

XVI

There are things that should be done, people to be contacted, phone calls to be made. But, for the moment, he still sits in the grey – not dark, not light – room and watches a sliver of sun run from the window across the wall and along the floor. She has not moved. He knows that she will not move, but he hopes that he has somehow imagined it all and that she will sit up and straighten her almost formless, blue and white dress and stroke her hand over his face with a soft, **Mīļo, Andrit!** before filling the kettle with water and taking the black bread from the cupboard.

Nothing moves in the room. Not even time. He wants to remain here, holding her cold hand in his own, but death has taken possession of the room, and his stomach baulks at the heavy, sweet odour that fills all the spaces and forces him to open the windows and to accept the fact that the kettle will not be filled and that the bread will eventually mould in the cupboard.

He sits for a long time, caught up in his thoughts, then he finds the telephone directory and dials the first number.

XVII

Mentally pulled between Rīga and Orsha, Rozalija wrote almost daily to Zacharias. She needed to hear that she had made the right decision. If that was impossible, she needed to know what she should do next. She prayed for an end to the war, wanting only to see and hear the words: War Ends!

But, more than twelve months after they had left Rīga, Orsha was becoming less safe, and still there was no sign of her prayers being answered. Sounds of fighting, though still distant, were already commonplace, and there were often planes overhead. People would stop their work in the fields to look up at the small grey shapes moving across the sky. Everyone knew that the Germans were advancing on Belorussia; it was only a matter of time.

Some people continued to focus on the present, pushing away worrying thoughts of the future, while many others were already making plans to flee. Those who had earlier fled from elsewhere doubted that any place was safe any longer. They had learnt that the war was not about them, even if it was tearing their lives to pieces; it was a game being played by people still clinging to boxes of tin soldiers.

Then, as 1916 was turning yellow with the autumn, Rozalija received another letter from Hermanis. He began: 'My dearest little Mother,' and he finished: 'so very much love to all of you, but especially to my darling Nika.' He wrote nothing about himself, except that he was well and that he hoped that they were not worrying about him. He said that he missed them all, and that he also missed his violin. He wrote that two of his friends had been killed, but their names had been blackened out, and the fact that someone had been killed was just a jarring line in the middle of all the other words.

In September, the school was forced to close when the only two teachers, anticipating the Germans, fled back to Russia. Nina's teacher took her colourful footstool and returned to her son and family in Moscow. There was no one who was able to take over the school, so it remained closed, and a feeling of desolation spread through the empty rooms and the silent school yard.

September moved into October, and Nikolina woke one morning to the familiar sound of rain against the windowpane, mixed with the sound of her mother's voice calling to her. As she dressed, images of cold, muddy fields and potatoes waiting to be dug up filled her mind. Beyond the foggy window, she could see only grey, misty rain. She wrapped herself in an extra shawl and walked over to the kitchen area. There was some thin rye porridge in a blue bowl on the table; Maksis had left for the railway well before dawn, and both Jānis and Rozalija had already eaten. Nina sat down at the table, still struggling with all the images, while Janis, having already pulled on his boots, lit a cigarette, no doubt contemplating much the same images as his sister.

The potato field, already dotted with wet, grey figures, was about half a kilometre from the house. Jānis took a shovel and walked further along the field to an untouched row. He wiped the rain out of his eyes with his arm and then began digging up the wilted plants, throwing them and the potatoes into the ditch next to the mound. Nikolina, Rozalija and Maria joined other women walking along the ditches, picking up potatoes and placing them in large wicker baskets.

The misty rain continued to fall, and Nina's boots and the bottom of her skirt were soon heavy with rain and mud. She had tied her two shawls across her chest, leaving both hands free to loosen the potatoes from the tangled roots while she cringed at the coldness against her fingers and the mud and dirt that had already caked her hands black. All the time, tiny rivulets of water were drawing cold, wet lines down her face.

As the morning became older, the rain stopped, and a pale sun looked down from a grey-white sky. Nina stood for some moments, wiping her face with the corner of her shawl, listening to the quiet chatter of people across the field and the dull thud as potatoes landed in the baskets. She noticed that she was now all alone; her mother and Maria had moved to rows further across the field.

The whirring sound of a plane was heard overhead, and, although Nina could hear the people on the field calling to each other, she could make little sense of what they were saying. Instead, she continued to pick up muddy potatoes, her hands now shaking with some unexplained fear. Then the plane banked, and it flew past a second time.

Then there was machine-gun fire.

She immediately dropped the potatoes she was holding and covered her ears with her hands. She screamed, but her scream was silent, being swallowed up by the awfulness of the sound above her. Her body froze; the world was coming to an end. She instinctively knew that beyond that instant of noise and light, there would be nothing. She was aware that people may have been calling to her, but the sounds had to fight their way through some invisible wall, and they were disintegrating long before they actually reached her. She could no longer see either her mother or Maria.

The plane had flown in a wide circle, and, as it flew back across the field, it fired again. It was much closer this time; she was caught in a vacuum where there was only herself and the plane above, and she knew that there was no one left on the field. Terrified, she threw herself down in the wet, muddy ditch and covered her head with her shawls.

There was more gunfire. The sound was all around her, but she could not see anything. She hoped that she was as invisible to the men in the plane as they were to her. She wanted to keep screaming; instead she made herself think of a song her mother sometimes sang, and the familiar words, making small hops and jumps, ran through her head. It was a song about spring and birch trees, and she tried to concentrate on the words, attempting to keep them in one long line while, above her, the stuttering noise continued.

Then, suddenly, it stopped.

She dared not stand up; she dared not move. From under a corner of her shawl, she could see someone running across the empty field.

She knew that it was not easy to run across a partially dug up, muddy potato field, but Jānis seemed to be flying towards her. As she stood up unsteadily among the mud and the potatoes, he reached her and wrapped his arms around her. He did not have to say anything. There was nothing to say. She was safe.

XVIII

"Jānis!" called Rozalija. She was standing near the front window, looking out at the street. The rains of October had already merged into November sleet. It was still early afternoon, but she knew it would soon be dark.

"Jāncis, come quickly."

He had been in the barn with Viktor all morning, bagging potatoes, and had come home to eat. Now he was sitting at the table, finishing his meal. He wiped his hands on the back of his trousers and walked across to the front window, wondering what could have happened.

There were two officers coming out of the house next door. From the window, Rozalija could see not only the officers, she could also see as far as the bridge, and, near the bridge, she could make out more uniformed men and a small group of boys. One of the uniformed men appeared to be talking to the boys – boys with hands plunged into threadbare pockets against the stinging, penetrating cold.

One of the officers had already lifted the latch to their gate; Rozalija's stomach slowly tightened.

"Why are they here?" Her voice was scarcely audible. The question was irrelevant; she already knew the answer. "What are you going to do, Jāncis?" She turned around to look at her son, her hand still on the window sill.

Jānis shrugged. What could he do? He had seen the two men in their long, double-breasted greatcoats, their shiny boots and peaked caps, and he could even imagine the black, white and orange in the badge on their caps. The Romanov colours. He was not surprised, just disappointed.

He sat down on one of the couches near the window while Rozalija remained where she was, still looking out of the window. He had been eighteen for several months now, and he had not dared think about why he had not been called up; he just assumed that he had been lost somewhere among the piles of papers and a filing system that did not work. He would have preferred to have remained forgotten – at least for the moment – but perhaps there were people who did not want that to happen. Or perhaps it was just fate.

Rozalija moved away from the window, already anticipating the knock on the door, unsure whether to sit down or not. Jānis smiled slightly, looking at his mother. He still felt that the war was being fought for all the wrong reasons, and he was still waiting for the Bolsheviks to take power. He knew that it would happen, but it had not happened yet.

There was a registration centre on the town square, but those who let themselves sink into the eddies around it, hoping to disappear, were usually picked up off the streets. Occasionally men were collected from their homes, like this. He told himself that it did not have to be so bad: he would ask to be placed with the Latvian Rifles. He might even see Ermonis. He stood up, squeezing his mother's hand.

He smiled at her. "It had to happen, just a bit too soon. But, things will change. I'm sure of it."

Rozalija did not answer. She did not know what she thought any longer, but she did not want another son going to war. So many went away, and she wondered quietly how many would be coming back. She heard voices downstairs and then heavy, confident steps on the stairs. She stood up, and, as the knock was heard, she went to the door and opened it.

As the two officers were entering the room, there was the sound of running on the stairs behind them. Nina threw herself through the door, her mittens and shawl covered with small icy flecks of almost-snow, a book half-hidden under her woollen coat. When she saw the two officers, she stopped abruptly, looking first at her brother and mother and then at the two men. For a moment, no one said anything.

Then one of the officers coughed.

"But Jāncis…" Nina threw her arms around her brother, the book falling out from beneath her shawl, her boots and her coat leaving patches of icy water on the floor.

She thought of Hermanis, and how he had left her, and how she had so desperately wanted him to stay. She looked at the two uniformed men, feeling angry that men like them had taken Hermanis away. And now they were going to take Jānis.

The officer who had coughed took a step further into the room and put his hand uncomfortably on Nina's shoulder, but no one knew what he might have been going to say because the other officer, who had children of his own, shook his head.

Jānis had stepped out of the world that had been his reality until only a few moments ago. He felt that he was now on the edge of an enormous crater that stretched across the universe where, until recently, his world had spun around the sun. Hovering so close to the crater, he could feel its depth and its size, and he could also feel that he was being pulled closer and closer to an edge that was not even or firm and that, in parts, fell away in sheer, endless perpendicular lines. Somewhere, along the edge, there was a flickering light. It was the only light in all the darkness of this strange world, and Jānis knew that he must not lose sight of it. He stepped back from the edge and hugged his sister very tightly. He thought it was strange that they were in two different worlds, and yet, somehow, they were still together.

"It will be all right, Nika. Don't worry." He wanted to tell her about the light, but he was not sure if she would understand. He said, "Things will work out. Just wait and see."

The light would become stronger. He wanted to be able to tell her that, but she was not standing on the crater, and she could not see the light that was in the distance. He would fight with the Rifles, and he would fight for Latvia, and eventually the Bolsheviks would take power, and the war would come to an end. When that happened, Latvia would be free. He knew that he had to believe in that happening, otherwise there was no point to anything any more. He kissed her lightly on the forehead.

The officer with children was talking to him now; he needed to be leaving, and, while he was possibly thinking of the impending darkness and the cold, he may have also been thinking of his wife and his children somewhere in Russia. Or else, he may have been thinking about endings and new beginnings, or perhaps he had stopped thinking altogether, after all the orders that had been given, and all the men who had died.

Then the officers and Jānis were gone. Nina listened to the steps on the stairs, following the sound of her brother's steps as they faded into the distance behind the sound of the front door closing. It was quiet in the little room after they had left and after the door had closed. Nina and her mother stood wondering if perhaps it had been a dream, and Jānis would burst in through the door and ask why they were both standing there, looking so serious. But, when they looked out the window at the officers and Jānis disappearing into the dark-grey afternoon, they knew that it had not been a dream.

Nina remained at the window for a long while, wondering how long she would have to wait until everything, as Jānis had promised her, would eventually 'work out'.

XIX

In late December 1916, the Latvian Riflemen managed to break the German line of defence along the Daugava river. This was the chance they had been fighting for: the chance to force the Germans out of Latvia. Rozalija heard that the fighting had been very hard and long and that both the Latvians and the Russians had lost many men. While she tried to think of her sons, her mind insisted on creating images of the devastation, until her every thought was crowded with frightened men and startled horses converging into a confusion that spun around and around in a never-ending commotion of sharp, blinding sounds, and she could think of nothing else.

She was standing at the scrubbed table in the kitchen, making sausages. She closed her eyes, breathing in deeply, wanting to rid her mind of all the other thoughts. But they held on tightly, refusing to let go. Was Hermanis at the Daugava? Were they both there? She did not expect that Jānis was there: the front was long and troop movements were slow. Was she trying to save Jānis by putting him somewhere else? She was almost sure that Hermanis was there; she was not able to imagine him somewhere else. She took another deep breath, thinking of the long thin fingers that had only ever wanted to make music, now wrapped around a rifle stock, now pressing a trigger. Had he killed anyone? Had he himself been killed? She did not want any more thoughts; she opened her eyes and tried to concentrate on the pig-meat as she continued pushing it through the heavy mincer into the long slippery intestines.

December had long since moved into January 1917, and reports in Russian newspapers spoke of tactical Russian victories in the face of an overwhelming enemy. But letters from home told how the Riflemen had expected the Russians to use the breakthrough on the Daugava to their advantage but that Russian officers had dallied, and the Germans had been able to regain their original position. The letters also told of the thousands of soldiers who had died because of the lack of leadership.

Rozalija reread the letters, searching for assurance that her sons were still alive. But the words on the flimsy pages only told her what had happened and not what she wanted to know. She prayed silently while she wrote to her sister Paulina and also to Auguste, always with the same questions: 'Have you heard anything at all of Ermonis? Do you perhaps know where Jāncis is?' She really wanted to ask if anyone knew if they had been at the Daugava, but she dared not. She was too terrified of what the answer might be. Then she thought of Jānis saying that things would change.

"But, Ermonis? Jāncis?" Nina asked, looking quickly from her mother to her brother. The three of them were sitting in the area beyond the kitchen that Rozalija liked to call the sitting room, and Rozalija had just finished reading a letter from her sister Paulina – the pages still spread out in front of her.

Maksis reached over and took his sister's hand. What could he say? If he had been Jānis, he might have said that people were already turning against the Tsar. But he was not Jānis, so he simply held her hand, wondering if things would work out the way Jānis had predicted: that the Bolsheviks would take power and that the war would come to an end. He thought how Jānis had always condemned the war while he hoped that something positive would come out of it. He agreed with him, but he did not agree that the Bolsheviks were the answer.

"They'll be all right," he said.

Nina withdrew her hand. "You are sure?" she asked. "You are quite sure?"

He had no idea, but he hoped, and he thought that if he hoped and prayed enough, then it would be true. He nodded while Rozalija pursed her lips and tried to believe that he was right.

As the Germans advanced across Belorussia, a sanctuary became a new battleground, and people were once again moving even further east.

It was February, and the strange half-light of winter sliding into spring was filling the window-space. Rozalija sat wondering whether or not she should get up and light the lamps; she knew how important it was to honour the twilight. *Svētīt krēslu* her mother had always said. And her mother before her.

She was sitting on the couch, the same one on which Jānis had sat the day he had been taken away; she was thinking that she had only had one letter from him, in late January. He had not written much, but he did write that he had finally transferred to the Rifles. When she received the letter, she understood that he had not been at the Daugava, but she still did not know if Ermonis had been there. Jānis said nothing about where he was. He wrote about the cold and the bad food and left her to imagine the horror and the boredom and the killing. She was thinking of the letter as she sat darning socks, wondering whether she should light the lamps. Maksis was sitting in the only armchair, reading, and Nina was sitting at the small table, writing to her father.

Eventually, Maksis closed his book. Leaving it on the chair, he got up and crossed to the window at the front of the room. He remained standing there for a moment, without saying anything, just looking out at the town.

He said, "Things are beginning to close down here; people will soon be leaving." He turned around and stood, dark against the window. "They told me today that I'm to be moved again; I'll be working in Petrograd." He walked over to the couch, sitting down next to his mother. "They want me to start there as soon as possible."

Rozalija looked at her son without saying anything. She was

thinking how she had not heard from Zacharias for some time, and that her son's news could be the answer for which she had been praying. Already in her head she was returning home. She stuck the needle into the sock she was darning and then placed it in the basket on the floor.

Maksimiljāns looked at his mother, knowing that she was worried about his father, knowing that she would want to return home. At the same time, he was aware that things in Latvia were dangerous, with the Germans still pushing towards Rīga.

"I could take Nika with me. To Petrograd," he said.

Rozalija glanced at her daughter sitting at the table. Would she be safer in Petrograd? It was further from Germany, but who knew any longer where it was safest. She certainly did not.

Nina listened to her mother and Maksis while she tried to concentrate on her letter. No one had thought to ask her what she felt, but even if they had, she would not have known what to answer. All she knew was that she wanted her two brothers back home. She wanted everything to be like it had been that midsummer, before everything broke into thousands of small pieces. No one could give her what she wanted, so it was easiest to let other people decide; she would do whatever she was told.

The days strung themselves into long knotted strings, and the strings tied themselves around so many hastily made decisions and, finally, around the goodbyes wrapped in promises to write. It was decided that Maksimiljāns and Nikolina would travel to Rīga with Rozalija and then continue on to Petrograd with the same train. Nina's hopes of seeing her father faded before she even had time to believe that it might have been possible. She sighed, reminding herself that she was simply doing what everyone else felt was best.

Everyone was moving, but the Elskys said that they would remain where they were; they had always lived in Orsha; it was their home. They knew that the war would eventually have to end. Everything had to have an end. While they waited for the end that had to come, Maria and Rozalija wrote letters to each other, sharing the heartache of loss and ruined lives. But, as the years fell upon each other, gathering the dust of memories, and life became entangled in other patterns with new players, the letters became less frequent, until one day, without anyone fully realizing, they had stopped altogether.

XX

Rozalija arrives back in Rīga only days after Tsar Nicholas II has abdicated – the resulting empty space now coveted by both the Russian Provisional Government and the Petrograd Soviet. But Rozalija cannot believe that the Tsar has stepped down; he is, after all, the Tsar. She does not feel that she can trust the Provisional Government. While she thinks about everything that has happened, she also thinks of Jānis.

She knows that she is not alone regretting the deposition of the Tsar. Caught up in the turmoil sweeping across Russia and her territories, there are many who are fearful of the future. The Provisional Government wants to continue fighting, but the Petrograd Soviet does not, and lots of soldiers, siding with the Bolsheviks, are beginning to leave the battlefields in protest. She wonders if Jānis is among them. She has only had that one letter from him, and he would not even know that she is now back in Rīga.

While she understands that this may be what Jānis has always been hoping for, she is not sure if it will be the beginning of a free Latvia. She knows that many Latvians have already joined the Latvian Bolsheviks, but, as she sees Russia sliding towards chaos, she is convinced that there must be another way.

She knows that Jānis had always been a revolutionary. While others around him accepted life as it was, he only ever talked about change, and she understands now that his idea of a free Latvia had never just been a dream. For him, it had always been a real possibility. She thinks back to when she was still a girl, and how there were people who argued, even then, that ordinary people also had a right to freedom, and, while she thinks about such things, she hears Jānis: 'We haven't the slightest notion of what it is like to be free. We have never been really free!'

When he said such things, she had always tried to quieten him. But, perhaps he was actually right. Perhaps they never had been free. She is not sure any more. She remembered once, when Jānis had been talking about change and freedom, Zacharias had said: 'But Jāncis! Tsar Nicholas is a good man. Since he came to power, we have always had food on the table and a roof over our heads. It was not always so. There is a lot of talk about change, but that's all it is, just talk.'

Now she is wondering who is right.

Zacharias knows nothing about the revolution or the abdication. His cough has worsened over the past few months, and, when Rozalija returns home, she finds him lying in an untidy, sweat-drenched bed. The house is dingy with dust and the smells of forgotten food, but Zacharias knows nothing of that either. He is too ill, existing in a dimension that is neither the present nor the past; it is a place of shadows moving across a layered confusion of greyness. Rozalija, exhausted after the trip back to Rīga, is still assessing the situation while accusing herself for leaving.

Most of her letters from the last few weeks are piled inside the door, unopened and unread. The tired envelopes are already turning yellow. From the front door to the back door, smells of stale food and sickness have wound in and out of rooms, settling behind cupboards and under sofas or between tightly closed windows and drawn curtains. In the kitchen, some grey rats have built a nest in the darkness behind the dresser, and their small dried-out black-brown droppings crunch beneath her boots.

She shivers slightly, not from the cold but from the horror of what she has seen, and she flings open the doors and the windows, letting in the sparkling cold air of early spring. A lark is singing somewhere high in the pale blue sky. At the back of the house, she can see the first snowdrops, green and white against the snow-patched, brown earth. She stands on the back steps, wanting to embrace both the singing and the snowdrops, looking for something that will erase all the sad, leaden-coloured images that have claimed her house.

She looks beyond the house, thinking that the barn is now empty, except for the cats. She wonders briefly what happened to the hens. In his letter, Hermanis had mentioned Mrs Baloda. He wrote that he had given her money to look in on his father. Perhaps it was she who took the hens. Angrily she returns to the house, leaving the door wide open. She will speak with Mrs Baloda – there is time for that – but first she needs to clean the house.

It had been several months since Zacharias had worked as foreman, and he had all but stopped turning up at the big white house at the centre of the estate. His illness had smashed into him, pressing with all its weight on his chest, draining him of energy. On days when he was able to force himself beyond the impossible, he was given light work in the yard or in one of the workshops. The German had known Zacharias for many years; he tried to be kind.

But eventually kindness had to be put to one side as the vaguely possible became, for Zacharias, more and more impenetrable. The German knew about beginnings and endings, and he also knew that nothing was certain any longer, not even for him. It was like walking on the ice at the end of winter, not knowing whether it could still hold, not knowing whether there might be an end already fused into the next step. He stopped with his foot above the ice, and he told Zacharias that he would no longer be needed.

"You're ill, Kindahls, and you need to rest. You'll kill yourself." He wondered if he was sufficiently sympathetic. The ice held. The German sighed, glancing momentarily at his hand resting on the top of the heavy, dark timber desk. "You've been a good worker, Kindahls. And your father before you." He put his hand behind his back. "We would like to thank you for that."

Zacharias nodded several times, without speaking, trying not to cough. He was standing in the polished-brown office at the side of the big house, part of the big house and yet separate. He could only think about lying down somewhere, anywhere. He nodded again, turning his brown chequered cap in his shaking hands – his bowler discarded many months ago – looking down at his boots.

"Do what you have to do to get better." The German walked around to the front of his polished desk and pushed a few roubles into Zacharias's hand, knowing that the money would not help and that they would not meet again. At the same time, he was wondering about disease and contagion and whether or not they would all get ill and possibly all die.

"Look after yourself, Kindahls!" The German would have offered him his hand, but this was one of his employees: one of his most loyal employees, but an employee nonetheless. He held his hand by his side, not sure of the etiquette. Not sure of the risk.

Zacharias, with the notes now clenched in one hand and perceiving the thin layer of blue water across the top of the ice, bowed his head. "*Schönen Dank.* Thank you, sir," he said, the words barely audible. Then he shuffled from the room, his cap still grasped in his other hand.

Out in the cold, winter-white air, a cough burst his lungs, filling him with pain, taking away his breath, forcing him to stand for a long moment supporting himself against the wall of the carriage-house. The German stood, watching him from the window, his thoughts still contemplating the other side of the river. Then he sighed and returned to his desk. Should he have been more worried about the etiquette? He picked up his pen and dipped it into the ink. Zacharias Kindahls was no longer his concern.

Weeks later, Zacharias was so weak that he could no longer get out of bed. The fever had taken a secure hold, and the coughing was much worse. Hermanis had been and gone, months ago, but time had lost all meaning for Zacharias; sometimes he did not know that Hermanis had left. Most of the time he was no longer sure who he was or where he was.

He was alone now, except for Mrs Baloda's visits. At first, Mrs Baloda – a widow who lived with her son and his family in a drab stone cottage further along Kalnciema iela – looked in on him each day. Most of the time she had a little food with her, whatever she could spare. Hermanis had given her money when he came home in the spring of 1916. It was a business arrangement: she needed the money. Everyone needed money to buy food, but it was food that everyone needed, and there was so little food anywhere.

Then Zacharias became much worse, and Mrs Baloda was frightened by the coughing and the blood. She saw how thin and feverish he had become; she was sure he was going to die, and she decided that she did not want to die as well, and she refused to go into the house. She had heard that lung sickness was spread by coughing and blood, even by contaminated air.

Later, she brought food only when she remembered – she was doing her best not to think of Zacharias dying a few doors from where she lived – and she placed it just inside the front door, together with the letters and the shirts. The shirts had belonged to her husband, and she had put them there when her conscience had worried her too much, reminding her of the money she had already received. But Zacharias, now sleeping on the couch under the window at the front of the house, was no longer able to walk. He would use his walking-stick and try to pull the bowl of food towards him. Often the food spilt. Most times, exhausted by his efforts, he moved in and out of consciousness while the food became cold and was left there uneaten.

When Rozalija arrived home, she blamed herself, the war, Mrs Baloda and herself again. She sighed and she wept. She ranted at Mrs Baloda. She comforted her husband. She visited Auguste and then she wept some more. Finally, she cleaned the house and Zacharias and, opening her mother-in-law's bottles of herbs, she made teas and potions and spent all her time trying to make her husband well again.

XXI

Hermanis had not died. He had miraculously survived the Christmas battles of 1916, though he still did not understand why. The fighting had been terrifying; he knew no words to describe it. His mind constructed walls, trying to pretend that it had never happened. But the walls were flimsy, and he knew that thousands of Russians and Latvians had died, while he was still breathing and walking. He found it incomprehensible that all the death and the chaos were already in his past, while for others that is where the end came: in the middle of everything as it happened.

Now it is his past, but then it had been his present. As walls topple between that which is and that which was, he sees how he is sent with his unit to force back the German front at Tīrelis swamp, west of Rīga.

On the very first day of fighting, the Riflemen gain ground, managing to break through the heavy German fortifications. The Germans had not been expecting such an assault, and they begin to retreat westwards while the Latvians and the Russians wait in vain for reinforcements that never come. It is cold, it is snowing, and those making the decisions lose themselves in a maze of inefficiencies and are unable to find their way out.

The Latvians have no choice: they continue fighting and capture the hill Ložmetējkalns, within the German area of fortifications. But the retreating Germans have now had time to reassess the situation, and, as the Imperial Army dithers, the Germans regain the ground they had lost. They have been able to reassemble, and they have also received many additional troops.

The Latvians cannot let the Germans win – the Baltic nobility is already looking forward to the reinvention of Latvia as a German province – and they do not want that to happen. No one is prepared to give in. Not the Latvians and not the Germans.

When it was all over, Hermanis wanted to forget the noise and the killing that still pressed so tightly around him like a taut, colourless skin. If it had been possible, he would have torn it off, but it had already fused to his own skin, becoming part of him. Instead, he tried to close his ears and eyes to the screams and the blood and the fingers frozen to rifle butts, to the images of men dying in front of him and beside him. But, no matter how he tried to forget, Ložmetējkalns remained with him, even as it became his past.

Afterwards, like other survivors, Hermanis remained trapped in the nightmare of what had happened, unable to forget while searching desperately for some way out. While they looked, there were many who began to question the Imperial Army and its commander-in-chief, and, when they finally found a small opening, many of them fell into the arms of the Bolsheviks.

Imperceptibly, forces were pushing people closer and closer to the eye of a storm, which, though possibly offering a moment of respite, would eventually throw everyone on to a path that no one had envisaged and no one would have thought possible.

XXII

At the beginning of March 1917, after Mother had returned to Kalnciema iela, Maksis and I stepped off the train in a freezing cold Petrograd. The Tsar had abdicated and was now imprisoned with his family; somehow I knew that things would probably never be the same again.

I remember Maksis swinging down from the train carriage, being careful not to slip on the ornate metal step before putting his arms around me and lifting me down to the ground. We stood for a moment looking at everything that had become part of the icy cold line between winter and spring. Along the sides of the tracks, there were still high mounds of dirty, frozen snow looking tired and spent, anticipating obliteration.

When I was older, I learnt that the escalating unrest in the city finally exploded at the end of February. The people had been starving, the winter had been long and bitterly cold, there was no fuel, the war was unpopular and millions had died. In February, everything surged together into one cause, and the people rampaged through the city, demanding food while condemning both the Tsar and his German wife.

Some of the demonstrators were killed, before hundreds of police and soldiers, realizing that they wanted the same thing as the demonstrators, changed sides and joined the demonstration. Buildings were looted and many prisoners were set free, while those police still loyal to the Imperialist Government were set upon by the crowd and hanged from metal lamp posts – their heavy grey shapes twitching awfully between a sky and an earth of the same colour before, at last, becoming part of the frozen landscape.

The Tsar, who was away from the capital, had not believed that his people would revolt nor that his troops would abandon him, not until it was too late, and then he had no choice but to abdicate.

Vitebsk station was very large, and the entry hall towered above us, with a few red flags filling spaces while looking awkwardly out of place. Maksis said something about Bolsheviks as I looked around quickly at the many Russian soldiers, hoping to see Ermonis or Jāncis. Still aware of the flags, I held tightly on to Maksis, and we continued through the station – the ornate decorations and wide staircases forming hazy patterns behind the faces of the soldiers and people hurrying in all directions.

Once out of the station building, we climbed on to a tram. I had seen that there were people huddled on the top in the cold, and I was thankful that we were able to sit inside. The world moving past the small window looked dismally grey-white and cold, and, as we moved closer to the centre of the city, I could see buildings where broken windows had been boarded up. I asked Maksis about the flowers lying in the street, but he just squeezed my hand and continued smoking and looking out the window, not saying anything.

While the conductor, in his long coat and fur hat, collected fares and pulled the cord that rang the bell, I remembered what Maksis had said about the Tsar and his family. Then I remember sitting back, looking at buildings and parks and statues, still not completely convinced that I was really in Petrograd.

Not long after we arrived in Petrograd, we received a letter from Mother telling us that Ermonis had been sent home.

She wrote: 'He had not been well since January'.

I thought: No, not Ermonis! Then I thought: January. That was so very long ago when we were still in Orsha.

She wrote about the fever.

"The fever? What does she mean?" I asked Maksis, who was

sitting across the table from me, reading the letter aloud.

He looked up from the letter and said that it could have been scarlet fever.

"'Many died.'" Maksis stopped reading, possibly thinking of the dreadful rash, the vomiting and the constant swing between being too cold and too hot. Possibly wondering how much he should tell me.

"What happened to Ermonis?" I asked, not wanting him to stop. "Why did they send him home?"

Maksis looked back down at the letter, and then he looked at me, reaching over to touch both my hands across the table. "He's getting better, Nika. You mustn't worry. Mother writes here that lots of men caught the fever, but it was when Ermonis developed pneumonia that they sent him home.

"'When Ermonis got pneumonia, they sent him home. He was very ill; they did not…'"

Maksis skipped a few lines, looking at me over the top of the letter, but I had already begun to worry.

Then he continued reading: "'Ermonis said that they were somewhere south-east of Rīga...'"

Maksis quickly skimmed the letter. Then he looked at me and said, "Mother will make him better. She writes here about teas and herbs."

"Think how wonderful it would be to see him, Maksis!" I said, wondering if it might at all be possible. Hoping that Maksis would say that we could return to Rīga.

Instead, he shook his head. "Yes, it would, Nika, but we can't leave. We have only just arrived, and we will have to stay here, for the moment at least."

I did not say anything. At least we knew that Ermonis was safe, that Mother would make him better, and that soon we would return to Rīga, and that he would be there waiting for us.

XXIII

The new Provisional Government announces that it will continue the war against Germany. But the people are tired of fighting, and they withdraw their support, looking around for some other possibility. Strikes break out around the country as hungry workers struggle against diminishing employment opportunities, poor wages and stagnant production. More and more soldiers, many without weapons to defend themselves, continue to walk off the battlefields.

After almost twenty years, Soviets once again begin to appear across Russia, with the Bolsheviks emerging in the minds of many as that other possibility. In April 1917, Vladimir Lenin returns from exile in Switzerland, and the players begin to take up their positions on the stage.

In June, the Military Office in Rīga sends Hermanis a letter, requesting him to attend a medical examination, and, when he does, the doctor decides that he is well enough to return to his regiment. The letter was not expected; no one had thought that Hermanis would be recalled. Beneath all her anger, Rozalija is frustrated but not surprised. She knows that Hermanis is still weak, but she also knows that, with so many men deserting and dying, the Russians have begun to recall men like Hermanis. They have also started recruiting older men.

By August, the Germans have reached the outskirts of the Latvian capital, setting their sights first on Rīga and then on a clear passage through to Petrograd. The Latvian Rifles have been attached to the Russian 12th Army, but, as the Germans prepare to enter Rīga, some of the Russians break their positions and retreat east and north; they have caught a glimpse of the future, and they cannot see the point of dying when victory is so close and the war is about to end. As they retreat, they burn houses and farmlands. And they loot and rape.

The Latvian Rifles inadvertently become a wall between the retreating Russians and the advancing Germans, and, while they try to hold back the Germans, they know nothing about what is happening in the east of the country. The Rifles, too few to hold back so many Germans, are decimated.

The German military force, with its horses and trucks and flags, moves into the capital, and grey uniforms and spiked helmets soon spread out across the city to fill and change the spaces. Competing against the sounds of foreign boots hammering against cobbled streets, the news from the east slowly trickles back into the city.

In the late autumn of 1917, Rozalija receives a letter from her eldest son. As she opens it, sliding the knife along the top crease of the envelope, she thinks back to the spring when he came home, and she remembers how ill he was. She knows that she should have held on to him and refused to let them take him a second time.

There are two thin pages covered with his familiar writing, small and almost indecipherable. As she holds the pages in her hand, the thought that he would have died had she not made him better refuses to leave the outer edge of her consciousness, and she finds herself wondering whether or not she had done the right thing. The idea is frightening, and she tries to rid herself of it, forcing herself to think of other things. But the thought clings to her stubbornly. Eventually, she allows herself to look at it through half-closed eyes, knowing that that she does not want to think of him dying in some strange place, surrounded by noise and chaos and pain, without her, without anyone.

She sees that the letter was written in August, two months earlier. The letter belongs to his past, and she has no way of knowing if he is still alive. She looks at the letter for a long time, willing it to answer all her questions, but it remains silent.

She glances quickly through all the usual greetings, wanting more. Wanting to know everything and yet, at the same time, not wanting to know anything.

'... After I was sent back, after I left you, we were moved to Russia (*here some words have been blackened out*).'

Rozalija thinks about the pointlessness of it all.

'... and I've been here in (*thick black line*) for some time. There has been some heavy fighting. Arturs, Hugo, Igors – do you remember Igors? All of them dead now. And here (*three lines of black*).'

She puts down the letter and looks out of the window near the table where she is sitting. This is all she has received from her son in months, and there is nothing left to read. Black lines and greetings. She runs her hand over the paper, thinking that at least he had touched the paper before all the others.

Outside the window, she can see that most of the leaves have already fallen from the trees and that the ground has become a mat of yellow and brown. The autumn storms have begun, and soon it will be winter. She thinks of all that he had wanted to say between the greetings and the blackened-out words. Life is hard for him, she can tell that. She knows he is not happy. She knows that he hates the killing and the senseless misery that everyone calls war. She just hopes that he will remain safe, and that the war will soon end, and that he will be among those who eventually will be returning home.

XXIV

In September, before Rozalija had received her letter, and while she was wondering whether Ermonis had been at the Battle of Rīga and whether he was still alive or not, Alexander Kerensky, the leader of the Provisional Government, entered into a coalition with the Mensheviks and the Socialist Revolutionaries. His grasp on power was extremely fragile, and, with the Bolsheviks on the rise, he was unable to do anything to alter his hold. He knew that his government could only survive with support from the Left, but it also needed the army, and no one wanted to fight any longer. Everyone had expected Russia to pull out of the war once the Provisional Government came to power. But that did not happen, and men continued to desert in their thousands.

The web was sticky: Kerensky knew that Russia would not survive without the economic support she was receiving from countries like France and England. Russia had her obligations, and she knew that she could not withdraw. Yet, if she was to continue fighting, she needed soldiers, and the soldiers were all leaving.

Kerensky was caught in a complicated tangle of virtual fibres from which there seemed to be no escape. Anticipating an attack by the army, he distributed weapons to the workers, ordering them to defend the city. But, by that time, it was already too late; most of the workers had joined the Bolsheviks. Kerensky was on his own.

At the end of October, Maksis wrote home, but it took many days for his letter to reach Rīga; by that time, news had already spread out from the Russian capital to the rest of the world. Lenin had stepped on to the stage, and the Bolsheviks were now in power.

Maksis wrote: 'A few days ago, Kerensky finally confronted the Bolsheviks. It was quite a desperate move; I believe that he may have cut the telephone line to their headquarters, but the Bolsheviks responded, almost immediately, by attacking the Winter Palace. That was when Nika and I were near the river. We were hoping to buy bread – there was a very long queue but, as it turned out, no bread – then suddenly we heard shots.

'There weren't many shots; most of Kerensky's supporters had already seen the sense in switching sides, and there were only a few Cossacks and women left. Can you imagine? They must have understood that they were on their own, because they quickly gave in. I heard that the Bolsheviks later spent hours searching the Palace, looking for people who might have been hiding in the rooms...'

Rozalija read the letter, trying to placate her growing anxiety. She had already heard what had happened. It had been on the front page of the newspaper, and there had also been a photo of Vladimir Lenin. Beyond all the reports and images, she was wondering about her children. The paper was still lying on the table. She pulled it towards her and unfolded it.

Zacharias was sitting with her at the table. "Can you read it for me?" he asked.

She had read the article to him once before, but he would not believe what had happened. He had been hoping that his beloved Tsar would return to power. He looked at her, waiting for her to read.

She skimmed the first couple of paragraphs of the article, and then she continued aloud:

> "... the jubilant Bolsheviks swarmed into the Palace. If many of them had perhaps imagined the moment, nothing could have prepared them for the magnificence behind

those heavy doors. They surged into the lower halls and rooms, stopping as they came face to face with all the blatant and undisguised wealth, staring at paintings, tapestries, statues, gold and silverware, beautifully hand-crafted floors, wall coverings and exquisite furniture. Then the spell broke, and they pushed their way noisily up the wide staircases, wanting only to plunder and destroy.
There was a crash as something fell to the floor. This was the signal the crowd had been waiting for, and the destruction could have been complete but for one of the Bolsheviks taking control. He stood at the top of the main staircase and demanded the people to be silent: 'All of this belongs to us now. Nothing is to be taken or destroyed'. "

Rozalija stopped reading and looked across at her husband. "It could have been much worse."

She folded the newspaper noisily and returned it to the table. "Zacharias, where will it all end?" She was upset and angry. Was this what Jānis had been hoping for?

Aloud she wondered, "What good can come of it?"

Zacharias shook his head without saying anything. He was also angry. His beloved Tsar was gone. Even the new government was no more, and nothing was any longer as it should have been. He felt as though his part of the world – the only part he had ever known – had somehow broken away from the axis and was speeding into some undiscovered region of space. He sensed a raw, primitive thrust behind everything that was happening, and he feared that things could only get worse.

Rozalija picked up her son's letter again and turned to the last page:

"'I don't know if they found anyone in the rooms, but I do know that there were guards placed all around the Palace to stop any plundering. So you can tell Jānis that there are both good Bolsheviks and not-so-good Bolsheviks.'"

Rozalija looked across at her youngest son sitting in a chair by the stove. It was only a couple of weeks since he had come home, and he sat with a blanket around his shoulders, his eyes closed. At the mention of his name, he opened his eyes.

"Just like Maksis!" he said, the slightest suggestion of a smile appearing on his face. "'Good Bolsheviks and not-so-good Bolsheviks'. At least he has begun to realize that some of them are good."

Rozalija said nothing. She looked down at the letter and then continued reading, wanting to find some reason not to worry.

"'Lenin is now chairman. We can only hope that he will be a good Bolshevik, and perhaps he will be able to bring some order to all the chaos. It would have been better if things could have remained as they were, with the Tsar in control, but that was not to be. We don't know anything about Kerensky, though some say that he may have fled the country...'"

The Provisional Government was no more, but many of those who had been part of the government quickly reunited to form the White Guard. When elections were held in November, the Bolsheviks, failing to get a majority, dissolved the Assembly and put themselves in control: the Russian Civil War had become a reality.

It was a miserable, grey, wet-windy day in early October when Rozalija opened the door to find him standing outside on the step, leaning on another man in uniform. She was not expecting him; she did not even know that his unit was stationed outside the city. She stood there for a moment, forcing herself through layer after layer of opaque incomprehension, while the sergeant helped him through the doorway and on to a chair. The stranger then stepped back, tipping his cap, looking slightly awkward and out of place.

Later, Rozalija could not remember much more than the man helping her son inside and the hand touching the cap. She wondered whether or not she even thanked the man. She had an incomplete memory of the door opening and closing and steps fading away in the distance; she had only been concentrating on her son, trying to find the point of connection between the immediate past and the present.

Jānis has consumption, like his father and his grandfather, and Rozalija knows that he is not expected to live; just as Hermanis was not expected to live. Rozalija is sure that she can cure him, but then she thinks of Hermanis, and she shudders at the insanity of it all. Now that she has Jānis home again, she does not want to think of him leaving; she knows that she should never have let Hermanis go.

XXV

The doctor, a middle-aged man with a constant worried look and tired-looking shoes, makes careful note of that which is obvious before retiring to the small kitchen.

"I can't say why she died," he says, looking out the window on to the children's playground below. "Admittedly, she was no longer young. Eventually, everything stops and then..."

Perhaps he is going to say that that is when we die; instead, he turns around from the window, almost as though he has suddenly lost interest in the seagulls arguing and the children throwing sand while mothers, rocking prams and talking with neighbours, pretend not to notice. He looks at the man in front of him, hoping that he might understand.

Andris nods, thinking about everything stopping. Without warning? Or did she know? He thinks how difficult her life had been and how she had never complained.

The doctor has already gathered up his papers from the kitchen table. "I am really very sorry for your loss," he says.

Andris nods again and shakes hands with the doctor. He listens to him closing the door and descending the stairs. He listens to the quietness once more taking charge. He remains in the kitchen for a while, and then he returns to the bedroom. The men from the funeral parlour will soon arrive, and then she will be gone. Is there something, anything, he can do to prevent the inevitable? Should he reach out to someone and say: 'Stop!' before it is too late? He is not sure. He sits on a chair with his own thoughts. And waits. Soon she will be gone, and then the little flat will be completely empty.

XXVI

As 1917 slowly moved into 1918, snowstorms swept across the landscape, and temperatures dropped suddenly like heavy metallic stones thrown down dark, bottomless wells. Birds – small ice sculptures that could no longer fly – fell dead out of the sky. People huddled in inadequate buildings, without food or fuel, where the choice between life and death had been all but obliterated.

Spread out across this cold, white world, where birds had forgotten how to fly, the small spider-web cracks of deserting soldiers gradually widened into deep fissures as more and more men left the battlefields to join the Bolsheviks. The old Russian army had been disintegrating into these cracks, and then fissures, for months, and most of the Riflemen, spurred on by the idea of a 'free Latvia in a free Russia', were now part of the Red Army. Other Riflemen, who did not not agree with the Bolsheviks, had joined aristocrats and officers from the Imperial Army, hoping to stop the cracks from spreading further.

Hermanis agreed with those who wanted a free Latvia, but he abhorred all the years of killing and destruction; all he wanted was for the war to end. But, despite what he may have wanted, and as winter was turning everything into one continuous frozen instant without any connection to time, and as lines in the spider web became more and more distinct, he and the men remaining from his unit were ordered to move north-west to Moscow.

They climbed on to trains when trains came, and, when there were no trains, they waited at railway stations or along the track. When the waiting became a long, unrelieved intake of breath, they tried to focus on life after the waiting, wondering if they would be able to breathe out again, or whether the air would remain locked within them, wrapped tightly around their only remaining need: to survive. Sometimes, driven solely by that need, they walked through deep snow and across frozen waterways, the cold often fastening sharply in their noses, making it difficult to breathe. As they moved north and then east, they were aware of all feeling being sucked from their fingers and toes; it had been easier if it had been summer, but it was winter, and birds could no longer fly.

When they finally arrived in Moscow, they understood that the people were now in charge, yet, everything seemed to be suffocating under innumerable layers of confusion and chaos.

As some of the layers were peeled back by people searching for order in the confusion, the Rifles found themselves assigned to an area south of the city where a small scattered contingent of the White Guard had spent weeks trying to create its own solution to the chaos. But the Whites were disorganized and without strategy, and, within days of arriving in the area, the more regimented Riflemen had established a different solution. Then, without warning, the fever struck again.

XXVII

In Petrograd, we lived in a narrow, forlorn-looking brick house in a narrow street running off Nevsky Prospect. The house was hidden from the street by a large wooden door and a small courtyard. The door had a black metal latch, to which, in the winter, my snow-covered mittens would sometimes stick as I tried to force it open. Our landlady, Mrs Makarova – a stout lady with lots of very blonde hair – owned all the rooms on the third floor. She once told us, while checking the red, glossy polish on her nails, that the rooms had belonged to her husband but that he had gone away to war, and he had not come back. She did not expect to see him again. It was very sad, she sighed, but it was life.

After her husband's assumed death, Mrs Makarova became the owner of the rooms, and she let out one large room to Mrs Bērziņa and a small room at the front of the building to us. Mrs Bērziņa was Latvian and quite young, and she had also lost her husband. I often wondered how she had lost him and whether he had also gone to war and whether perhaps he was together with Mrs Makarova's husband. Whether their husbands knew each other or not, Mrs Makarova and Mrs Bērziņa were very good friends. They would often sit together in Mrs Makarova's sitting room, drinking pale-coloured tea and laughing a lot. I knew that I would have liked to have sat with them, but I always had to remain in my room with my books after school. I knew that Mrs Makarova was watching me, somewhere between the tea and the laughing.

Mrs Makarova occasionally had gentlemen visitors, though

she assured me that it was all very proper. At the time I was not sure what she actually meant by the word *proper*, and I once asked Maksis, but he just shrugged and continued reading the newspaper. Years later, I realized that the word could mean so many different things and that, for some people, Mrs Makarova's *proper* may not have been proper at all. But that was many years later; by then, it really made no difference what the word meant.

Like most people in Petrograd, we thought constantly about food, simply because there was none. Very little was reaching the city and that which did was often offered at prices that few could afford. Thousands fled to the country, hoping that things would be better there, but Maksis and I remained where we were. For some unexplained reason, Maksis usually knew where to find food at a reasonable price, and the proper gentlemen sometimes had food with them. We all shared what we had; none of us starved, but the watery soups and the grey, tasteless porridges did little more than keep us alive. Hunger had become part of life: I had already forgotten what it was like not to feel hungry.

A new year had rolled around, and Lenin's Peace Treaty with the Central Powers was not yet signed. Trotsky was supposed to get it signed, but he was waiting for the workers of the world to unite. The workers were still hesitating, and the Treaty remained unopened and unsigned. Trotsky knew what could be achieved if workers everywhere were to join together into a single powerful force. He could not understand why people refused to see what he could see.

When Trotsky was alone, he argued with himself, standing in front of the small mirror in his room, admiring his thick, curly hair and his short, black moustache. If Russian soldiers could lay down arms, then German soldiers should be able to do the same. And the French and the English. He smoothed the ends of his moustache and ran his hand through his hair, enjoying its thickness while continuing to think about all the workers still fighting an imperialist war.

But how long could he wait? Trotsky knew that Lenin was getting impatient; the civil war was demanding all his attention. He was prepared to give up the three Baltic countries and other territory, just to be free of the war with Germany. Lenin was desperate to put that war behind him, so that he could concentrate on Russia.

Trotsky continued looking at himself in the not-perfectly-flat mirror, thoughtfully. But if other soldiers lay down arms, then there would be no one to fight, and there would be no need for a treaty. And Russia would not lose her territories. He had it all worked out. It was just a matter of waiting.

Then, with the Treaty still unsigned and the world's workers still indecisive, the Germans began to close in on Petrograd.

XXVIII

The fever had quickly swept through the camp, leaving in its wake many exhausted men who, as the days collected together into weeks, were thankful that they had finally been able to pull themselves back on to flat, even ground. But there were others, like Hermanis, who knew that such a feat was beyond them. They were the men who, after days and nights of cold whiteness filled with fever and confusion, could no longer imagine themselves anywhere else; some of them had even lost sight of the longing that was still wrapped somewhere tightly within them.

When the fever struck, randomly selecting its first victims, they had made camp in a deserted farmhouse on the outskirts of the city, and, having buried their dead, they did what they could for the wounded and comforted the sick, knowing that the respite was temporary and that soon they would have to move on again. They had seen the tiny lines beginning to appear across winter's frozen face, and they wondered if perhaps the landscape was trying to decide whether or not it would be able to start breathing again. Those who had managed to pull themselves back from the abyss wondered if perhaps there would be a spring after all.

Through the haze of fever that had once again taken over his body and was now burning his skin and muddling his thoughts, Hermanis tried unsuccessfully to locate some form of logic in all the insanity around him until his thoughts wandered off aimlessly across tinder-dry, parched sand before falling into bottomless blackness. Occasionally, he tried to fix his mind on images of his family, and especially his little sister, but the images were all fleeting, and his mind could follow only some of them a short way before again falling into darkness.

Lying in the corner of a strange room, watching men moving shadow-like between the light and the darkness, listening to voices fusing into strange, new realities and absurd, unconnected dreams, Hermanis tried to find some answer to what was and what had been. But, for him, the present was just one instant, incorporating everything that had ever happened; he was no longer sure where he was. Then there were the pinpoints in that one instant when everything suddenly went dark like a shutter closing sharply.

The men gave him water from a tin mug and tried to make him comfortable. When he became incoherent, they sat with him; when he had moments of clarity, they talked to him: about a free Latvia and how he would soon be going home. And, when he slipped behind that shutter for the last time, they sat quietly with him, praying learnt prayers to a God who no longer seemed to be watching over anyone. Or, perhaps, He was watching, but He had simply given up.

In Petrograd, in February, Nikolina said to Maksis. "Last night, I dreamt about Ermonis; he told me that he was going home."

XXIX

It was the same winter that, like sheets of ice-dipped, silver-white steel, had wrapped itself around Hermanis and his men, removing life and obliterating the horizon. In Petrograd, it filled the spaces between buildings with a cold whiteness that covered the ugliness of a hungry city while temperatures sank far beyond the bottom of that cold, dark well, and it seemed as though everything had died. Breathing was painful, with white breath-clouds turning into thousands of small ice particles before settling on exposed eyelashes and the woollen fibres of scarves. Sometimes it even hurt to move.

The civil war was raging, and thousands of people were leaving the capital in any way they could, lured by the promise of food in rural districts. But Maksis and Nikolina were still in Petrograd; Maksis knew that trains to and from the city had all but stopped running, and that those trains now stood somewhere else and would most probably never reach their destinations. Like the minute ice particles sticking to clothing, frustration and despair had become an integral part of the winter scene around which everything else clung tightly, having no other option.

Then, when everyone thought it was impossible, the winter let out a long, almost inaudible, sigh and slowly began to make its retreat, rolling back the frozen landscape while beckoning to the sun. But the people had scarcely had time to fully comprehend the promise of spring before news reached Petrograd that the Germans were approaching the city, having crossed from the Åland Islands to Finland. Petrograd waited. Maksis also waited, thinking of the Germans outside Petrograd and the Germans already in Rīga. He had his sister to consider; he did not know what to do.

Then the trains stopped completely, and no one was able to move into or out of the city. Lenin shifted the capital to Moscow further away from the Germans. His Peace Treaty was still not signed, and, while he continued to worry about the Germans and the workers and the civil war, the German army moved even closer.

Maksis was being pushed into a corner; he knew that he would have to act.

At the beginning of March, Trotsky, finally despairing of the world's workers and knowing that he could wait no longer, had the Treaty signed. Before the ink had had time to dry, Russia pulled out of the war, and the German troops fell back from Petrograd. Trotsky could only shake his head, wondering why others had not been able to see what he had been able to see. The cost was significant: Russia lost many of her territories, including the Baltic countries, the Ukraine, Poland, Finland and the Åland Islands.

Maksis decided that he and Nina would stay where they were.

XXX

When I was still a child, Jānis would run races with me along dirt roads and cobbled streets or across fields. Sometimes he won; many times I won, and it was not until much later that I understood why I had won, but, by that time, everyone was running, and there could be no winners.

As the war exploded into, and then past, the October Revolution, and thousands of Russian soldiers and many Riflemen joined the Bolsheviks, it seemed as though even Latvia had a chance of winning. But although Lenin may have been dependent on the Latvian Riflemen for victory, he did not want independence in the Baltic. He had no intention of letting the Balts win.

Jānis was still at home in Rīga, and occasionally he wrote to us, short letters where the beginning was already anticipating the end. We learnt that he had joined the Latvian Bolsheviks, and I imagined meetings in bare, bleak rooms with rows of chairs and speakers talking about Peace, Land and Bread; I could almost hear subdued cheering. But, as we moved into 1918, there would already have been many Latvians questioning what the Russians actually meant by Land. They would have listened while trying to connect what they were hearing with what they wanted to hear. Everything was orbiting Russia, a sun in a new universe. Yet, the Latvians had always believed that the universe would have remained the same with the same sun, looking out on autonomous planets, each following its own elliptical path. They had always believed that a victory for Bolshevism would have also been a victory for Latvia.

By April 1918, Jānis was well again, and he told Mother that he would be rejoining the Rifles. She wrote to us and said that she wanted him to stay at home; she had not made him better to send him off to be killed. Maksis said that there was not much to be done if Jānis had made up his mind. I said nothing, but I agreed with Mother. I did not want Jānis to return to the army either.

Jānis wrote to us and said that he would be fighting alongside the Bolsheviks. He had been thinking about it for months; if Latvia was to be liberated, then Russia had to be liberated first. He also told us that he had married Marija.

Marija was one of the people in those small back rooms, listening to the speeches about land and the possibility of peace. She was a Russian from Petrograd, and, after her parents died of influenza in 1917, she moved to Rīga to live with a cousin of her father's. Marija's older sister, already married with three small children, remained behind in Petrograd, arguing that things were certainly no better elsewhere. But Marija missed both her sister and Petrograd and was on the point of returning home when she met Jānis, and then everything changed.

Like Jānis, Marija believed in the Bolsheviks, but, while she was hoping for better conditions in Russia, Jānis was only looking forward to a free Latvia. They may have discussed their hopes and what was really meant by freedom and land, and, perhaps, in some ways, their hopes were similar. They were both very young, neither of them had yet turned twenty. Jānis wrote to us of Marija's dark-brown eyes and fair hair that almost touched her heels. When I finally met her, I decided that I had never seen anyone quite so beautiful.

XXXI

In July 1918, months after the Revolution and the Peace Treaty, the Tsar and all his family were executed at night in a cellar. It was said that they had been calm and dignified right to the very end, almost as though they had been sitting in their own sitting room without men with guns. It only took a couple of minutes, and they were all dead, lying on the floor of a strange cellar. Could the people celebrate now – now that the Tsar was dead?

Rozalija thought again of the snake. Finally, she knew what her dream meant.

XXXII

With Jānis in the army, Marija, already pregnant, returns to Petrograd to be with her sister. Jānis writes to her saying that she should remain in Rīga with his mother; the situation in Petrograd is far too flammable. But their letters pass each other, somewhere between Petrograd and Rīga.

Rozalija follows her daughter-in-law to the train, wondering if she will ever see her or Jānis again. She stands on the railway platform, her thoughts filled with Hermanis and Jānis and an opaqueness, which she knows is the future.

The Latvian Rifles are fighting with the Red Guards against the Whites, who are now receiving support from Britain and America. The Russian people do not want a return to the past, which is what the Whites signify. Jānis, like other Latvians fighting someone else's war, knows that victory will mean a free Latvia. Lenin, still reliant on the Latvian Rifles and desperate for victory, has promised that a socialist Russia will definitely support an autonomous Latvia.

Then, in November, the war that everyone said would only last a few months finally comes to an end. The armistice signed by Germany cancels the Treaty drawn up between Russia and the Central Powers earlier in the year, and the Baltic countries, as well as other countries covered by the Treaty, find themselves free.

While the Germans are digesting defeat and the Russians are coping with civil war, the Baltic States hasten to have their independence internationally recognized. The Latvians paint a picture of what the Baltic could look like with Soviet Russia in charge – a sombre painting that the Allied Powers are quick to appreciate – and on the 18th November 1918, Latvia proclaims her independence.

Then, only days later, a Provisional Latvian Soviet government appears in Rīga as a prelude to the Red Army marching into Latvia. The Army is made up of both Russian units and Red Latvian Rifle units. The Latvian people are told that the Soviets have come to liberate them, but the people are confused. They are already liberated. They even have a paper to prove it.

On the sidelines, the German barons have formed their own government, and the Russians tell the Latvians that they will need help to fend off such an Imperialist attack. The Soviets are there to help them, but the Latvian people are divided: some want to believe the Soviets while others are more cynical. Many are beginning to realize that the Russian Bolsheviks do not want Latvian autonomy, they want Latvia to be part of the Soviet Russian dream.

There are now three governments in Latvia: the Provisional Soviet, the Baltic German and the Latvian, each with its own agenda. Soon, the Red Army controls all of Latvia with the exception of German-controlled Liepāja, the port city on the west coast. The Soviets talk about liberation while they confiscate private property and conscript young Latvians who had begun to believe that the war was over. More people become cynical, and many Latvians in the Red Army desert, no longer wanting to fight for someone else's dream.

Jānis is not among the Rifles sent to defend Latvia. He and his unit are still outside Petrograd, the shadow of what is yet to come already stretching itself across the city. He believes in the Revolution; he also believes that the Soviets are in Latvia for all the right reasons. He now knows that Marija is in Petrograd, and he has been able to visit her in the small flat on the third floor, where her sister and his brother-in-law and their three children live.

The Allies have left some Germans troops in Latvia as a buffer against Russia, and the Germans now join forces with the

Latvians. Ostensibly, the Germans are there to stop the Russians, but secretly they dream of claiming Latvia for the Baltic Germans and for Germany. The Latvians watch in silence while any hope of independence slides further and further from their grasp.

XXXIII

We met Jānis and Marija in Petrograd on a sparkling freezing white day towards the end of January 1919 when the snow talked to us from under our boots, and minute, dancing pieces of cold filled the air around us. We took the tram to the other side of the city, and then we walked the last few streets to where they lived. There was no door to the courtyard, but an opening, more like a short tunnel, joining it to the street. Near the stairs, leading up to the three floors of flats, there was a door and a few steps going down to a tea house. Jānis had told Maksis that we would meet in the tea house – there was so little room in the flat. And so many people. The man who owned the tea house, Sergei, had very little left to sell, but he remained open because he knew that people needed somewhere to sit and talk. Sometimes he was able to offer tea or ersatz coffee; other times, he sat on his stool, joining in the conversation and offering advice.

As we pushed open the door, a small bell tinkled somewhere beyond the door and the cold. We stamped the snow off our boots before we walked in and closed the door behind us. The room was dark after all the whiteness outside, and it took a while for my eyes to adjust. Then I saw him.

He had been sitting at a table on the other side of the room, but now he stood up and walked towards us. I noticed that he was in uniform and that he seemed older and more serious than when I last saw him, almost two years ago. It is possible that there was an instant when I wondered at all the things he had seen and all the things he had done, but I was already running towards him, my shawl trailing behind me, my arms outstretched. As he caught me in the middle of the room, he was smiling. I thought: Were his eyes really that blue? Then I burst into tears as months of loss and disappointment reached the top of the precipice and tumbled over. I was powerless to do anything, except hang on to him. I knew that I wanted to tell him how much I had missed him, but I was not able to speak. As I held on to him, I was also thinking of Ermonis, thinking how I had not been able to tell him how much I had missed him. And still missed him.

Perhaps Jānis understood. He hugged me back, and some of the sadness and longing of the last years fell away, melting in slow patches, like the snow from my boots.

With tears running down my face, I knew that I had not felt this happy for months. With both Maksis and Jānis next to me, I felt that there was now a chance the world might return to something resembling normal. Without Ermonis, I did not feel that it could ever return to normal.

Maksis had picked up my shawl and now he wrapped it around my shoulders before hugging his brother. I unbuttoned my coat and removed my mittens as I looked around the small room. Sergei was sitting on his stool, looking at us. He was smiling sadly; perhaps he also understood about longing and loss. He stood up and walked over to us. Today he had tea; would we like some?

Then, as we sat down at the table where Jānis had been sitting when we first came in, I noticed Marija. She had pushed her coat back, and I could see the plain grey dress underneath and the bulge of her stomach. Her fair hair had been plaited in a long thick plait, which hung over her shoulder and rested in her lap. Her face was a perfect oval, and her eyes were brown. She was probably only a few years older than I was, eighteen at the most, and I found that I was staring at her without wanting to, knowing that it was wrong but being unable to take my eyes away from her.

Jānis put his hand on my shoulder. "This is Marija," he said.

I thought that it was strange that he would need to say something that was so obvious.

"You are very beautiful," I said, still looking at her.

She smiled at Jānis, before kissing me on both cheeks. "I have so looked forward to meeting you, Nika." she said.

While they drank tea, Jānis explained that he had been given two days' leave. He did not talk much about the war or the fighting. He said that he was certain that the Bolsheviks would be victorious but that there was still a lot of fighting ahead of them. He spoke with Maksis about the Whites and the support they were getting from abroad. He said that it was a problem; then he laughed and said that the Bolsheviks had the support of the Russian people. No one wanted to return to a pre-revolution Russia.

Maksis wondered about the Red Army in Latvia, and Jānis was silent for a few moments.

"Latvia is so vulnerable at the moment," he said, turning his glass between his hands. "She needs support."

Maksis shook his head and lit a cigarette. He was not sure that his brother was right; then again, he could not prove him wrong. He was worried that Soviet Russia had another agenda that idealists like Jānis had not yet realized.

The conversation turned to other things while Sergei wiped down tables and pushed precious wood into the small stove in the middle of the room. Some more people came in and sat at a small table on the other side of the room. They took out a chessboard and started playing chess. A woman from one of the flats upstairs came down to talk to Sergei.

The afternoon closed in quickly. Though the only windows were small, narrow rectangles near the ceiling, it was possible to see that outside it was already dark while, inside, the four of them sat at the little table, pulled together into a soft, almost yellow, glow from the oil lamps hanging from the overhead beams. Maksis, a cigarette held between his fingers, watched the almost imperceptible movement of light across their table. It made him think about life, which caused him to ponder the inevitability of death. He was also thinking of the long trip home. Finally, he took out his watch and looked at it, then he stubbed out his cigarette in the ashtray and stood up, buttoning his coat at the same time.

He looked at his brother as Jānis pushed back his chair, and everything that had been said and not said pushed together into one single compact moment. They did not say anything but hugged quickly before Maksis bent down and kissed his sister-in-law.

Nina, holding her shawl in one hand, waited, not wanting there to be an end to what had been. Jānis wrapped his arms around her and whispered, "This is just the beginning, Nika. You wait and see!"

She stood back and looked at him for a moment, trying to smile, and then, having said goodbye to Marija, she followed Maksis out of the tea house.

XXXIV

At the end of March, Rozalija wrote to Maksis and Nina: '... and they are calling her Iskra Ivanovna Kindahle. *Iskra*! How could anyone be so unchristian as to name a poor child after a newspaper – a revolutionary newspaper at that?'

Maksis and Nina had already heard from Marija, and Maksis shook his head and smiled as he read his mother's letter. He admired his brother's unwavering belief in everything that was happening, but he had to admit that he also understood his mother.

Months later, when Jānis was back home on leave in Petrograd, he wrote to his mother: 'All that is needed is a single spark.'

Rozalija had then reluctantly decided that if *Iskra* stood for everything in which Jānis and Marija believed and hoped, nothing she could say would ever change her son's mind.

The Baltic Germans and the Germans and the Latvians fought together against the Russians. The Estonians moved down from the North, defending both Estonia and Latvia, and, by late spring, the Red Army was already in retreat. When Maksis heard about everything that had been happening, he thought back to the afternoon in the tea house in January and Jānis saying that Latvia needed Russian support.

The Allies, greatly relieved that the Russians had finally been defeated, ordered the Germans to leave Latvia, and many Latvians began to think back to November 1918. Perhaps Latvia would be liberated after all.

But the Germans had other plans; they argued that it was still too soon for them to withdraw, and England relented. By April, the German army was once again moving on Rīga. Most people no longer believed in a free Latvia, but they did not want to be part of either Russia or Germany. They had come very close to independence before their dream had gone into another orbit; obviously, their dreams were not part of the equation, other people seemed to be in charge of arranging the variables.

It was late April 1919, and Petrograd was holding its breath before the storm that had to come. The Whites, with support from Britain, Finland and Estonia, were moving closer to the city, intent on destroying the Red Army. Maksis told me that we could not stay any longer; soon it would be impossible to leave. I thought of March 1918 when he had talked about leaving and had then changed his mind. I also thought of Jānis and Marija and Iskra.

Very occasionally trains ran, but there was no guarantee that we would be able to leave, even now when we had made up our minds to do so. Maksis said that if there was no train then we would have to walk. I looked at him, wondering how long it would take to walk from Petrograd to Rīga. Wondering if it was even possible.

It was April, and it should have felt like early spring, but there were only greys and browns and the ugly shapes of barricades being built across streets and along the river. Maksis was anxious to leave before the Whites attacked, but he suspected that things were probably not much better at home.

Mrs Makarova, with her red lipstick and plucked eyebrows and red, shiny nails felt that we should stay in Petrograd, and she told us every day how much she was going to miss us. It is possible that I thought that I would miss her as well. She had been part of my life for so long, and she had always been kind to us.

Maksis still went to work at the railway although, most days, there was very little for him to do. He smoked cigarette after cigarette and studied the arrival and departure lists of the few trains still running. On the day he saw that there was to be a train leaving for Rīga from Vitebsk station that same evening, he left work early, knowing that he would not be returning.

We said goodbye to Mrs Makarova and Mrs Bērziņa, and both ladies cried and hugged me several times. Mrs Makarova kissed Maksis emphatically on both cheeks, but Mrs Bērziņa did not kiss him. I think that, secretly, she quite liked Maksis, and she would have been too embarrassed to have kissed him now when he was leaving, knowing that she would never see him again.

We had squeezed everything that we owned into one large bag. Maksis picked up the bag, and we descended the stairs for the last time. When we walked across the courtyard, I could see Mrs Makarova and Mrs Bērziņa standing next to each other, waving to us from the window.

As we left the courtyard through the heavy wooden door, the sky was already turning a darker shade of grey, and lights – almost like small blinking stars – were beginning to appear in windows. We hurried along the cobbled streets, walking all the time in a south-easterly direction. Soon, we crossed Nevsky Prospect. There were people on the streets, but no one paid us much attention. We cut across a confusion of small streets to the canal. I had to run to keep up with Maksis; it was so important that we did not miss the train – if there was to be a train. He slung the bag over his shoulder, and he held on to my hand tightly. We crossed the canal; then we saw the dark shadows of other people heading towards the station. Perhaps there would be a train after all.

I was wearing thick knitted grey stockings and my brown boots. Beneath a heavy dark-brown coat, my grey skirt skimmed the top of the boots. The coat was the only coat I owned, and I had worn it all winter, but now it was not as cold, and I had left the buttons undone, letting the coat fly open, revealing the rough linen shirt that Mrs Makarova had so kindly given me. I think it may have once belonged to someone else, possibly her husband, but she had carefully taken it to pieces and then re-sewn it to fit me.

As we approached the station, I let go of Maksis' hand, trying to catch my breath as he hurried on ahead.

Beyond the cavernous entrance and station area, we could see the train standing dark and quiet against the sky. We could also see people near the train, but no one was boarding. Maksis asked one of them if the train was running.

The man shook his head and spat on to the platform. "Just another bloody rumour," he said.

Disappointed, we stood looking at the man until Maksis took me by the shoulder and led me into the large waiting room. We sat down on one of the benches, and Maksis put his hand on my knee.

I asked Maksis what we should now do, thinking of the long walk back to the flat and Mrs Makarova and Mrs Bērziņa. Wondering what we would say to them and if we would ever be able to leave. I remembered Mrs Makarova telling us that trains did not run any more and how much she wanted us to stay with them in Petrograd. For some reason, I thought then of Mrs Makarova's sitting room, where I knew that the gentlemen used to sit, and where Mrs Makarova and Mrs Bērziņa used to share cups of tea.

Maksis took out a cigarette and lit it, the bag on the floor. For a long while, he said nothing; then, with his cigarette almost finished, he said we would stay where we were. Eventually, the train would have to leave the station. With my feet tucked under me on the bench and my head in my brother's lap, I pulled my coat closer around me and, very soon, I was sound asleep.

Maksis was right. As the first glimpses of morning light began to appear in the east, the engine crew appeared from somewhere within the depths of the station, and slowly the engine began to come alive. Nina looked around her and saw that there were others like themselves in the waiting room, and that people were now beginning to board the train. Maksis took her hand and, hoisting the bag on to his shoulder, led her out of the building and on to the train. Finally, they were going home.

They returned home to a house that was not the same as the one they had left all those years ago. Hermanis was dead, and no one knew when or if Jānis would be coming home. Nina had been away for five years. People had changed; the world had changed; the past had slipped well and truly beyond everyone's grasp.

She visited Aunt Auguste in the little house not far from St Peter's church, re-acquainting herself with all those things she had once known and had continued to remember, breathing in the reality of her aunt's presence, thinking about Ermonis. And even Jānis. While she attempted to pull together the memories and realities into something that she could perhaps pretend to understand, it was Aunt Auguste, and not her mother, who remembered with her and who comforted her.

Later, in the summer, instead of proceeding east after the retreating Russians, the Germans moved further north, intent on defeating the Estonians. The Russians had been vanquished, and the Germans were preparing to claim Latvia as their own. But the Latvians and the Estonians managed to push the Germans back towards Rīga where they were defeated with the help of British troops.

With the Germans finally on the retreat, the Latvian army was able to concentrate on the remaining pockets of Baltic Germans who were still hoping, against all odds, to form their own state. With each victory, the Latvians moved a little closer to regaining their freedom, and people began, yet again, to run their tongues around words like *autonomy* and *liberation* and *freedom*.

In that same summer, while the Latvians and the Estonians were trying to overpower the Germans, Zacharias fell ill again. The disease had returned, and now it was stronger and more aggressive than before. He no longer had any will left to fight it, and he wondered if there was actually anything left to live for. He put the question to Rozalija and Maksis and even Nikolina, and they all told him that life was on the edge of a new beginning. He did not know how that could be possible: he knew that the Tsar would not be coming back; he was still bewildered by the demands for an autonomous Latvia; he abhorred all the killing; he mourned the son who had died, and the son who was still fighting for all the wrong reasons. At the end of August, he gave up wondering and he died. A year later, the Peace Treaty between the Soviets and Latvia was signed. Latvia was finally free.

Two

I

Everyone has now left. Even she has left. Two men came and took her away, and the small child within him wonders if she will return.

In spite of the warm day, the flat suddenly feels cold, yet he does not feel that he can close the windows. There is something without substance lingering in the rooms, hiding in the shadows, moving across the timber floors, pulling lines tightly around all that has been. He walks into the small lounge room that runs off the other end of the hall. He sits down on one of the chairs, his view of the window practically obliterated by a large green plant. He is thankful to the plant; it makes him feel safe, hidden and anonymous.

A book lies open on the table. He wonders if she had been reading it before...

He thinks: Why didn't she phone? Perhaps she didn't realize? Perhaps it all happened too quickly?

He touches the book as if to close it and then changes his mind. He stands up and walks out into the hall. He bends down and pulls on his shoes while he thinks: She didn't phone because there wasn't time.

However, he is still not quite sure as he leaves the flat, quietly closing the door behind him. She had always said that what she feared most of all was being on her own at the very end. She had always asked him not to let that happen.

II

In the early 1920s, the war in Russia finally ended, and clouds, heavy with the dirt and decomposition from years of fighting, slowly dissipated to reveal millions of bodies. The survivors looked around, wondering why just they had been saved, and, while they were wondering, disease and starvation brought up the rearguard, and even more died. Death's scythe swung low and wide across the country as thousands were either executed or slaughtered. Many fled. The economy gravitated downwards. There was no longer any industry, and farmers, frustrated by the many requisitions, refused to work the land. The government saw that there would have to be radical change. The country could fall no further; it had touched the hard rock surface at the bottom of the abyss. The only way forwards had to be up.

Most of the Latvian Riflemen who had survived the fighting in Russia had now returned home. Some were confronted by people straddling a virtual chasm between Red Riflemen and the concept *hero*, unable to decide on which side to stand. Many of them left their indecision lying on both sides of the drop, naked and vulnerable. But the Riflemen knew that there had been no other alternative. They had only ever wanted to free their country from Imperial Russia and to eliminate the threat of German occupation. For them, the way to achieve their goals was to liberate the Russians. They had seen Bolshevism as the first rung on the ladder of Latvia's own liberation. The sun might well be blood-stained for a time, but they had always known that it would eventually rise.

When the other Riflemen returned home, Jānis remained in

Petrograd. He wrote to Maksis and said that they hoped to return to Latvia one day, but, for the moment, they would remain where they were. Maksis was not completely convinced that this was what Jānis really wanted.

After Independence, Maksis began studying. The old Polytechnic Institute, for ever entwined with memories of Hermanis, had passed through several reincarnations before being reborn as the University of Latvia in 1923. By then, Maksis was well into medical studies. He was also married to Beatrise. After all the years of chaos, he felt that he was finally in control.

But such feelings are sometimes no more substantial than white foam clinging to the sand at high tide. He thought he knew where he was going – his sketch of the future had already begun to fill out with small details – but then, on a bright autumn morning, he read a notice pinned to the board in the Great Hall. He saw that there was to be a lecture by a French professor of chemistry from the Sorbonne. As he stood in front of the noticeboard, his sketch began to disappear like the foam into the wet sand.

Looking for a place at the back of the lecture hall, weaving his way past people already seated, he was only vaguely aware of the dark timber panelling and the high windows. From the windows, shafts of white light drew patterns over haphazard groups of students while shoes scraped and echoed on the hard parquet floor. Then the lecturer walked up on to the stage, and the subdued buzz came to a sudden halt.

The professor, a balding man who had already passed that point in life where the past and the future were still somewhat in balance, knew that chemistry was the reason, the answer and the reality. The sun, with its atoms and molecules, was part of his universe, but chemistry was his god.

"*La chimie*," he began in his soft voice, launching quickly into the wonder and mystery of chemistry, brushing away the complexities while highlighting the simplicities. Everything, he claimed, was dependent on chemistry; in fact, everything *was* chemistry. The whole world and every organism within that world was built on matter, and all matter was in a state of change.

Maksis took out his pen and wrote in his notebook: *matter,* the black ink glistening for an instant on the page.

The man on the podium talked about the relationship between various types of matter and how these relationships then create new matter with new behavioural patterns and new structures. He talked about breaking down matter to its smallest component. He became almost lyrical when he talked about energy. Then he spoke about entropy. He mentioned separation and joining, reactions and systems.

Maksis sat in the hall, listening. Nothing was new; yet, everything was new. It was as though he was hearing it for the first time. He was amazed at the connectedness and the simplicity of everything. It had always been so while he had been looking elsewhere, doing other things. His head whirled with the sudden discovery of a universe at his very own fingertips, and of his own place in that universe. He was captivated by the verbalization of a world he had never before considered. By the time the lecture had finished and the students were swarming out of the hall, Maksis had made up his mind: he would change his course of study.

His friends asked him to reconsider. "Why, Maksis? You've only three years left! Why now?"

Beatrise was not particularly interested.

Rozalija was apprehensive. "But you have responsibilities, Maksis!" she said.

And he thought how his whole life had revolved around responsibility.

Only Nikolina agreed with him. She had already learnt that life is fickle and unreliable. It was important to grab the moment; there was nothing to say that the moment would still be there in another week or another month.

He did not concern himself with anxious admonishments: he

had already made up his mind. He had been so sure of his path, but he knew that paths can veer to the right or to the left, without warning. He also knew that sketches were just sketches and could always be erased and redrawn. He believed that both he and his country were on the verge of wonderful things, and that the new anthem, *Dievs, Svētī Latviju!* (God Bless Latvia), sung beneath waving maroon and white flags, only confirmed what he already believed.

He first met Beatrise in 1920, only days after Independence. Everything felt positive; everyone was celebrating. They met at a party and, discovering some kind of a connection with each other, they later moved through the city, latching on to other joyful revellers while breathing in all the giddiness of freedom and opportunity. The following day, still riding on a wave of excitement, he proposed, and Beatrise accepted.

Before the giddiness and the euphoria had completely settled, Maksis was no longer sure that Beatrise had been one of his most responsible decisions. But his whole life had been about making responsible decisions, and he felt swept up in the thrill of being able to do exactly the opposite.

Rozalija did not agree.

"But Maksis!" she exclaimed when Maksis told her that he was getting married. "We don't even know her!"

Maksis thought that he did not know her either. He said: "But you'll get to know her. I'm sure you'll like her." Though, in fact, he was not that sure at all.

Beatrise was brought home to meet the family, but Rozalija had already made up her mind that she did not like her. When the tall, thin girl with the short fair curly hair and blue eyes stood in front of her, she did not waver in her decision. Beatrise, too tall to be called pretty and too skinny to be attractive, exuded some kind of an untamed, irresponsible excitement that pushed convention and tradition to the corner of the room and replaced it with something else. It was the *something else* that Rozalija did not recognize. Did not want to recognize. She was polite, but she had made up her mind: nothing would make her like the girl.

Beatrise, sitting in the small living room on Kalnciema iela, suspected that her future mother-in-law did not like her, but she decided that there was very little she could do about that. She moved closer to Maksis and placed her hand on his knee. She knew that it was important to establish ownership at an early stage. Rozalija pursed her lips and said nothing.

The following summer, Maksis and Beatrise were married, and it was the only time Rozalija was to meet Beatrise's family: her parents and an older brother travelling all the way from Jēkabpils by train. She discovered – not that she had expected otherwise – that she had absolutely nothing in common with any of them.

After the wedding, Beatrise moved to Kalnciema iela, and Rozalija, resenting some subtle loss of authority, retired further behind her wall of pain and confusion and concentrated on her work at the Jewish Women's Centre.

But, when Maksis talked about changing courses, Rozalija finally was forced to concede that she no longer understood her son. She shook her head; she needed security in her life after all the unreliability. She knew how important it was to hold on to a single strand and follow it through, not letting go. If she had not done that, she would never have survived. But Maksis would do as he wanted; she knew that as well.

Rozalija was now fifty, but she seemed much older. Her hair had turned white some years earlier, and beyond the green-grey of her eyes were the memories of people she had known and loved. People she could no longer reach. So many people had left her, and each person had taken with them a small part of her. Her father had died in 1916 while she was in Orsha, and her mother had died in 1921. She went to her mother's funeral and mourned both parents while, at the same time, she remembered Hermanis and Zacharias. Her sorrow had become part of who she was. She wore the same round steel-framed glasses, but they seemed to sit differently. Perhaps her face was thinner and her nose longer. She looked smaller as though the difficult years had pressed down on her too heavily. There were some lines on her forehead like an entry in a notebook or a diary: this was what happened. This was what it was like. This is what it is like.

III

It was the spring of 1924, and I had just turned eighteen. Maksis came into the house, holding a letter in his hand.

"Nika! A letter. From Marija."

The bright, fresh air, with a hint of summer, rushed into the house behind Maksis, through the open door. He was turning the envelope around as though he was trying to guess what it might contain.

I gave him a kiss on the cheek as I took it from him. We had given up expecting letters from Jānis; he did not like writing, and it was nearly always Marija who wrote. Holding the letter in my hand, I thought briefly of Iskra, who was already five.

"Well, are you going to open it?" Maksis smiled, pouring himself some tea from the samovar next to the stove before sitting down at the table. Mother was somewhere outside in the barn; Beatrise was visiting her parents in Jēkabpils.

Marija had written on sheets of thin blue paper that smelt of summer, though it was only April. On the very first page, she wrote that Jānis was dead. They were the first three words I saw when I opened the letter: Jānis is dead.

"Oh, my God, Maksis!"

For a very long moment, everything stopped. There was no movement; the world had stopped turning, and there was no sound. It was as though I had been thrown into some kind of a vacuum. Then the moment passed, and I saw myself clambering to the surface. I heard myself so very far away.

"No! It must be wrong! It's not possible!" Tears beginning to throb behind my eyes.

"But, Nika!" Maksis took the letter, read the same three words, pushed back the chair and took me in his arms.

It made no sense. The war was over. I stepped back from my brother and leant against the kitchen cupboard.

"Jānis can't possibly be dead. It's a mistake, isn't it? Tell me that it's a mistake." I was fighting against something that was trying to push me into the darkest corner of the room.

Maksis took my hand and sat me down on a chair. Then he sat on the edge of the table opposite me, still holding my hand with one of his, while he looked at the letter in his other hand.

He read quietly and quickly. Then he looked at me; he was also fighting the vacuum and the darkness.

He shook his head, searching for words. He put down the letter. "He was shot."

"No, Maksis, it isn't true! It can't be!" I remembered when we last saw him in Petrograd all those years ago. His smile was still imprinted on my mind, and my body had not forgotten the feel of his arms around me. Somehow, the whole room was filled with him, though I knew that he was not there, and I was beginning to realize that I would never see him again.

While Maksis held me tightly, part of me rushed headlong towards the end wall of a long, blocked-off tunnel, and the other part remained locked between my brother's arms. I knew that both parts were me, but they did not recognize each other.

"But, why, Maksis? Why? Ermonis and now Jānis."

Maksis did not say anything; there was nothing to say.

Our sorrow spread through the house and then, even further, until Auguste and Paulina and the rest of the family and friends dressed in black, and each of them remembered Jānis in his or her own, often strangely unfamiliar, way.

Aunt Auguste held my hands in hers and said: "But Nika, he is with God now, with God and Ermonis."

I envied Auguste her indomitable faith while I continued to wish that both my brothers were still with me. As far as I was concerned, God could have waited.

The April days and nights joined together into a long band of greyness that was broken only by diffused memories of Jānis and Ermonis. I could not understand why they had both been taken from me, and when I asked Maksis, he would take me in his arms and tell me that he was there and that he would always be there. While I held on to him tightly, I thought how Ermonis had also been there, and how then he was not. I thought about Jānis and his dreams for a free Latvia, and I decided that Life, pre-destined or not, was terribly unfair.

No one ever knew exactly why Jānis died. He was walking along the Neva one evening in early April, and an elderly Russian, who had been some steps behind him, said later that Jānis stopped to light a cigarette but then remained standing where he was, looking out over the river. As the man walked past, Jānis greeted him briefly, and the man soon turned away from the river into a side street. Behind him, he had already seen a couple of Bolsheviks approaching from the opposite direction.

The man had not walked very far when he heard a shot. Shots were still commonplace, but this shot was quite close, and it came from behind him. He retraced his steps hesitantly. When he came to the river, the soldiers were nowhere to be seen, but Jānis was lying on the ground. The man removed his coat and put it under Jānis's head. He knew that the boy was dying. He held Jānis's hand, and he thought of his own son who had not had anyone to hold his hand. The cigarette was on the ground, still burning, and he found that remarkable. He knew that he did not want to extinguish it, because it suddenly stood for something that he was unable to put into words.

It was chaotic in Petrograd, and there were new Bolsheviks rising in the ranks. They wanted to sweep away the past. They would not have known that Jānis had fought to give them the freedom they now had, or perhaps they did not want to know. Perhaps they were just two drunken Bolsheviks with a pistol. They were never found; no one really bothered looking for them.

So many people had died, it really did not matter if there was one more death. The elderly Russian came to the funeral and stood a little apart from Marija and her family. He had many things to mourn. He knew that the cigarette was no longer alight.

IV

By 1926, Latvia has been independent for six years. The Peace Treaty, with its twenty-two articles, was signed in the summer of 1920, but, if it was an attempt to draw a thick line through all the years of war and exile, everyone knows that there is no way of completely obliterating them. The treaty declared an end to hostilities, established Latvia's sovereignty, confirmed borders and even wrestled with questions of compensation. The words used in the second article, 'Russia recognizes without objection the independence and sovereignty of the Latvian State', have managed to erase the anxiety of some of the people, but for others, who have lost the ability to trust, it has merely incited suspicion as to how the words could later be interpreted, and whether, in spite of all the transparency, Russia could still be hiding something.

Despite all these formless suspicions, hope is becoming more tangible as democratic elections are held, reassuring the people that the future of Latvia is finally in their hands. But the democratic process is complicated, with voters being courted by a plethora of new and old political parties, each vying for power while collectively fracturing the power of the parliament to make any reasonable decisions. Frustration is unavoidable. Everyone wants progress and stability. But, with the kaleidoscope of perspectives on offer, it is becoming obvious that the way forward will be both steep and slippery.

Nina is now twenty. She is no longer sure if she actually had a childhood, for that time is all but obliterated by everything that happened since. The blonde pigtails have long since disappeared and with them many other thoughts and ways of acting that, in her memory, will always be tied up with the past. She smiles when she remembers how she used to wonder about the sun.

She is of average height and build and wistfully attractive while her well-formed mouth and grey eyes reflect all those things that have happened and cannot now be forgotten. Her skin is smooth and her face, slightly more oval than round, is framed by her hair which has now darkened. For a time, she wears it pulled back from her face, gathered into a thick, soft bun on the nape of her neck until, one day, she takes the scissors and cuts it short. Then she steps out of her long skirt into one that is not quite so long. It is called *change* and *moving with the times*. But, in spite of all the anticipation and optimism, the change does not quite eradicate the sadness in her eyes. The suffering and the pain of the past will remain with her, even as she is being pulled into the chaotic promises and the hesitating excitement of the post-war years.

Maksis has already turned thirty. While the difficult years may have sketched him with angular, hungry lines, he has now had several years to partially erase those lines, although silver hairs around his temples remind him that not everything can be completely erased.

He and Beatrise are no longer together. After Jānis's death, the dislike and the tension that had been smouldering between Rozalija and her daughter-in-law finally broke through the surface. Life in the small cottage became unbearable. Beatrise packed her things and left. Maksis wondered if the relief that filled the house after her departure was due to the automatic influx of peace and quiet or whether, deep down inside himself, that was what he had always wanted. He met up with Beatrise in a tearoom in Rīga a few days before the divorce, and they talked about some experiences being short and intense. They decided that the very essence of such experiences is their transiency. Beatrise returned to Jēkabpils, and Maksis never saw her again.

The Gregorian calendar has been adopted in Latvia, and Nikolina's birthday is now the eighth of April. Like everyone else, she is the same person, but, like them, she now has two birthdays. At first it is confusing, but eventually the *then* and *now* dates become part of life, and a new generation comes into being where there is no *then* and only *now*.

There are other changes as well: the Bolsheviks call themselves Communists, and, since Lenin's death two years earlier, Petrograd has become Leningrad. The biggest change of all is a free Latvia.

Since finishing school, Nikolina has helped her mother at the Jewish Women's Refugee Centre, an old house in the centre of Rīga. The tide of those who fled to Russia during the war has now turned; as it sweeps back towards Latvia, it collects some of the Jews who were forcibly exiled. The Jews return as refugees. They have lost everything, and Rozalija knows that nothing she tries to do can ever be sufficient. She helps them find shelter, provides food and gives hesitant comfort. She feels a close connection with these women who are confronting their own walls and their own nightmares. Like Rozalija, many have lost spouses or children or both. Each of them attempts to join together the few remaining pieces of a past into a new life. Many of them move on; some leave Europe altogether.

When Nina is not at the Centre, there is always work to be done at home. During the spring and summer, their new cow grazes on the green grasses behind the barn. In the field alongside the barn, there are potatoes, turnips and a grain crop. This year they have sown rye. Near the house, they have kitchen vegetables and a few bushes of flowers: pink and white peonies and white marguerite daisies. The sow and her piglets share the barn with the cow as well as some noisy hens and several cats.

Other times, she goes to the university and sits in on lectures; it is accepted practice. She is interested in both philosophy and literature, but occasionally she joins Maksis in one of his classes. She enjoys the atmosphere and all the new ideas, but she has no intention of studying seriously; change, described by cropped locks and shorter skirts, hesitates, standing on one foot, pulled back by centuries of prejudice and a paternalistic society.

V

Only a month before Zacharias passed away in 1919, Nina's Great-Uncle, Jānis von Korff, died of a heart attack. It was sudden; unlike Zacharias, no one was expecting him to die. He owned a house on Ūnijas iela, which was on the opposite side of the Daugava to Kalnciema iela, but he left no Will. Documents concerning the ownership of the von Korff house did the rounds of the Courts for four years until it was decided that his daughter Auguste had the greatest claim. In the spring of that same year, she and her son, Ernests, moved from their small flat near St Peter's church to Ūnijas iela.

By 1929, Auguste and Ernests have lived on Ūnijas iela for almost six years. It is summer and the house is painted brightly with July sun. Sunflowers, leaning against the stone wall of the house, hold satisfied faces up to the shimmering, white ball of warmth. Auguste has placed coffee cups and a plate of cottage cheese cakes on the table in the living room. Dressed in summer-white, Nina sits on the edge of the armchair.

It is now fifteen years since Auguste's husband, Ernests, died, and sometimes Auguste finds it difficult to remember what he actually looked like. He appears like a grey shadow on the edge of her mind, just beyond her grasp. She misses him, but she knows that he will not be coming back to her. She still visits the cemetery once a week and talks about what has been happening, and sometimes she tells him about her thoughts and her fears. She often berates him for leaving her on her own. She feels that he has merely changed his address.

"I really don't know what Ernests could be doing." There is a slight note of impatience in Auguste's voice as she calls up the stairs after her son and then sits down opposite Nina. She is a few years older than Rozalija, and, although she seems to have grown smaller with the years, her hair still retains some memory of its original colour. She leans across and pats Nina on her knee. "Have I told you how wonderful it is having you home again?"

Nina knows that she has said it many times, but she always loves to hear her say it yet again, amazed that anyone could have missed her that much.

"All those years..." Auguste's voice trails off as Ernests enters the room.

Like Nina, Ernests is now twenty-three. At some point, he grew past her, and round, steel-rimmed glasses accentuate the seriousness, which is now so much part of his face and his entire physique. His nose is prominent but not disproportionate, his eyebrows are high and rounded, and his lips are well-shaped, almost sensuous. There is a vague aesthetic feeling in the way he holds a glass or a cigarette – his fingers long and thin as though they would be more suited to making music or holding a paintbrush. His hair is dark and straight and he wears it swept back from his high forehead. Occasionally, it falls forward across his eyes, and then he brushes it back with an almost unconscious gesture that has become part of who he is.

Nina half rises, and Ernests gives her a kiss on the cheek.

"It's wonderful to see you, Nika." He smiles at her while he sits down in the only remaining armchair. "How is Aunt Roza?"

"She is well," answers Nina, her hand resting in her lap, vaguely aware of the softness of the fabric in her skirt.

"And Maksis?" He reaches into the pocket of his brown jacket and removes a thin cigarette case. He offers it to Nina who shakes her head; then he takes a cigarette and, while he returns the case to his pocket, he places the cigarette between his lips.

Nina notes the thin, white finger of paper held between his barely-moist, barely-closed lips and watches as he takes a small box of matches from his pocket. He removes a match from the box and strikes it: the sound, sharp and short, the flame, sudden and yellow. She watches while he holds the match between his long fingers and lets the flame connect with the cigarette. As he blows out the match and drops it into the ashtray, her eyes trace the line of his lips, making a detour around the cigarette. She becomes absorbed by the experience, forgetting where she is.

She notices that he is looking at her. Questioning her. Then he breathes deeply before removing the cigarette from his mouth, letting it rest loosely between his fingers.

She blushes, wondering if he is able to read her thoughts. "Maksis is also well," she says, folding her hands in her lap. "He will be graduating soon."

Ernests nods and pours coffee for the three of them. He is studying architecture and still has two years left. Sometimes, he sees Maksimiljāns at the university.

Aunt Auguste hands around the small cakes and returns the plate to the table. "Do tell Maksis to call by. I haven't seen him for several weeks." She thinks for a moment. "Not since Pentecost..."

Nina notices how the black fabric of her aunt's summer skirt draws a line between the chair and the floor as she sits down again opposite Nina and Ernests.

Nina promises Auguste that she will speak to Maksis. Then, while Ernests talks about a lecture he had attended a few days ago, her thoughts push well beyond the room and everything in it.

There was a boy she sometimes saw at the university when she was sitting in on lectures. Krišjānis was somewhat older. Tall and dark. Several times, he had waited for her outside the lecture hall. She looked at him and, for some reason, was reminded of Ermonis. He looked at her and saw someone special. He took her to a concert. Afterwards, filled with everything that they had heard and experienced, they walked through the park, holding hands. He wanted to see her again, but Nina knew that the relationship was as doomed as twigs in the swirling waters of the Daugava. She knew that both her mother and Aunt Auguste wanted her to marry Ernests – her mother going so far as saying that she had to marry him. But Nina was really not sure what she wanted. She would have liked to have seen more of Krišjānis, but she knew that any chance of that happening had already caught in branches overhanging the banks.

"You will, won't you?"

Nikolina becomes uncomfortably aware that Ernests is talking to her. "I'm so sorry, I... "

A dead butt is already lying in the ashtray on the table, and Ernests is wondering whether or not he should light a new cigarette.

"We're thinking of going to Sigulda next month," he says. "We'll take the train, and we'll be back the same day. Rikards wants to look at Turaida, and there are a lot of walks..."

"So it will be you and Rikards and myself?" she asks, interrupting him.

"And Aija and Ilze and Mārtiņš."

Nina sits for a moment thinking. She has been hesitant about meeting Ernests on her own. She knows that he will eventually ask her to marry him – it is inevitable – but she still does not know what her answer will be. She searches among all the emotions that are pushing their way to the surface. She thinks again of Krišjānis, and she wonders what she really wants. She knows what Auguste and her mother want, but she and Ernests are cousins. They have always known each other; they have always been part of each other's life. She pushes aside all the unanswered questions; a trip to Sigulda might help her think of other things.

"Yes," she says. "Of course, I'd love to come."

It takes about two hours on the train. It is a warm day, and they stand at the open windows, laughing at the breeze on their faces, breathing in the sharp smell of smoke, closing their eyes against the minute particles swirling towards them while the countryside rushes past. Occasionally, they wave to people in the fields, wondering momentarily at the gulf between *us* and *them* and the transitional shape of the gulf.

Ernests and Rikards lean back on the wooden benches and smoke thin cigarettes, their white shirtsleeves contrasting with their summer-brown skin, their jackets lying on the polished seats. Ilze sits with her basket of freshly baked pirogi next to her, and Mārtiņš reads a book, his elbow resting on the window sill. At some stage, Aija takes out some cards, and everyone, except Mārtiņš, joins the game.

It is hilly around Sigulda, and the sun is shining, accentuating shadows, rounding off hill tops, covering everything with a soft, glimmering whiteness. They climb the long path to the castle ruins, and, as the others space themselves in ever-changing patterns, Nikolina and Ernests find themselves together in the rear. She feels breathless from the climb, but she is also full of a strange anticipation and anxiety. She has never before felt like this with her cousin. She feels that something is expected of her, yet she is not sure what.

The silence and the whiteness and the heat mix together with thirteenth-century footsteps no longer obvious on the path. She wonders about the footsteps while she talks about trivialities. He nods and continues walking, his eyes on the dusty path. For some minutes, they walk in silence, barely aware of the white and yellow flowers stretching towards the forest. Even the lark's persistent song and the cuckoo's intermittent calls do not seem able to penetrate their thoughts.

As the path makes a sharp turn, Ernests stops and, taking Nina by the arm, says, "Nika."

She looks at him, the breathlessness and the silence coming together in one overwhelming moment. She thinks that if she were to cry out in some kind of response, there would be no sound.

"I must ask you something," he begins.

The tension is suddenly expelled. Nina laughs cautiously. "But Ernests, you can ask me whatever you want." Thinking that she knows what he is about to ask.

He looks uncomfortable. "I was wondering..." he begins,

removing his glasses and wiping them on his coat sleeve. "I would like to marry you, Nika."

For a moment everything stands still, and the silence that has surrounded her for the last half-hour becomes an enormous waterfall; the water is surging towards the drop, and she is on her way down. At least the tension has subsided, and she can start to breathe again, but everything has changed. She catches a glimpse of transparent sheaths of blue-white water obliterating round, black stones. Water above, water below. How far down? She does not know.

She loves Ernests. For so many years now, it has been Ernests and Maksis and herself. Ernests has always been like a fourth brother; he is part of Kalnciema iela in the same way that she is part of Ūnijas iela. But marriage? She is still not sure. Her thoughts keep going back to Krišjānis.

She looks at Ernests and wonders what she will say, thinking again of her mother and Aunt Auguste. She knows that her mother will equate a refusal with imminent disaster, and she attempts to grapple with what other people expect while wondering what she really wants.

Her head is bursting with what everyone else thinks and wants. Somewhere beneath the noise and the arguments, she wonders if she may want something else quite different, but she is not sure, and her thoughts cannot be heard above the thunder of the water. They drift off and disappear in tight whirls of white water to some place where she is cannot find them. She really does not have a choice.

"Yes," she says. "Yes, Ernests, I will marry you."

VI

In the autumn, Maksis graduated, but university had been part of his life for so many years that he was unable to turn his back on it completely. He decided to study for a master's degree in chemical engineering, and, at the same time, he started his own business – he found a couple of rooms in an old warehouse near the river, and Nikolina agreed to be his assistant.

"Fireworks?" Rozalija's face quickly dissolved into a pattern of questions when Maksis told her of his intention. "What a dreadful waste of time!" she exclaimed, a frown creasing her forehead. "Making things for others to destroy!" Her practical nature recoiled from the idea. They had just dragged themselves through years of fireworks.

Maksis had shrugged and stretched out his legs in front of him. They were in the kitchen, and Rozalija was standing on the opposite side of the table, pickling gherkins. A large ginger cat was weaving itself in and out of her skirts.

He placed his fingertips together and looked at his mother. He smiled slightly before pulling his legs back under the chair and placing his hands on the table. The manufacture of fireworks was both science and art, and Maksis could see no connection with the devastation of war; his fireworks were only about celebration. He painted his mother a picture of the stars in the sky and asked her if she still thought of desolation and ruin. He spoke of the joy and happiness that could build up inside a person, and then burst forth in words or actions or both. And he compared these outbursts to the colours and sounds of pyrotechnics.

From the heights, he dropped quickly to the valleys. To the

practical. He talked about the composition of fireworks, about chemical reactions and the packaging of the different combinations. He pulled a notebook from his coat pocket, and, quickly removing the top from his pen, he roughly sketched different fireworks before and after ignition.

"They come in so many different shapes and sizes," he explained. "It's all about colour and sound impacting together at the same time. Of course," he said, pointing at his sketches, "there has to be gunpowder for the explosion, and all the particles have to be just the right size – just the right amount – otherwise the result will be wrong. If you use copper in the mix, you'll get blue, and barium will make green." He only had the black ink from his pen to conjure up all these colours, but he was so involved in the excitement of it all that, for him, the black lines on the page were no longer black.

"And the red..." He leant back in his chair, suddenly aware that technical details were of little interest to his mother. He stopped speaking and placed his hands behind his head.

Rozalija had stood watching him, a cucumber in one hand and a knife in the other. She felt she knew Maksimiljāns, and she knew that once he got an idea in his head, he would follow it obstinately. Thinking of Beatrise, she was not sure if this was extremely admirable or extremely stupid.

"And you know that you will be able to sell these things, these fireworks?" she asked, deftly slicing the cucumber.

Maksis exhaled audibly. "Of course! Of course!" He was relieved. He wanted his mother to accept the idea; though, had she opposed it, he would have gone ahead anyway. The idea had surged ahead of him. He had already found interested buyers in Latvia, Lithuania and Denmark, and he had not yet given up on England.

He swung to his feet and embraced his mother. "Why not Kindahls' Constellations?"

He laughed quickly, then taking one of the uncut cucumbers, he disappeared through the door.

VII

At the beginning of the war, Latvia's industry was packed on to endless lines of rolling freight and was moved across the border into Russia. Consequently, when the war ended, Latvia was left without any significant industry. But there was land, and Kārlis Ulmanis and his government drew up a programme of radical land reform where most of the large estates were subdivided. Thousands of new farms were created, and peasants became landowners. The reform worked, optimism swept across the country, production overtook demand, and the beginnings of an export industry emerged. Soon, other industries, many connected to agriculture, began to reappear.

With Latvian farmers now working their own farms, there were too few hands left to work the larger estates, and migrant workers were brought in, mainly from Poland. Kārlis Ulmanis intended to eliminate the need for these outside workers by further division of the estates, but history intruded. In 1940, an oversight with the constitution was to push the country and its people into a place that no one had foreseen and where all thoughts of migrant workers and subdivision were completely superfluous. It was an error that could have been corrected; by 1940, it was already too late.

However, in the early 1930s, no one was thinking about flaws in the constitution. The economy was improving; people were beginning to enjoy a better standard of living. The future was bathed in sunlight; hopefully, all the heartache was now in the past.

Walking along the grassy verge separating the university

buildings from the small canal, Nina and Ernests would have agreed about the positive future, but they were not thinking of either the economy or politics. It was a beautiful summer day in 1931. The sun was warm and white, splashing the trees with a multitude of green tones, while, beyond the grass, ducks were floating lazily on the water, occasionally making their soft quacking sounds. Nina watched as a couple of them clambered clumsily out of the water on to the grass. While she watched them, her thoughts wandered back to Sigulda.

In the beginning, she had continued to wonder if she may have wanted something else, but, as the months passed by, such thoughts became weaker and less insistent until, eventually, they simply faded away. She decided that her mother and Aunt Auguste may have been right all along; she freed Krišjānis from all the overhanging branches, and now there was only Ernests. She squeezed his hand. She knew Ernests; she had known him all her life.

But Ernests did not want them to get married yet. He needed to graduate and then to find work. Auguste was impatient with him. She had been waiting so long. 'Wait and see!' she had said to her husband all those years ago, and now he was no longer there to see that she had been right all along.

Ernests was talking about the Schubert Impromptu; it was like water slowly flowing downwards from a great height. Had she possibly thought the same? He looked at her quickly, and she smiled at him. Perhaps rain on flat, polished stones, she suggested, thinking of them both sitting on the grass with its imperceptible film of evening dew, and of the orchestra with its back towards the river. Perhaps that was the connection with water? She thought of the piano, lifted out on to the grass for the concert, and the pianist completely lost in his music, oblivious of the people sitting on the grass, listening to his music; music that was water.

Ernests had moved on from Schubert; he had recently discovered Schopenhauer and Nietzsche. As the verge became wider and more park-like, Nina realized that he was talking about the futility of desire.

She listened with half an ear. He enjoyed talking, and she enjoyed twisting her mind around his thought-patterns. Sometimes agreeing, sometimes disagreeing. He once put forward Schopenhauer's theory that women, foolish and short-sighted, can never rise to the same heights as men. He had then added, with a smile, that he definitely did not agree with Schopenhauer on just that point. She had laughed and said it was just as well. She had also read what Schopenhauer had written about women, and she did not agree with him either.

She was tempted to respond, but it was a beautiful early summer day, and she did not feel like listening or talking. She raised her face to the sky, letting the warm sun caress her face. In one hand, she had a parcel she had promised to post for Maksis, and the other hand was firmly in Ernests' grasp. She liked the warmth that moved from his hand into her own, and she enjoyed the secure feeling of belonging.

Two young girls passed by, laughing at something they were sharing of which no one else was aware. Nikolina nodded at them and then looked at Ernests. He was saying something about desire causing suffering; she wondered for a moment whether she would say something, and then she decided not to give it too much thought.

VIII

I loved dancing. When I danced, I was pulled into the sound and the movement, and, for that moment, I became a long drawn-out tone, without weight, drawing hypnotic arcs across some wonderful, breathtaking dream.

Almost every week, I went dancing with my two girlfriends, Karla and Hermine. There was a dance hall in the centre of Rīga that had reopened after Independence. The building was quite large, with wide stone steps leading up to double doors where the doorman, resplendent in a grey and red uniform, usually stood.

He was an elderly man with white hair, and he would smile at me, past all the other people on the steps.

"Here again? And your girlfriends? Will they be coming as well?"

Barely a thought behind me, they would wave at him, and we would pass through the doorway into the room beyond. In the distance, at the end of the room, we would see the stage where the members of the band would already be taking their seats, and we would hear the sounds of chairs scraping discordantly on timber flooring, providing a background to the tentative sounds of instruments being tuned. Then we might note the polished floorboards sprinkled with powder, and the few dancers already testing the floor, trying out new steps, waiting for the music. From the floors, our eyes would move to the almost-pink walls with Grecian idylls in relief, linked by garlands of roses and flying birds.

Every week, I was swung out into a space that was infinite – a space that was music like the ocean was water – and, as it filled my body and my mind, propelling me before it, sweeping me along in its currents, I was sure that there was nothing else. Sometimes, I wondered if God knew how to dance.

In between the dancing, there was the laughing and the talking while the men in the band moved away from their instruments and smoked hand-rolled cigarettes, and the doorman opened the doors wide to let in the cold night air.

During the week, we altered our clothes, wanting to believe that our wardrobes were limitless. Once a hemline had been lengthened or shortened, or a collar had been carefully removed, we would add pieces of lace, or necklaces of small beads or brooches of richly coloured glass. Maksis would patiently resole my shoes, shaking his head and sometimes sighing while I sat next to him at the table, holding the small tacks, telling him about the last dance, attempting to recreate that wonderful intangible moment of freedom.

For Ernests, there was no division between life and music; they were so intertwined that the one was completely dependent on the other. Yet, while he loved music, he did not like to dance; instead, he preferred to skate. Sometimes, I asked him about the difference, and he would brush his hair back from his forehead and smile, or he would shrug and turn away, and the difference, if there was one, hung cobweb-thin in the air between us. We moved around the ice like separate entities, shadowing each other while I longed to feel him close to me on the dance floor. Every so often, when I was moving over the floor, my body filled with the music, feeling my partner's hand on my waist, feeling him moving with me in time to the same music, knowing that he was part of the arc cutting across the room, I would think of Ernests, and I would try to imagine that the hand on my waist was his.

I once said to Hermine, "You know, Hermine, I want to soar with birds, while Ernests..."

Hermine interrupted me, putting her hand on my arm. "You fly when you dance, Nika – so do I – but Ernests doesn't need to dance; music is what he is."

In spite of what I might have wanted, I knew that she was right. I remembered Ernests once saying to me that if music did not exist, it would have been God's biggest mistake.

"When I am dancing, I can sometimes forget that there are other ways of flying, and then I ask myself why everyone is not dancing. But you are right, Hermine, Ernests doesn't need to dance: he dances inside of himself."

Then I remembered Ermonis and his music, and I thought: for dancing to exist, there must first be music.

By 1931, Nikolina's days were completely filled with rockets and sparklers and bangers and firecrackers. Sitting at a small brown desk in a corner of the warehouse with a view of the river, she wrote letters in a neat hand, with blue ink from a white porcelain well on her desk. When she was not replying to correspondence or ordering ingredients, she packed fireworks into brown paper bags or cardboard cylinders, which she then carefully labelled before placing into boxes. When there was nothing to do, she talked to her brother, laughed at his jokes or made tea while Maksis leafed through notebooks or mixed the different chemicals with small piles of black powder.

"It's not a matter of just throwing everything together." he would say. "It's an art! Do I want an explosion? Do I want a slow burn? This is where I decide." And he would explain to Nikolina how one chemical reacted in one way with the gunpowder and how another reacted in a completely different way. "Big grains of chemicals will slow down the reaction, and even bigger grains will make sparks. Add aluminium, and we have the sparkler!"

She may not have understood the chemistry, but she enjoyed the sharp, earthy smells. When Maksis tested the fireworks, she was entranced by the colours and the small explosions, and, although she knew that there was always an element of danger present, with her brother nearby, she felt remarkably safe.

When there was little to do at the warehouse, Nina would sometimes cross the river to the university where, sitting at the back of the hall, she might listen to a lecturer explaining philosophical theories in the light of contemporary thought, or to a tutor discussing Russian literature or enthusiastically dissecting the Latvian *daina*.

Other times she would meet up with Ernests at the Laima Clock – the tall white pillar with the four clocks, each looking in a different direction – and they would walk through the streets or along the canal arm in arm. On wet, cold days, they would often sit in the library, talking softly until abrupt coughs and raised eyebrows would force them out of the warmth into glistening spaces between the stone buildings.

Back at the warehouse, Maksis was no longer just thinking about fireworks and explosions; he was also thinking about Elza.

Elza Kenkera, with her fair hair and blue eyes, was a year younger than Nikolina. When she met Maksis, she was living with her father and an aunt in the upstairs flat of a grey timber house in central Rīga, and, from her window, she was able to see church spires and the river. While the church spires may have caused her occasionally to wonder about the afterlife, the river reminded her of life itself, though its reasonably straight path contrasted greatly with all the twists and turns her life had taken so far.

Her father, a short, though somewhat solid, man with a heavy black moustache, was the doorman at a middle-sized factory on the outskirts of the city. Around his waist, he wore a leather belt with many jangling keys, and no one could enter the building without Jānis Kenkers first opening doors; in the evening Jānis was always the last to leave.

Barely a month after giving birth to Elza, their fifth child, Janis' wife died, leaving Jānis alone with five young daughters. Distressed by his wife's death and overwhelmed by the prospect of caring for five small children on his own, he turned to an unmarried cousin for help, and Sofija moved in immediately, willingly accepting the task of looking after the girls and running the household. But, in spite of her best efforts, two of the children died from tuberculosis before the outbreak of war in 1914.

As the war pushed itself into Latvia, Jānis Kenkers, who was working for a Russian company, was moved with the remnants of his family and Aunt Sofija to Russia. They were four, not counting Aunt Sofija, who fled into inland Russia but only three who returned, yet another sister having died while they were in Russia. Only a few months after their return to Latvia, Elza's remaining sister, Anna, also died, leaving Elza and her father the only survivors from a family of seven.

As each child died, there had been more food to be divided between the survivors, until there was only Elza left, and Sofija was able to keep her chubby and healthy while she continued to mourn the deaths of the other sisters, especially her favourite, Anna.

While Aunt Sofija enclosed the surviving child, Elza, in a protective bubble of food and love, Jānis continued to open and close doors, and around them the newly independent Latvia slowly began to spread her wings.

Thanks to her Aunt Sofija, Elza thrived, and, when she was twenty-three, she met Maksis. Two years later, they married on a snowy, white Christmas Eve, and, afterwards, Maksis brought her to the house on Kalnciema iela. Maksis knew that a line had to be drawn between the past and the present, so he moved out of the room that had been his and Beatrise's, and moved into one of the rooms upstairs. Hermanis had lived there before he had been conscripted. It was a room at the back of the house with a view of the chestnut tree.

When Maksis brought Elza to the room, he took her to the window and showed her the chestnut tree, completely covered with soft, silvery hoar. For him, the tree was strangely important; it tied together his past and his future. He would have liked to have explained this to Elza, but he could not find the right words. She smiled at him and said that it was a beautiful tree. She felt strangely relieved that she had been able to leave the spires and the river behind.

Beyond the tree, and leaning against the wall of the barn, there was an old wooden cart hidden under layers of snow, no longer looking like a cart but like a small, soft mound. He reflected on how deftly snow wiped things clean, changed them and gave them new identities. Perhaps that was what life was all about: change and new identities. Or perhaps it was just about change? He was not sure, but he felt that all the changes in his life had brought him to this moment. He turned away from the window and his thoughts and all his previous identities and put his arms around Elza.

He knew that his present was now with Elza, and he was thankful for both Elza and the fact that he had a present. Before the chestnut tree had shaken off its winter clothing and before the snow between the house and the barn had turned grey and brittle, Elza was pregnant. Maksis felt that he had a foot in both the present and the future, and, of an evening, he would stand at the window, looking at the chestnut tree, noting the changes and the permanence behind those changes. It told him that there would be a winter after the autumn and a spring and a summer after that.

When his tree, dark-green with summer warmth, was sending heavy shadows across the ground and the walls of the barn, Nikolina and Ernests circled the seventeenth of September as their wedding day. Maksis thought about his little sister. He felt he knew Nina, and he trusted that this was what she wanted. He really liked his cousin; he loved his sister. He finally decided that things happened in certain, predestined ways, similar to his tree changing its leaves.

IX

It is late afternoon by the time he leaves the flat, and the sun has lost some of its warmth. There is a faint evening breeze coming in from the lake, and the children who had been outside playing earlier have long since disappeared. He feels in his pocket for his car keys. He has moved from one side of a chasm to the other; nothing will ever be the same again. He wonders if the house and the gardens should now look different and that the street should show that something has happened – like in some films where a change in the lighting and the music indicate just that: that something has happened.

He reaches the car and opens the door. He sits down and rests his hands on the steering wheel. For a moment, he wonders what he should do next; then he puts the key in the ignition and turns it. The engine bursts into action; he indicates with his left blinker and pulls out from the kerb.

X

"But are you sure?" She looked at her brother, who was standing, one hand on his bike, waiting to swing his leg over the bar. "Are you quite sure?"

Maksis had said that the baby might be on its way.

Nina had spent the night before her wedding with her best friend, Lucija. They had sat up late, talking about then and now and free will. Thinking of Maksis and Ermonis and Jānis, Nina had argued that there was no free will; it was obvious that everyone is pushed in certain predestined directions. Lucija had disagreed. Then Nina remembered Ernests saying that happiness cannot be experienced without first accepting the pointlessness of desiring it, but she was not sure if this was an acceptance of predestination or an acceptance of indifference.

Nina knew that paths could easily swing off in unanticipated directions, but she had hoped that the path she was following might have continued straight ahead on her wedding day. She placed her hand on the handlebars and looked at Maksis.

"How is she?" she asked.

He was not sure; he should be getting back to her.

Nina let her fingers rest on his hand, still on the handlebar. "She'll be fine, Maksis." Not perfectly sure but wanting to reassure her brother. And herself.

Maksis smiled just a little and squeezed his sister's hand. He sighed. "Of course she will!" He positioned himself on the bike. "But today, everything must be perfect." Thinking about the wedding.

Elza had woken that morning with an unfamiliar sensation of pain. She had lain perfectly still, watching the shadow patterns on the wall from the chestnut tree outside the window. The grey-black shadows were moving slowly, almost rhythmically. For a moment, she almost forgot about the pain. Perhaps she had just imagined it; the baby was not due for another three weeks. Until that morning, she had felt in control of the space between herself and everything around her. But now the control was slipping away; in its place, there was a growing sensation of pain and fear. She wondered if there was anything she could do to halt the sensation, but the thought had barely formed itself before she discarded it, knowing that she was being swept into a place from where she could only move forwards, not backwards.

She also knew that she would miss the wedding.

She swung her legs over the edge of the bed and sat, her back towards the window, her face towards the large brown wardrobe in the corner of the room. The wardrobe door was slightly ajar, and there was a dress hanging against the door. She noticed how the colour of the dress cut across the monotonous brown of the wardrobe while her thoughts remained locked in the wall of pain that was slowly moving closer towards her. There was no door in the wall, no way out. Would she find a way out or would the wall close in on her until she was unable to move and unable to cry for help? The soft blue material broke into her thoughts, almost taunting her. It had been Nina who had helped her choose the material, and they had then sewn the dress together.

They had bought the material one day in summer, at a little shop near the park. It had been a clear, blue day with sunshine dancing across the dark-green bushes lining the paths. She remembered the children flying a kite and the woman with the pram. She also remembered thinking that soon she would be a woman with a pram. They had stayed in the little shop a long while, looking at different materials, letting silky fabrics run through their fingers like water, exclaiming over beautiful patterns, watching while the shopkeeper lifted down the heavy bolts on to the shiny timber surface of the counter, each time with a muted thud. It had been difficult with so much choice, but eventually they had chosen the blue material that was full of summer and sun.

She turned her face from the dress. Picking up her dressing gown from the chair near the bed, she wrapped it around her. More than anything, she had wanted to go to the wedding, and now she knew that she would not be going anywhere. She wondered if the baby could feel her disappointment and her fear. She was afraid, but if only the baby could have waited. She was not sure how long the baby should have waited; she just knew that she was not ready. And she had been looking forward to wearing the dress. She sighed, thinking that life was really quite unfair.

She could hear Maksis downstairs, and Rozalija was in the kitchen making tea. It was nice to be able to hear them moving around, fetching glasses, pouring water. Perhaps she had nothing to worry about after all. Then the wall seemed to move just a little closer, and she was no longer quite so sure.

After Aunt Sofija arrived later in the day, Maksis and Rozalija took a tram to the city's centre and then crossed a labyrinth of small streets to the small Lutheran church where Ernests and I were to be married.

Inside the church, the high, narrow windows split the outside light into long, thin fingers, running geometrically across highly polished pews and the grey, rectangular stones of the floor. Near the altar, white candles flickered with yellow light as people moving nearby caused small breezes to caress the flames. I can remember watching the wax slowly sliding down the sides of the candles, collecting on the black metal of the candelabra.

I wore ivory silk that brushed against stockings of the same colour. I also wore lace gloves, and, in one hand, I carried small purple and white dahlias. My other hand was in Ernests', a sensation of nervousness running from his hand to mine.

I remember feeling completely absorbed by destiny as though I was being carried along on the top of waves. I felt secure, knowing that the waves would take care of me. Perhaps that was when I turned away from the candles to look at Ernests, or it may have been when the Lutheran minister was reading from his prayer book, but I do remember Ernests smiling back at me while clutching my hand. I thought he looked handsome in his dark suit and white shirt. With his free hand, he brushed back his hair.

The organist, an elderly man with long white hair, played the Chorale-Prelude by Bach and then two serenades by Mozart, and the music filled the church, pulling everything into one memory. Even as we exchanged rings and, later, listened to the vicar's congratulations, the music continued to add multiple layers to that one memory, until we were signing the Marriage Register, Maksis and Lucija were adding their signatures, and I was no longer Nikolina Edvīna Kindahle but Nikolina Edvīna Āboliņa.

The river with its branches had long since disappeared, and all that remained were the never-ending waves and my hand holding on to Ernests'.

As we left the church, the organist was playing again. It was a well-known hymn, and the words kept moving around inside my head: We raise our hearts to you, O Lord. Around and around they ran, following us outside to where relatives and friends were pressing in on us, congratulating us.

We raise our hearts. I can still hear the words in my head, and then my mind stumbles over the continuation of the verse: Bless their future, bless their home... Standing outside the church on that autumn day, we could only be thankful that we knew so little about the future.

Two days later, on the nineteenth of September, Ilona Kindahle was born.

XI

In May 1934, the President, Karlis Ulmanis, frustrated by countless small parties and impossible coalitions, deposed the government. Since Independence, he had watched while twenty different governments passed from one side of the stage to the other. After fourteen years, he felt that he had no alternative other than to replace an unworkable democratic system with an autocratic system. He had a vision for Latvia, and he believed that he could realize it, but to do that he would have to have unlimited power.

There was no physical opposition. No one died. Life continued much the same as always with the difference that Latvia was now an authoritarian state. Two years after the coup, Ulmanis also took over the position of Prime Minister and became the most powerful man in Latvia. People were divided; many welcomed someone taking charge, others regretted the loss of democracy. Prosperity blossomed. Stability was introduced. The standard of living rose steeply to compete with that of other European countries. The dissenters began to wonder if perhaps Ulmanis may have done the right thing after all, while the believers felt that he had been sent to them by God.

The Constitution was discarded to make way for a new one that was to strengthen the government and prevent the rise of small independent parties. Ulmanis also intended to revise the part concerning the rights and obligations of citizens and the annexation of the country. Unfortunately, nothing was completed – an omission that would impact on the country and its people, for more than half a century.

Even in the mid-1930s, there is the smell of fear on winds blowing from all points of the compass. Europe is once again becoming cautious and suspicious, fearing the possibility of another war. In Latvia, many shake their heads: life is positive. People have work, and there is plenty of food. War is a dark memory relegated to the past.

Ernests reads the newspapers and runs his fingers through his hair. He cannot believe that Latvia will float in a protected bubble while the rest of Europe descends into chaos. Nina laughs at him. While she listens to his reasoning, she will not accept that Europe could once again be plunged into devastation and death. She opens the window and lets in the smells of early spring.

She moves more carefully now. Her hand lightly touches her stomach where the life she carries is almost visible. Only a few more months. She draws in a deep breath, feeling intoxicated by the heavy, earthy smells of spring grass, the familiar smells of Auguste's cooking and even the metallic smells of the tram rumbling past their house.

She closes the window, excluding some of the smells, and walks across the room. She wraps her arms around Ernests' neck. "People will come to their senses before it is too late – you'll see. 'Never again!' they said before, and we must believe them."

Ernests sighs. "Perhaps you are right."

She is so positive and so hopeful, while he is more realistic. He folds the newspaper and puts it on the table alongside his chair. He turns his head and smiles at her, letting his hand slide along her arm to her hand.

"At least, I hope you're right, Nika."

She leans over and kisses him.

XII

'Sigulda, September, 1935.

'My dear, dear Ernests,

'The weeks have passed by in such a haze, and I live only for your letters. I should have been holding her in my arms by now, and we would have been looking at the future together, all three of us. But that is not to be. She just passed by, and my arms are empty. For your sake, Ernests, I am trying...'

She sat with the pen still in her hand, thinking back to that day in mid-June when the wicker basket had overturned as she had crumpled to the ground. She had been fetching the washing from the line behind the house. For a moment, she had been part of the garden – the trees, the flowers, the line at the back of the house – and then, suddenly, she was no longer there. Auguste had seen her fall and had run out of the house, the back door slamming behind her. It had been a warm day.

'... to accept what happened. But do you think she knew how much we loved her and wanted her? In your last letter, you wrote that it is only the suffering of human beings that can reach such depths. Why must we suffer so? Do we become better people? I have thought a lot about what you wrote in your last letter: about the depth of suffering and about suffering caused by others being worse than suffering caused by chance.'

She put down the pen and remembered how Auguste had helped her inside, and how she had lain on the couch in the sitting room, feeling both cold and hot, with perspiration beading across her forehead. Lying there, watching the white lace curtain moving in front of the open window while it caressed the green leaves of plants in brown pots, she had wondered about the cramps and the nausea. The baby was not due until September. She kept telling herself that everything would be all right; then Auguste went next door and phoned Ernests.

'Of a night when I cannot sleep, I sit at my window. It is so very dark outside now, just the stars and practically no moon. There is a large lilac bush near the window, but all the leaves have been swept away, and the bare branches tap against the glass; sometimes I wonder if it might be our little girl wanting to be let in.

'I miss you so much, Ernests. It is lonely here with so many long empty corridors trailing off towards closed rooms, and the constant smell of antiseptic. Often when I am walking along the corridors, I imagine meeting you around the next corner, and then I can almost feel your arms around me and hear your voice.

'The gardens are beautiful, but, with the weather turning colder, I do not go very far from the house. Yesterday, I sat on the veranda with my book. There is such a beautiful view of the hills from there. I dozed off, and, when I woke, I thought for a moment that I was in Switzerland. Not that I have ever been there, but, for some reason, the hills appeared like mountains, and I found myself looking for small chalets and sheep with bells. Or is it cows with bells? Of course there were no chalets or sheep or cows, and then the bell rang for supper, and I remembered that I wasn't in Switzerland at all but in a sanatorium in Latvia.

'I want to come home and be with you, Ernests. I need to feel your arms around me, to hear you say that everything will work out and that you love me. You do still love me, don't you?'

Ernests wrote again about suffering and that life was all about finding some kind of meaning in the suffering. They had to move beyond their loss, put it behind them and learn from it. Their daughter's path was very different to the one that they would have willed for her. They had to let her go. They had not possessed the power to keep her with them when the very essence of her existence was non-existence.

He told Nina that he thought about her every minute of every day and that he loved her. He wanted her to get better. They would move on from this together.

While he wrote, his thoughts kept going back to that day in June, after his mother had phoned, and he had cycled home from work, narrowly avoiding trams and pedestrians, thinking only of Nina, willing her to be all right, willing the baby to be all right, willing everything to be the way it had been that morning before he had left for work, and Nina had stood at the gate, waving to him.

At the hospital emergency department, Nina was quickly led away by an efficient nurse and a tired-looking doctor, leaving Ernests and Auguste waiting on hard wooden chairs, listening to the cold echo of shoes on wax-polished floors. There were no explanations: just worried looks and a sense of haste.

Ernests lit a cigarette. She had been well when he left in the morning. He could not understand what had happened. Why it had happened. He got up from the hard, uncomfortable chair and walked the length of the hall and back. He did not want to leave. Perhaps they would call his name and tell him that it was a mistake and that she could go home.

When he sat back down on the disagreeable chair, his eyes rested on a small painting in a heavy frame. It was a painting of a river – it could have been the Daugava – with green trees and grass and flowers, and the light in the painting said that it had to be summer. There was something special about the painting that drew his eyes to it as it hung on the wall not far from the door. He had not heard of the artist, but he studied the painting until he felt he knew every line, every colour, every shape. Then, when he turned his head and looked at his mother sitting next to him, he realized that he had forgotten everything except Nina.

Eventually, they did call his name, and the tired-looking doctor showed him into a small examination room. He sat down, indicating an empty chair. Ernests sat on the edge of the chair, unsure of what the doctor was about to tell him. He felt in his pocket for his cigarettes.

The doctor sat in front of his cluttered table. "I'm sorry." His hands moved across some papers. He picked up a pen, turning it around and around in his hand. "Your wife is ill. Very ill."

Ernests had been trying to convince himself that things would be all right, and now the doctor's words crashed into his flimsy convictions, scattering them about the room. While he watched everything disintegrate, he wondered why the doctor should be sorry. Was he sorry for what he had done or not done, or was he just sorry? For everything?

The doctor said, "It's the placenta". He paused, looking at Ernests dubiously, but, when Ernests said nothing, he continued, "It has separated from the uterus." He looked down at the pen in his hands. "It is not common, but it does happen."

Ernests thought he may have understood why the doctor was sorry.

"Unfortunately, there is absolutely nothing we can do." he said, "We will try to save your wife, but..." He was silent for a moment; Ernests knew what it was that he did not want to say.

There was nothing left to disintegrate. "But you can't save the baby?"

The doctor looked at him and sighed. "Our greatest concern is for your wife, Mr Āboliņš. The baby is still too immature; it would be a miracle if it survived."

He looked past Ernests, possibly wondering about miracles. "We have induced labour, but your wife has already lost a lot of blood." He stood up, leaving the pen on the table. "If there was anything else we could do, we would do it." He looked resigned, almost sorrowful, as Ernests shook his hand and moved towards the door. He said, "Perhaps if you believe in a god..."

Ernests nodded without saying anything and left the room.

The doctor had told him that his baby would most probably die and that Nina might also die. There was nothing he could do, nowhere he could go. Auguste took the tram home, and Ernests returned to the hard chair by the window. He lit another cigarette and looked at the painting, trying to remember prayers to a God whose existence he doubted, and he waited for the miracle in which the doctor no longer believed.

Nikolina remained at the sanatorium until the end of September. When she came home, she walked slowly from room to room, absorbing the emptiness, wrapping herself in the grey chill that hung over the house. It clung tightly to her, though the fire was lit in the stove, and the heavy curtains were drawn against the cold and the darkness. Auguste came with blankets and glasses of hot tea, and Ernests told her that things happen, at times, over which no one has any control. He also told her how wonderful it was to have her home again. She took the blankets and drank the tea and tried to understand what was so wonderful while images of her father and Ermonis and Jānis and her baby daughter rushed past behind her eyes, and she wondered why people were always being taken from her. She did not have any answers. Rozalija told her that she could have another baby. Ernests said that he had almost lost the most precious thing in the world. There would be no more children.

At the workshop near the river, Maksis was branching into other inventions. He was experimenting with colour and the use of colour with different materials; he was also working on an idea for a pen with its own ink source. He made prototypes and experimented with different inks; he knew that the idea was unique, and he was excited by the possibilities.

The business had expanded long before Nina's life moved in another direction. Even before his sister left, Maksis had already employed two assistants, both with degrees in chemistry. Now he had more time to experiment though, after Nina left, he knew that he missed the neat letters that she used to write and the jokes they used to share. But Maksis was satisfied with his life: he had a beautiful wife, a baby daughter and a flourishing business. The country was prospering; at last he felt that he could put the past behind him.

Occasionally, in those long evenings, before summer and autumn turned into winter, he and Elza and Ilona would take the tram to the river to look at the boats. Many were moored in neat lines along the river's edge, while others sent out smaller or larger ripples as they cut through the water on their way to or from the Gulf of Rīga. Maksis enjoyed the sense of stillness and peace and the feeling of being part of a whole that stretched out beyond him in all directions. He liked to think that everything around him was safely protected beneath some enormous, invisible glass cover – a bubble that pushed all the devastation of earlier years beyond the boundaries of what was now considered acceptable.

They would walk slowly along the river bank, his arm around Elza's waist; he would smoke a cigarette or two while he thought about all the things within the bubble, and then they would take the tram back home.

Rozalija still lived in her room at the front of the house. The Refugee Centre had finally closed, and she spent her days cooking and cleaning and helping Elza with Ilona. Although they were now four people living in the house, for Rozalija it would always be filled with everyone who had ever lived there. As she moved through the rooms, she could see Zacharias, Hermanis and Jānis, Marija and Iskra. Sometimes she could hear Jan and Anu in the upstairs room. Very occasionally, she even caught a glimpse of Beatrise. While everyone else was forging a path into the future, she was still coming to terms with the past.

Sometimes, when she was alone, she would walk through the house, listening to her shoes echoing on the timber floors, sensing all the people who had once walked on those same floors while listening to the same sounds. She had lived there for more than forty years. She had been a young girl when she had moved in, and now she was an old woman. With the years swimming before her as she moved from room to room, she could see a younger Anu, and there was Jan. She was unable to make out his features, but he still had his cap on his head. Perhaps he had just come home from work? And there was Zacharias with his bowler hat and starched collars and his moustache. She sighed. He was a good man, she thought. A kind man.

Near the back door, she saw Hermanis standing with his back towards her. 'Turn around', her thought cried out. 'Please turn around.' But he did not turn around. He was looking at something she could not see and would never see. 'Was it really that dreadful, Ermonis?' she wondered. She did not expect him to reply; she already knew the answer.

Jānis was sitting at the table. He was laughing as he explained something for Marija sitting next to him. She had Iskra in her arms. Rozalija could not hear what he was saying, and she could barely see Marija and Iskra, but she knew that they were there. She wondered where they were now. Were they safe? Were they happy? Would she always remember how it had been? Did she want to remember? Everything?

XIII

In the barn, beyond the cow pen and just before that cluttered corner where there were gardening tools, a couple of old, broken chairs, a bike that no longer worked and some boxes covered with dust and cobwebs, there was a shelf. It was not very long, but it was deep and it clung to the inside of the barn wall, about a metre from the ground. Over the years, it had become home to the empty, coarsely-woven bags and the tired, old blankets that were used to cover the hen house in the winter when it was very cold. Mice lived there from time to time. And also cats.

I remember being in the barn one spring before Orsha. Before Petrograd. Before Ernests. Before so many, many people had died. It must have been late afternoon, and both spring and light were streaming in through the open door. There was no one else in the barn, and I stood there enjoying the feeling of being on my own. In the distance, I could hear the muffled sound of people talking in the house. As I watched minute pieces of dust dancing across the light-path, I breathed in the barn's earthy smell mixed with the smells of animals and feed and manure.

The cow had been let out earlier in the day to feast on the green nettles that were pushing their way through remnants of dirty winter-snow, already mixing with spring's bare earth. I could hear her moving outside the barn; inside, I was aware of the hens talking earnestly with each other as they scratched in the soil or sat guarding their small eggs. A pig grunted, and then a dove cooed somewhere in the darkness of the roof space above me.

I stretched out my arms and tried to catch the dust swirling past me. Someone had once said that it was not dust at all but tiny pieces of the sun that had broken away and had finally fallen to Earth. It was somewhat worrying to think of the sun disintegrating out there in space. Perhaps, eventually, there would be no sun left – no light, no warmth. But, whether it was the sun or whether it was just dust, it did not want to be caught, so I ran along the path of light to the back of the barn.

It was near the back of the barn that I heard the miaowing, and it came from the shelf beyond the cow pen. The side of the barn was in half-darkness – the shapes of all the things within that half-darkness painted in tones of grey – the light from the door not able to reach so far. As I knelt down level with the little shelf, pushing away the corner of some bags, I could see our black cat, Minna. She was lying down, looking straight at me, and, attached to her, along her length, were four small, wet things that I knew were kittens. They made tiny sounds as they blindly nuzzled closer to their mother. Minna and I continued to look at each other, sharing the wonder and the stillness and the pieces of sun that had fallen into our barn.

XIV

Since Independence, the State Historical Museum in Rīga has been housed in some rooms in Rīga Castle. Overlooking the Daugava, the castle is an imposing, fortress-like building on Pils laukums; it is also where Ernests began working after qualifying as an architect in 1932. Part of his work consists of photographing buildings and artefacts – photos that must then be carefully numbered and archived. Most of the time he works on his own or together with Valdemārs Ginters, the director of the museum.

In one the brown rooms behind the museum's exhibition area works a man called Roberts Dzirnis. He is tall and dark-haired and only a couple of years younger than Ernests. They are very similar, Ernests and Roberts: they are both serious and efficient. Occasionally, they work on projects together, but most of the time they work on their own, greeting each other with a wave or a few words when their work takes them into each other's space.

When Ernests raises his head from his work, he sees the river. In the summer, it is kissed by sun, and glimpses of it are caught between the many small boats jostling for space on its surface, while, in the winter, it is a long stretch of white, snow-covered ice. The photographer in him enjoys the view from the window; the architect is intent on preserving the past for the future. The castle has become a mixture of the past, the future and the present.

In his present, Ernests sometimes stands on the banks of the river, looking up at the stone walls of the castle that contrast with the black, wooden spire of St Peter's Church in the background. He leans his bicycle against the wall and stands for a moment, absorbing the pattern of buildings and shapes, somewhat in awe of the history surrounding him. Valdemārs Ginters likes Ernests. He likes the work he does and his attention to small details. He has invited Ernests and Nikolina to his home, and they have become friends both at work and outside of work.

XV

"Pleurisy is an inflammation of the membranes surrounding the lungs. It is not a disease in itself, but it indicates other diseases, usually tuberculosis. These small membranes, or pleura, which assist in the inhalation and exhalation of the lungs, are separated by fluid. Pleurisy occurs when this fluid disappears, and the membranes rub against each other causing inflammation and pain..."

Hospital. Hospital smells, hospital sounds. I was being flung out into space, and there was nothing I could hold on to. Ernests had insisted – I had been so ill for several days – but I needed to be able to hold on to something. I did not want to be pulled apart from him. Not again.

We had arrived at the hospital early in the morning, and now we were sitting in the doctor's surgery with the dark-brown bookcases full of books and the small window with no curtains. On the red-brown, polished floor, there was a thin rectangle of bright, white sunlight. The doctor, a short, corpulent man in his late fifties with grey, receding hair and small wire-rimmed glasses, sat at a desk to the right of the window. I resented him and his brown-red surgery. I even resented the light painted across the floor. I thought about my breathing, trying to breathe as little as possible.

He was still talking to Ernests. The words clumped together like cold porridge somewhere on the table between them. I had stopped listening. I was in too much pain, and it hurt to breathe.

The doctor broke off his medical evaluation, looking across at me where I sat in a straight-backed chair near the window. All I wanted was a soft armchair in which I could curl up and go to sleep. Yes, sleep would be so wonderful.

"Has anyone in the family had tuberculosis?"

He was obviously talking to me now. I shifted slightly, and the sharp, cutting pain of my next breath caught me unawares.

My father and a brother. My answer was staccato, the few words being forced out with as little breath as possible. They both died. Then I added that my brother was shot. I really do not know why I said that. It was hardly relevant. Ernests was looking at me. Curiously. I was thinking about the soft armchair.

The doctor nodded slowly. "As I suspected," he said.

I tried to stagger my breathing, trying not to breathe, wanting only to avoid the shooting pain. Not enough air. Almost drowning, I reached the surface and coughed suddenly, my chest burning with pain. My hands gripped the sides of my chair; my knuckles white, perspiration on my forehead, wondering what it was he suspected. That Jānis had been shot? That my father died?

Ernests looked concerned. "She has a fever," he said.

"Fever, chills, cough, pain," said the doctor, moving some papers on his desk. "It will have to be the sanatorium." He wrote something on a paper; then he stood up and came over to where I was sitting and listened to my chest with his stethoscope, yet again. He shook his head. "Most definitely," he said. To me? To Ernests? He sighed. "I'll fill in the paperwork. You can go now."

He looked obliquely at Ernests. "We'll see to everything."

My heart missed a beat. Not again. Not months on my own in cold, sterile hospital corridors. I wanted to object, but talking was too painful. Breathing was too painful. My eyes welled up, and I looked at Ernests. Surely he would save me?

But what could he do? I needed that soft armchair or a bed or something that would breathe for me. I felt both hot and cold, and I was thirsty though I knew that I could not possibly drink anything. I could feel the room beginning to turn and turn and turn...

After four months at a different sanatorium, Nina returned home at the end of 1937. During those four months, she had been an invalid not capable of doing all the things that other people could do, and what she did was completely directed by all these other people. She ate when she was told, and she slept when she was told. She sat out on open verandas wrapped in warm blankets, because it was thought that the cold air would help her lungs. She endured hot baths and cold baths, exercise and massage, enemas and hot fomentations, herb teas and poultices. She moved from one treatment room to the next, from one veranda to the next, from one common room to the next. She did not make many friends; people came and went, and it was not worth getting close to anyone. Occasionally, someone died, and the immediacy of the death and everything afterwards lay like a heavy cloud over the sanatorium for a few days, oppressing the remaining patients, forcing them to consider and to reconsider. What, after all, was life?

She asked Ernests the same question. It worried him. If she was thinking of life, then she was probably also thinking of death. He wrote back to her and said that life was everything – there was nothing else. She replied that he was being unrealistic, which was not like him at all.

She read many books, and she wrote long letters to everyone she knew. She also wrote in her diary that she still longed for a child. As the weeks passed, she began to improve; the pain lessened, and she was able to breathe again.

When she finally came home, it was winter, and, beyond the snow-covered fields and houses, there were grey clouds building up on the horizon. They were not clouds that were visible, but they were there anyway. For two years, Ernests had been saying that they would not have any more children, and now the world was descending into chaos all over again. Even if Nina had been well, they could not possibly bring children into a world that was about to disintegrate, in spite of all the *Never agains* and all the promises. He was adamant; there was nothing more to discuss.

XVI

By the latter part of the 1930s, people were already talking about a new war, and the talk filled my mind once more with the bleak images I had only wanted to forget. Tensions, like fine threads in some enormous web, were again fanning out in all directions before trust, clinging awkwardly to the very edge of that web, finally let go and fell. Ulmanis saw it fall, and he knew how vulnerable Latvia would be without it. He had tried not to offend either Russia or Germany, yet he managed to make enemies of them both. Neither was interested in his compromises: their agendas did not allow him to straddle the fence; they both expected his full support.

Then, in July 1939, fearing an attack by Germany, men sitting behind heavy polished desks in France and England signed eggshell-white papers allowing Soviet troops to enter the Baltic countries. Germany countered by drawing up a secret pact with the Soviets. The stronger countries were playing a game of chess, in which smaller countries could be easily sacrificed. Perhaps they believed that the means would be justified by the end, but I now know that they all had a different idea as to what that end might be. Whether or not it would incorporate the Baltic countries as independent nations did not seem to be of any great concern to anyone.

Years later – when checkmate had been delivered, and the game had ended – I was unable to remember what I had been doing on the third of September 1939, when Germany entered Poland and England declared war. I may have been buying food at the market halls in the centre of Rīga, or I may have been walking along the river with Ernests. As a day, it was simply the first in an almost endless line of domino days, all of which would, eventually, fall upon each other with a muffled cry for help, a cry which would run unanswered from the beginning to the end. It marked the beginning of so much tragedy, and, since then, so many other memories have pushed in, crying for recognition. I know that I have no reason to remember exactly what I was doing that particular Sunday. Though, through the haze of all those uncertain memories, I do remember that it was early autumn and that the dahlias were in bloom.

Although we were already aware of the ground moving beneath us in some kind of seismic shift, we kept doing all those things that had to be done while the news slowly found its way on to the airwaves and into the newspapers. Afterwards, we shook our heads in disbelief, whispering anxious words over pieces of meat being wrapped in coarse, not-quite-white paper, or beside flowers lifted from buckets of water on to other pieces of paper, on other counters, in other shops. I remember listening to England's declaration of war against Germany and wondering how it had been allowed to happen. Again. All the rhetoric had obviously crumbled into dust, like pressed flowers within the pages of some old book.

Ernests assured me that I had nothing to worry about. It is strange the small fragments that one remembers so long afterwards. So many other memories discarded along the way – only black squares and rectangles remaining in their place – and all those other memories: the colour of a plate hidden at the back of the dresser, the smell of full-blown, pink roses wet with rain, a stranger's fleeting, parting glance – they remain. Like Ernests telling me that I did not have to worry, his hands lightly touching mine.

I was still thinking about dahlias: the multitude of colours and each petal repeating itself. They grew at the front of the house, a show of red and white and purple, and I remember standing near them, kissing Ernests fleetingly and saying that I really wanted to believe that everything would revert to normal and that people would come to their senses before it was too late.

I thought that there was a chance he may have been right when he said that there was nothing to worry about. I clung to his words like a survivor from a shipwreck holding on to a small piece of sodden wood. I had heard Ulmanis on the wireless at the end of August. He had insisted that Latvia would continue to remain neutral if there should there be a war. Other countries had already declared themselves neutral. I thought of the other two Baltic countries, and I thought of Sweden, Finland and Norway. Perhaps there would not be a war; perhaps there would be no one to fight. I had smiled then, in spite of myself. Perhaps the world had remembered the rhetoric after all.

Only days before Germany marched on Poland, there were rumours of a non-aggression pact drawn up between Russia and Germany; a lifetime later, I heard of the secret protocols attached to that pact. Protocols that divided countries and territories into two separate piles. When I learnt about the secret protocols, I wanted to be very angry. But, by that time, I was drained of all emotion. Instead, I wrote a long letter to Maksis, in which I questioned concepts like *justice* and *transparency*. Then I tore it up and sat for a long while looking at nothing in particular, until the room became dark, and I got up and lit the lamps.

The war became a reality. The newspapers talked about fatalities, bombed cities, refugees, military manoeuvres. Everything was painted in black overlaid with multiple shades of grey. Sometimes there were photos, grainy and slightly blurred. It became more and more difficult to believe that things were going to return to any form of normality, but I tried. Latvia was, after all, neutral. I felt sorry for the people in the newspapers, people who had been reduced to part of a number or to faces in a grainy photo.

My memory falters as it attempts to find a way past all the blockages I have built up over so many years. I recognize the jarring sounds of trucks and heavy boots. Then, as I push my way past the blockages, I see Soviet troops. Truckload after truckload of Russian soldiers in Latvia. Independent, neutral Latvia.

"Have we been attacked?" I remember asking Maksis, Ernests and Auguste.

Maksis lit a cigarette and dropped the match into the ashtray. "I suppose you could say that." He drew on his cigarette, looking at me. "They're here because of bloody Ulmanis. Thousands of them, and they're setting up military bases all over the country."

Ernests leant across the table, looking at Maksis intently. "But, what choice did he have? They'd have done it, whatever he did or didn't do!" He paused before continuing, "What would you have done? Do you really think Stalin would have gone away if Ulmanis had said *no*? Do you think the army would have gone away? By God, Maksis, it was a blatant threat: Do as I say or else we'll attack! Could he afford such an attack? I doubt it." He removed his glasses and wiped them on his sleeve before setting them back on his nose. "Twenty-five thousand troops! Can you imagine! He was actually trying to save us, but this dice is loaded and not in his favour!"

Maksis raised his hands in the air, the cigarette tracing a small line of smoke. "You're right, of course, dear cousin!" He smiled and then ashed his cigarette. "A Pact of Defence and Mutual Assistance."

I remember him emphasizing each word with a short pause in between.

"I hadn't heard that we needed assistance. Had anyone heard that we needed assistance?" He laughed and turned to me. "Do you need assistance?"

I looked at him, amused and confused at the same time.

Ernests was more serious. I think that he still felt that he needed to support the President.

"You know, he didn't agree." He was playing with an unlit cigarette. "He didn't *not agree* either. As I said, he didn't have a choice." He rolled the cigarette slowly back and forth on the smooth timber surface. "He was trying to avoid a bloodbath."

Maksis smiled again but said nothing.

He sat for a moment, looking at the cigarette, before finally shaking his head and pushing back his chair. As he stood up, he said that it was already late and that Elza and the children – they now had a son, Jānis – would be expecting him.

But Ernests had not quite finished talking. He turned to face Maksis, who was already standing. "Imagine if Ulmanis had disagreed! Imagine what would have happened then!" He lit the cigarette. "Stalin does exactly what Stalin wants to, and if he wants to lend assistance, in whatever form, then that is exactly what he will do, whether we want it or not."

Maksis nodded, his hand resting briefly on Ernests' shoulder. Then he pulled on his coat, kissing both Auguste and me quickly on our foreheads before leaving the room.

As the outside door closed behind my brother, I was thinking of Stalin needing to lend assistance. I was also thinking of Finland and of what had happened when she refused assistance.

Ernests drew on the cigarette and exhaled the smoke. "But this has nothing to do with assistance. This is the beginning of something else."

At this point, I began to doubt Ernests' assurance that life would return to normal. Perhaps this was the top of the spiral, and all that was left was an outwards, downwards curve. I looked at him sadly, almost accusingly.

Ernests finished his cigarette, and, as he stubbed it out in the ashtray, he put his arm around me.

I lived in a strange kind of twilight zone that was somewhere between being at war and not being at war, being occupied and being free. Russian soldiers became part of the landscape. They went about their business, and we went about ours. We saw them around Rīga, but most of them had been sent to other parts of the country, especially to the West where they were building military bases. Many of them were very young; some of them may have even wanted to be friendly, but there were too many things in the way.

An open-faced Russian youth, who was standing on a street corner with a sub-machine-gun slung over his shoulder, confided in me that he did not understand what they were doing in Latvia.

"We were told that we were being sent to save the Latvian people, but I don't know what we are saving you from."

Then he returned to guarding buildings and people, and I continued walking along the street, wondering why we needed saving.

Others were less friendly. They had come from inland Russia, where life was mainly about eating and sleeping and copulating and working. And dying. Their needs were basic. *Civilization* was too long a word for them; they knew nothing about running water and water cisterns. But Stalin knew that he could use them. He did not care how they coped with the gulf between themselves and civilization as long as they obeyed him.

In June 1940, as the trees were turning from spring-green to darker green, and the lilacs were beginning to fade, there was news of a confrontation on Latvia's eastern perimeter. Latvian border guards had crossed from Latvia to Russia and attacked Soviet guards. We listened to the news reports in disbelief: we knew for certain that someone was lying. The attack was said to be a violation of the mutual assistance and defence treaty, and Stalin was demanding permission for the Soviet army to enter Latvia and form a new government. Then I remembered what Ernests had said all those months ago: this is the beginning of something else.

It was Sunday, the sixteenth of June, and Ulmanis had been given only a few hours to make a decision. Like everyone else, I was anxious, almost physically ill. We all knew that, whatever decision Ulmanis made, the Red Army would still move into Latvia. It had already entered Lithuania. I did not believe that the Latvian border guards had attacked Russia. It did not matter whether we believed it or not; we were all being swept along towards towering rapids, and there was nothing to hang on to and nothing to stop our pace. In my mind, I threw out my arms to stop our flight, but it did not help, and I could feel the coldness and the blackness slipping past my fingers.

We took a tram to the centre of the city and then walked to Brīvības iela. There were a lot of people around the Freedom Monument. They were not talking, just waiting quietly. There were also a lot of Soviet soldiers. Everyone was waiting.

We left the Monument and continued on down to the river. It was strange how quiet the city had become. Surreal groups of people stood clustered on street corners, in parks and outside buildings. Everyone knew that there was only one answer to Stalin's ultimatum, but no one would accept it. We drank in images of our city: St Peter's Church, the Blackheads' House, the Opera House, the Museum, the Dome cathedral, the parks and the Daugava itself, the cobbled streets and the narrow alleyways, the castle, the market halls and the Freedom Monument.

I closed my eyes and felt the almost-warm air against my face. I wondered why life was so unfair. I wanted to pull all of Latvia into the safety of my arms, but I was just an ordinary thirty-three-year-old woman, and my arms were just not that long. Ernests was leaning against one of the pylons supporting the bridge, smoking a cigarette. Did he still think that there was nothing to worry about? I looked at him. He seemed tired and drained. We all did.

There was no decision to make, as it had already been made in Moscow. Most probably weeks in advance. On the Monday, Soviet tanks rumbled into Rīga. They met no resistance, only the frightened, confused looks of a subdued people. We had hoped for help from the rest of the world, but its eyes were still on Paris. Latvia was on her own. No one was watching, and no one was listening. No one seemed to care.

Eventually, when it was no longer of any importance to the Soviets whether we knew the truth or not, we found out what had happened on the night of the fifteenth of June. It was not a surprise; it was simply a confirmation of what we had known all along. Everyone knew, though no one said anything openly.

Soviet soldiers had crossed Latvia's eastern border during the night of the fifteenth of June. We remembered that it had been a cold night and that there had been a lot of mist. Under cover of the mist, the Soviets had opened fire on several border stations. The border guards had returned the fire, but their rifles were useless against sub-machine-guns and hand grenades.

Three guards and the family of one of the guards had been killed, and many others had been taken hostage and later sent to Moscow. Then the Soviets cleaned up after themselves before returning to Russia and accusing Latvia of breaking the mutual assistance treaty.

After June 1940, everyone spoke softly, almost in whispers. Most of the time, they avoided having to speak, and they learnt to communicate in other ways. They stayed inside, and, when they had to go out, they kept to the shadows, their eyes downcast, fearful of feeling a hand on a shoulder or hearing a sharp voice commanding them to stop. They were also fearful of seeing things they were not supposed to see.

But, no matter how the people may have felt, it was important that the world believed that this was no annexation, that Latvia had asked to be part of the Soviet Union and that her request had been granted. All of this had been very carefully planned and orchestrated, especially the elections in July.

It was a breathlessly warm day, when Ernests, Nikolina and Auguste walked to the polling booth to vote. Like everyone else, they knew what the result would be before they had even voted. People had been told that they had to vote, and they were also told how to vote. Russian tanks stood blocking off streets while Russian soldiers with sub-machine-guns watched the people going to vote.

Ernests held Nikolina's hand tightly, a cynical smile playing around his lips. "What do they actually expect us to do?"

The newspapers, now supervised by the Soviets, assured the

people that the election would be completely democratic; however, only one party list, the *Latvian Working People's Block*, could be placed in the ballot box, and no changes could be made to the list. During the days before the election, from the backs of trucks and on foot, imported agitators ranted into megaphones about the government, the state of the country and the expectations of its people. They organized marches and demonstrations, giving the impression that Latvians were disappointed with the government and that they were looking for change, a change to Communism, the only possible way forward. No one was able to object; there was no democratic discussion, because there was only one Party.

When they entered the large hall, now labelled a polling booth, they were confronted by Stalin framed by two Soviet flags at the far end of the hall. He looked down on the people in the hall with a sardonic, triumphant smile. The face of Soviet Russia. Had he been able, Ernests would have immediately left the hall, but, along both sides of the hall, there were soldiers with sub-machine-guns. He took his voting card for the *Latvian Working People's Block*. Then, having identified himself, he placed his card in the box. Nikolina and Auguste did the same.

On the sixteenth of July, the Soviet-controlled newspapers praised the well-run election and made known what everyone already knew: almost one hundred percent of those eligible to vote had voted and all had voted for the Communists. It was obvious that the Latvian people wanted change. The Russians would help them achieve their wish.

There were some Latvians – members of the Latvian Communist Party and some Latvian Jews – who welcomed the possibility of change. Many of the Jews did not necessarily accept Soviet ideology, but they were concerned about rumours coming out of Hitler's Germany, and they believed that Soviet Russia might offer them some form of protection. A number of them were very well-educated and were given administrative positions within the new government; as the months wore on, the horror of Soviet rule caused some Latvians to regard the words *Jew* and

Soviet as interchangeable.

However, the world was not completely convinced that the Latvians wanted change. America condemned the takeover, but she was sitting in safety, far beyond the sidelines, and her voice could not be heard. Germany had already given Russia *carte blanche* in the Baltic area, and it was no longer her concern whether the takeover was legal or not. England had been pushed off the continent, and France had been defeated. Everyone saw it for what it was, but no one could, or would, do anything about it.

XVII

While a person is walking through a dark, dank tunnel, he has no way of knowing whether it is long or short, not until he has reached the end. When he finally stumbles out of the tunnel into the daylight, he might then lie down on the grass near the opening, breathing in all the different smells around him. While he relishes the sight of brown earth and wispy clouds sketched across a blue sky, he will fill himself with the smell of green vegetation still holding the lingering memory of rain. He will wrap himself in such smells and sights while he thinks back on the humid darkness of the tunnel and the frightening images that moved on the edge of that blackness. He will remember the gaping holes and the labyrinth of secret passages, many without any exit, and he will offer thanks to whatever being he had prayed to for deliverance.

Latvia's tunnel was a long tunnel of dread; when it came to an end, it was called the Year of Terror. It had a beginning and an end, but the sunshine-bathed hill remained a mirage as new tunnels and new horrors scattered the people in the darkness, until any remaining sense of direction was completely lost.

XVIII

Although most countries did not want to recognize the Soviet Union's annexation of the Baltic countries, they needed to retain diplomatic relations with Stalin. Foreign journalists in Rīga kept their articles simple, writing that the new government of Latvia, the Latvian Soviet Socialist Republic, had requested permission to join the Soviet Union. They also wrote that the request had been granted immediately and that it had been formalized on the fifth of August. Lithuania and Estonia had lodged similar requests and had also been accepted.

There was not much else that they could write. When they returned home to their own countries and their own desks, they talked about sins against democracy and the frightening, burgeoning power of the Soviet Union. They had long discussions on the legality, or otherwise, of Russia's takeover of the Baltic countries. They referred to the Latvian Constitution that stated that Latvia is a democratic republic unless deemed otherwise by a plebiscite, without always realizing that the Constitution had been suspended. They thumbed through books on the history of the Baltic area. They knew that they had seen the opening of the tunnel, and they were thankful that they would not have to enter.

Gordon, a young English journalist, had been sent to Rīga to write an article on the election. He kept it simple; he was overwhelmed by what he saw. He could have written much more than he did, but he also wanted to retain his position with the newspaper. He also wanted to return to England, to his family and his fiancée. All the things he could not write about in his articles he wrote in his diary, a thick black book bound in leather. He wrote more in his diary than he wrote for the paper.

'The Latvian Home Guard has been disarmed,' he wrote in fine copperplate with black ink, 'and the Latvian army has been incorporated into the Red Army. I heard that the Latvian officers have been replaced by Russians and that the Latvians sent to Moscow, on the pretext of attending special courses, have either been shot or sent to Siberia.'

After the last sentence, he had crossed out several words, frightened of having written too much, even in a black leather book hidden at the bottom of his suitcase, beneath his underwear and his pale-blue pyjamas.

Once something was written, it was there for all to read. It was his diary, but he had given the words on the page a life of their own. With life, they could speak to other people. Gordon was cautious. If he could have written in code, he probably would have done so, but he had heard such dreadful stories of people being tortured to reveal secrets. He knew that people were being tortured in Latvia. In Rīga. Where he was just now. He shuddered and put the cap on his pen. He would write more tomorrow. He wanted to tear up his diary; at the same time, he felt that writing it was the least he could do. In some ways, he felt like a hero, and, when he finally fell asleep, he dreamt of receiving the Victoria Cross, 'for valour in the face of the enemy', from the hands of the King himself.

The following day, he left Rīga and returned to London. He had no regrets leaving; he felt that he had done his bit for the war effort.

XIX

Some tunnels are gloomy, but they are often quite straight without complicated turns, and the ground underneath is dry and hard-packed. Walking is easy, even though there is not a lot of light. Also, it is possible to stand upright and even walk two abreast. Air rushes past in sudden bursts while small pinholes of light talk about sun and grass. Then a spot of light grows larger: the tunnel is coming to an end.

The tunnel of 1940-1941 that ploughed through Latvia was not straight, nor was the ground pleasant to walk upon. People walked in single file through mud and filth, sometimes crawling because there was not sufficient room to stand. When the path opened into unseen chasms, people disappeared over the edge with muffled screams. Those behind stopped suddenly, trying to find a way around the chasm in the darkness. They could do nothing to save those who had gone over the edge because the chasm was too deep and the darkness too black. There was no fresh air in the tunnel and no spot of light showing an opening. For all they knew, there was no way out and they would all inevitably succumb to the oppressive blackness, and fall, almost thankfully, into one of the gaping, bottomless holes.

As August slowly moved into September, Latvia's farms, chequered with late-summer, beige-yellow crops and green and brown fields, changed owners and became the property of the Soviet Union. Some farmers were left with handkerchief-sized plots of unproductive land. Others were left with nothing. While this was happening, it was proclaimed triumphantly that all land and everything on the land now belonged to the people. Yet the people felt as though they had lost everything. In silence, they watched the changing patterns as Communism spread its expanding shadow over the country. Few dared complain; no one wanted the chasm to open up before him. Everyone knew that there was no way out of the chasm.

The trucks and tanks moving across the country imprinted the new ownership, obliterated the individual and annihilated God. Religion was past tense and subversive; only organizations spreading communist philosophy were permitted. The people took on one face, and everyone was expected to think the same, act the same and believe the same.

Everyone was confused and anxious. The Latvia that they had known was slipping away, and it was no longer possible to reach out and grab hold of those things that once had been safe and familiar. Colours had been pushed aside by all the blacks and greys of trucks and other heavy vehicles. People had forgotten how to laugh; they did not even smile. When they had to go out, they always chose the shortest path, and they hurried along the streets, keeping their heads down. They did not talk, and they did not ask questions. They were all trying to disappear behind empty expressions. At home, they learnt to keep the windows covered and the doors locked.

Kārlis Ulmanis and his government disappeared down one of the many chasms. It was said that they had been deported and that they had died somewhere in prison, but the tunnel was long and it was impossible to know exactly what had happened to everyone.

After August 1940, resistance groups began to take form in the passages of schools and workplaces, behind closed doors and darkened windows. They were both a connection with the past and the hope of a better future, but the People's Commissariat for Internal Affairs (NKVD) found the passages, obliterating the past, drawing black lines over the future.

In the beginning, when there was still a vague sense of light coming from the opening to the tunnel, the questioning, the imprisonment and the executions were often hidden beneath a heavy veil of silence. People saw the veil and became anxious and fearful. Then the entrance to the tunnel disappeared behind a bend, and darkness replaced the half-light, and the veil was discarded. The people no longer had to guess. Now they knew.

Professionals, government workers, authors, intellectuals, politicians, known dissenters, suspected dissenters and newspaper editors all disappeared. All kinds of people disappeared and nearly always at night.

Those who had said or who had written anything against Soviet ideology were collected, without warning. Their families disappeared as well. Sometimes it was sufficient only to have thought something, and it was difficult to stop thinking.

People were questioned, tortured and executed quickly at the NKVD headquarters in Rīga. Others were forced on to trains and sent to labour camps in Siberia. Families were broken up. Men were taken first, but their wives and children also ended up in Siberia, separately, often without shelter or food. Very few survived, while those women who did sometimes married Russians – their only guarantee of continued survival – and tried to forget about their past.

Those who were left were frightened and silent. No one dared talk freely. Nothing was safe. There was nothing to hold on to, and the tunnel was winding downwards, perilously steeply.

And all the time, people wondered why the rest of the world had not reacted. Was Latvia really that invisible?

In black trucks, they came with guns and dogs. Our neighbours – Peteris, Maja and the three children – were forced out of the house. Idris was only a baby. Peteris had a small job in the government: an office job. Nothing at all political. The baby was crying, and Maja was trying to hush him. The older children were frightened. I could see the fear on their faces.

More people had now been dragged out of the house. The soldier in charge had a list. I prayed that our names were not on the list. I looked behind the curtain and saw how the people were being pushed into trucks: the men into one, the women and children into another. One man hid himself in the darkness and tried to escape, but a sharp pistol-shot stopped him short and left him lying on the side of the road.

My body froze. It was as though I had been the one shot. Auguste beckoned me away from the window. The three of us huddled in the darkness. It was worse not being able to see anything. I thought that this was the way it must feel when a person is blind: knowing that something is happening but not knowing what. Ernests put his arm around me. I was shaking. Outside, we could still hear the voices, and the heavy boots on the cobbles. Ernests shook his head and said something about groups of people and insanity. Then, one of the trucks drove off with a loud, heavy sound, gears engaging. I wondered about the man. No one attended to him. No one dared, and I could only hope that he was already dead.

The trucks had gone now, and it was quiet. Strangely quiet as though people were holding their breath for fear of making a sound. It felt as though the quietness should have been followed by a scream, a scream to put an end to the silence and to avenge those taken away and those left behind.

But there was no scream. The silence melted into the darkness, and we sat there unable to go to bed, too frightened to light lamps.

And they came again and again. Always at night, always with trucks and dogs. Sometimes they were further away, but we knew that they were there. Everyone knew that the trucks were there, and everyone prayed that they would not be taken.

XX

In 1933, the State Historical Museum takes over ownership of Rundāle Palace. The palace is near Bauska in southern Latvia, not far from the Lithuanian border. It had been badly damaged at the end of the Great War, and the Museum's first task is an extensive restoration project that takes several years. When the work is almost completed, a permanent exhibition of art and artefacts is set up inside the palace.

Then, in 1941, Valdemārs Ginters, possibly remembering how much he likes the work his assistant has done over the years, asks Ernests to be curator for Rundāle Palace. There is much to be photographed and archived, and he wants Ernests to manage the programme. There is also a castle mound near the Mežotne Palace, which is close by and which they have already begun excavating. Ginters will be in Rundāle during the summer months. Ernests accepts, and he looks forward to leaving Rīga. It is only later that he realizes the extent of the position he has accepted. He has been placed in charge of the palace and its staff and, in fact, the entire Bauska area.

Ernests knows that the palace was first built in the fifteenth century, and that it was completely rebuilt three centuries later by Count Ernst Johann Biron. Ernests now reflects that the Count and he share names, and he wonders if they share anything else.

At the museum, he finds a thin book about the Courland region, which he takes home with him. He is sitting with Nina after dinner, and he picks up the book and turns to a page he has marked with a bookmark. Nina says that she heard somewhere that Ernst Biron actually came from a poor peasant family.

Ernests nods, and then he reads how Ernst eventually won the favour of the Russian Empress, Anna Ioannovna.

Nina laughs. "A very brave man or an ambitious man?" she wonders, thinking of the Russian court.

Ernests, holding his finger on the page, not wanting to lose his place, continues, "'... the Empress, as his lover and his patron, made him the Duke of Courland.'" Courland stretching across the south and the west of Latvia.

Ernests is also thinking of the Russian Court and its intrigues. Then he reads how the Count arranged for Rundāle to be rebuilt and for a new palace to be built at Jelgava, the capital of Courland.

"'... then, unexpectedly, the Empress died.'"

Nina says, "The palace. Rundāle. Isn't there some kind of a connection with the Hermitage." She is back in Petrograd, now called Leningrad, walking along the Neva with Maksis, looking at the Hermitage. "Something about the architect?" Knowing that Ernests would have to know.

"The same architect. Rastrelli."

Then he continues, "'After the Empress died, those with their eye on the throne saw Ernst Johann as an uncomfortable hurdle...'" He turns to Nina. "You know, they could have executed him, but they didn't. They exiled him instead. Twenty years."

Nina thinks that things have really not changed that much.

Ernests reads that work stopped on the palaces while the Count was in exile. Then, after the twenty years had passed, Ernst Biron returned to Latvia and finished his two palaces.

"He actually managed to finish them both before he died," says Ernests.

He closes the book carefully. He does not have to read any more. He already knows that, after Biron's death, Rundāle changed hands several times, and they both know that, in 1919, it was very nearly destroyed by Soviet troops.

Before we leave, there are the goodbyes. How different it is saying goodbye when the goodbye is held between four solid walls, and there is no chance of it escaping. We are not going far, and we will be coming back. We will still be in Latvia. We will write. Often. Such a goodbye cannot last for ever. At some point someone will come and retrieve it, unpacking it from its tissue and lavender. It will be dusted off and given another name. It will no longer be a goodbye, and it will whisper softly about new beginnings. But there are other goodbyes that will not be retrieved. They will remain tied up in small packets where no one can reach them. Sometimes they will be forgotten.

Between all the goodbyes and Rundāle, I pick out images of train stations and Soviet soldiers. The soldiers have pushed themselves into everything that I remember from that time. They stand like a long chain, holding all the memories together. Yet, while I can still see their brown uniforms and their boots and their guns, I do not remember their faces. There was the grey central station and the brown soldiers and the queues of silent, brown-grey people waiting to show passes and identification cards and letters of permission. Permission to travel. Somewhere in all the miserable drabness, I see Maksis at the station, helping us lift our luggage on to the train. Then he steps away from the train, and I cannot see him any more.

On the train Ernests is asked, yet again, to show that he has permission to travel, and he takes out the letter from Ginters from his inside coat pocket. The soldier looks at it and looks at Ernests, then he looks at me and hands the letter back to Ernests, who folds it and returns it to his coat pocket. I watch him folding the letter; when I look back, the soldier has moved on.

The memory fades, and then we are at Jelgava, and I can smell the fresh, cold-tipped beginning of a spring day. A man is standing near a polished, brown carriage, and the dappled grey horse is eating from a feed bag. The man's coat collar is turned up against the early morning cold. He rubs his hands together and looks hopefully at the people beginning to move out of the station. He waits until the pattern of moving people has broken up and all but disappeared, and only Ernests and I are standing in front of the station. Then he removes the cigarette from between his lips, and stubs it out beneath his boot. He moves towards us. His name is Eduards; he will be taking us to Rundāle.

The goodbyes and the soldiers and the train all push together as we seat ourselves in the carriage, with Eduards in front holding the reins. There is no continuity of thought. I remember large black wheels and grey-white hindquarters moving rhythmically, stretches of brown fields – some veiled with an almost-green colour – stone houses and, elsewhere, lonely, blackened chimneys where houses once stood, storks and their large clumsy nests balancing on poles, and, in other places, naked, white birches, firs and knotted oaks drawing strange moving shadows across the road. I see Russian tanks and trucks, and I think how tightly birth and death are plaited together. Ernests is leaning forward, talking to Eduards; I listen to the sounds of wheels and horse's hooves, the creaking of the carriage, the larks and the voices.

Bauska is bathed in the light of early afternoon. Ernests says that we are almost at Rundāle. I look at Bauska Castle and think about different kinds of castles. This one is compact, almost like a fort. Behind the castle, I can see glimpses of a moving, sparkling river. But the dull-brown colour that is now so much part of Rīga has spread out from the capital and has reached Bauska. I see a few red flags; on the town hall there is the obligatory photo of Stalin. I know that we are close to the Lithuanian border, but for the Soviets the border is just a line that someone else has drawn on a map. They are on both sides of that line.

The images begin to press together.

Ernests asks, "Eleven, twelve kilometres?"

Eduards nods. The horse turns west. More fields and scatterings of trees. We have turned on to a narrower road. I can already see the palace in the distance. We pass a collection of small cottages. Eduards points his cigarette at one of them, and I look at it, assuming that that is where he lives. Now we are on a tree-lined avenue, now we are crossing a small bridge.

We enter the outer area of the palace, with its stables and

outhouses; in front of us, beyond the enormous gates, is the palace itself.

I sit transfixed, amazed by its size and its omnipotence. Never before have I seen anything quite so magnificent. Eduards jumps down and opens the gates and then guides the horse to the front steps of the palace. The palace is now stretching across in front of us, but it is also all around us, and we are in a huge courtyard. When I look back at the gates, I see that they form the only section of the rectangle that is not part of the palace building.

In front of us, very wide steps lead up to three massive front doors. The central part has three floors, but the rest of the palace is on two levels only. Then, I am out of the carriage, and, as I turn around and around, I can see the tall windows, the architraves, the wonderful stonework, the lions sitting on the gate posts... I hear Eduards tell Ernests that there are one hundred and thirty-eight rooms. Then he and Ernests lift down the luggage, and we walk up the steps into the palace.

After Rīga, Rundāle is cold spring air rushing into a room where windows and doors have been kept tightly closed for many years. A door has finally been pushed open on stiff, rusty joints and has then hung heavily, as far as it has been pushed, while air rushes in and fills the room. Rundāle air. I want it to smell of freedom, but I know that it cannot be freedom. It chases away the darkness and the rot and the mildew, but there is still a smell of decay behind all the cold and freshness.

Even with this other smell, it is better than a closed, musty, dark room. If I hold my breath, I can almost believe that we are free. I stop waiting for knocks on the door, because I can no longer hear trucks and tanks and heavy Russian boots on the street outside my window. We are in the country, far from Rīga. I try to convince myself that we are safe, and sometimes I can almost believe that everything is exactly the way it once used to be.

But things can never be exactly the same. Perhaps the light

falls differently, or commonplace smells are no longer familiar, while those things that have always seemed *normal* suddenly appear strange and, at times, even perplexing. Ernests has been put in charge of the palace, and I am expected to take care of the people who come to discuss the dig. There are three women who cook and clean, plus a couple of men who work in the garden. Then there is Eduards and his boy who look after the stables and the yard; when she is needed, Eduards' wife helps in the palace. All these people are part of the difference, and they become part of my present.

When we arrive, we find that Ernests' assistant, Antons, has already settled into the palace with his family. Antons, a year older than Ernests, is short, energetic and very ambitious, and I soon become aware of a carefully-veiled resentment. I assume that Antons had expected to be placed in charge, but, when I suggest this to Ernests, he shakes his head and laughs.

One evening, shortly after our arrival at Rundāle, Ernests and I walk through the garden, arm in arm. I have decided to ignore my feelings about Antons: if Ernests is unaware of any resentment, then perhaps there is none.

When we are back at the palace steps, he turns and kisses me on the forehead. Then, lighting a match, he holds it between his fingers, and we watch the small flame flare up and then quickly disappear.

"A whole universe!" he says, looking at me. "Generations lived and died in that instant. Perhaps they were people just like us... Time is so relative."

He smiles at me as we enter the palace, and I feel that my concerns regarding Antons have been given a slightly different perspective. There are other things that are more important. I think of the initials worked into the main gate; they are Ernests' initials. It is his palace, and I am his wife.

We live in the palace in one of the enormous rooms on the second floor, a room divided into two living quarters. From the windows on that southern side of the palace, I am able to look down on the baroque garden below, where paths fan out from a fountain near the palace. Between the paths, there are large leafy trees and rose-bushes; beyond the garden, which stretches to another set of gates, there are more trees.

On the west side of the palace, past the stables and the entrance, there is a large kitchen-garden where we grow tobacco alongside potatoes and vegetables. When the dark-green leaves are fully grown, we pick them carefully, then we dry them on ribbed grates; after several months, we pack the pale-brown tobacco into barrels.

Sometimes, I visit the exhibition area to watch Ernests working, or else I help the women in the kitchen or in the garden. Occasionally, we organize musical evenings with those involved with the dig at Mežotne, and sometimes people come down from the museum to check on the project or simply to break away from the darkness that has covered the capital. Several times, Ginters accompanies them, and then he and Ernests and Antons disappear to Mežotne. In the evenings, we sit and talk about archaeology and the state of the world, and the darkness that is pushing everyone closer and closer towards extinction.

XXI

In the middle of June 1941, the constant trickle of lost people became a flood that washed down into the deepest of all the chasms. Where the flood was widest and strongest, fifteen thousand people disappeared over only two nights. Then, without warning, on the twenty-second of June, Germany broke her pact with Soviet Russia and attacked. Several thousand Latvians being held by the NKVD in Rīga, were either immediately executed and buried hastily in mass graves, or were packed on to trains and sent to Siberia. While Stalin was overwhelmed by an attack that he had not been expecting, the German army entered the Baltic countries.

The tables had turned; the Latvian people were still not free, but now there were other people in charge. After the Year of Terror, the people went out into the streets with flowers and open arms and welcomed the German soldiers as liberators. The Germans had come to save them. At last, someone had heard. Someone had been listening after all. A light had been shone into the tunnel, and they had finally been able to crawl out into the sunshine. The brown had been vanquished by a river of green-grey.

But the sunshine was only a break between clouds. As the vice once again tightened around the country, as the executions continued and as Jews and political prisoners were herded into camps, the people very soon understood that they had merely exchanged one tyrant for another.

In the November of 1941, Josef Goebbels travelled to the Baltic countries. While he was in Latvia, he and his entourage stayed at Rundāle, the palace allowing them access to both Latvia and Lithuania.

Nina had been told that the Germans would be coming, and she felt that she was being pushed back into that room again, the one with the musty air and the locked door. She would have run away, but it was not possible. There was nowhere to run to. She told herself that the Germans knew what the word *civilization* meant and that they were able to pronounce it. But then she remembered all the grainy images in newspapers, and she realized that *civilization* could mean different things to different people. She hoped that they would not stay too long and that the door would open, and she could leave all the mustiness behind her. Then she saw the black chauffeur-driven military cars with the swastika flags, and, later, she heard the shiny leather boots of the bodyguards sounding harshly unfamiliar on the timbered floors. And she heard the door slam shut behind her.

If it had been possible, she would have hidden herself on the back stairs. But it was not possible; she was the hostess. When the cars pulled up at the front of the palace, and the black-booted men clicked their heels and saluted, she stood statue-like on the steps with Ernests and Antons and his wife, in front of all the palace staff, ready to say *Willkommen,* ready to greet and direct.

She kept thinking of the word *civilization* and that it only needed a very small number of people to bring it to an end. She thought of the music and the literature and the philosophy, and she tried to ignore the swastikas. As they followed her into the palace, she told herself that the Germans had chased away the Russians. She knew that she was grateful, but if Latvia did not belong to Russia, it did not belong to Germany either. She knew that the door remained locked; as the boots echoed on the polished timber floors, she wondered if there was anyone left who would be able to open it.

There were the meals, and the evenings with music and song. As she listened to Beethoven and looked at all the German faces, she asked herself how it could be possible to soar to such heights, and, at the same time, sink to such depths. She argued with herself that some of the men in the room probably felt that they had no choice. She knew that life was complicated; sometimes, it was difficult to see the black and white amid all the grey. She also knew that devastation is always initiated by the few, not by the many.

The Nazis were interested in what Ernests was doing. They were very impressed by his photography; he was even using a German camera: a Leica. They were curious about the dig and the finds from the Middle Ages. He was an interesting diversion from everything else, but he was only a small diversion. They had too many other things to discuss, and most of the time they kept to the ballroom, making plans, looking at maps, drinking, smoking and talking.

One day, they all disappeared on a surveillance trip to Lithuania. They told her that they would be back in the evening. For dinner as usual. As they all disappeared out through the gates in their shiny, black cars, Nina felt her body relax. She stood at one of the long windows and breathed in deeply, enjoying the quietness and the sense of freedom. The palace was almost hers again. In the afternoon, she walked slowly from room to room, reclaiming her space.

When she reached the ballroom, which was on the same floor as her own rooms, she noticed that the large doors were ajar, and she looked in. Something was telling her that she should not be there; she knew that this was where they met and talked and planned.

The room, which was very large and very white, was empty. The weak November sun was slipping in through the tall windows, painting the polished parquet floor with bands of light, and there was a feeling of solitude in the room. She walked in, looking up at the beautiful ceiling with its reliefs, all in white, and then she let her eyes drop to the white walls where other reliefs danced across the tops of windows and doors. She reached up to an invisible partner and took a few waltz steps into the middle of the room. Her shoes were heavy, and she was not dressed for dancing, but the feeling of liberation was there. For a moment, she closed her eyes, imagining all the other people around her and the musicians in the corner of the room. As she moved across the floor, she could almost feel her partner's hand on her waist.

Then she stopped, seeing the large table at one end of the room. She remembered the warning that she had ignored. The table was covered with papers and maps, and around the table there were many chairs. She should not be here. She knew that. She turned and began to hurry back towards the door. But there was someone else in the room. She looked up and saw him leaning against the door, watching her.

She recognized the gaunt, almost aesthetic, face, with the cruel, intense eyes and the thin, unsmiling mouth. She had seen it so often these past few days, wondering what it was that drove him, what it was that could drive anyone into such a dark place. She was aware that his uniform, with the leather belt fastened securely around the light-brown jacket, was fastidiously correct. The leather boots were polished to a bright, even shine, and his cap was held lightly in one hand. On his left arm she could see the swastika.

"Doctor Goebbels!" she said. Politely. Correctly. Curtseying. Looking beyond him, beyond the door.

He moved away from the door and limped into the room. "Frau Āboliņš! How nice to meet you here. Like this." He spread out his arms, indicating the room. He was quiet for a moment. Then he said, "Frau Āboliņš enjoys dancing, I see."

She bit her lip; obviously he had been watching her for some time. Putting his hands behind his back, he laughed coldly, and Nina was reminded of a glass breaking against a stone floor.

"But Frau Āboliņš must know that this room is restricted?"

He was slowly eyeing her up and down. She felt that she was naked and that she should be covering herself with something – her arms, the papers on the table. Anything.

She shivered in spite of the sun outside the windows. "It was an oversight, Doctor Goebbels. A mistake. My apologies, it will not happen again." She knew that he had a reputation for being very intelligent; he also had a reputation for women. She heard voices from the courtyard below and footsteps in the hall. They must have returned earlier than expected. How stupid of her not to have realized; she had been so caught up in the feeling of being free.

She looked at him, and then she looked down at the floor, at his boots, at the space between them and the door. She thought how unreliable feelings of freedom could be. Everything was so subjective. She began to move towards the door.

He laughed. Again, a quick, cold laugh. "We all make mistakes, Frau Āboliņš, but some mistakes can have disastrous consequences."

As she reached the door, he was already bent over the table, but he turned and said, "I shall, of course, be meeting Frau Āboliņš again this evening?"

XXII

It is 1943, and there are many young boys hiding in the forests. Some of them have found caves or holes in the round, gnarled trunks of tall trees. Others have climbed into the trees, feeling more in control should anyone come. They have built precarious platforms between branches, and they lie there, hidden by thick, green foliage, praying that they will not be found. The boys' families and neighbours place food and blankets and clothing in places where they know the boys will find them. They have to be cautious, and they look over their shoulders, listening for sounds that should not be there. They are risking everything: their own lives and the lives of the boys. Some of the boys remain hidden in the forest for months until the danger disintegrates, and a new danger takes its place. Others are pulled out of the forest by German soldiers with black boots and large dogs. They are loaded on to trucks and are sent south. To labour camps? To concentration camps?

Germany is beginning to lose the war, but she is ignoring all the signs. She is concerned about losing her hold in the Baltic, for she knows that she must retain some kind of a buffer against Russia. She also knows that if she relinquishes her hold, Russia will walk back in. She does not want that to happen, nor do the Baltic peoples.

Hitler decides to form the Latvian SS Legion. It is to be made up of Latvian volunteers with only Latvian officers. By treating the Latvians as equals, he is hoping to strengthen his hold on Latvia. He believes that a Latvian regiment will appeal to the Latvians' sense of patriotism.

But there are almost no volunteers, and in March, notice is given to all men born between 1919 and 1924 to present themselves for mobilization. Their choices are abysmal: join the Legion, be sent to a German labour camp or be incorporated into the German Army as an auxiliary somewhere on the front lines. Eventually, the second two choices are removed, and there is only one choice: the Legion. Refusal is the same as deportation. Deportation usually means the concentration camps. Men claim not to have seen the notice. It does not help. Some of them hide in the forest.

Gradually, the Legion expands with the men who have no choice. In the beginning, they wear the Latvian Army uniform from the first war, but the Russians recognize the uniform and resent being attacked by other Soviet citizens. The Latvians in the old Latvian Army uniform, captured by the Russians, are horribly tortured and eventually killed. When the Latvians look down, there is one millstone, and when they look up, there is another; the two stones are moving closer together, and Latvia is in the middle. Later, they wear the German uniform with a small badge indicating that they are actually Latvians, but the new uniform does not make any difference; they are still caught in the middle, between two large, flat stones.

Then, in the summer of 1943, Nina unexpectedly becomes pregnant. It is what she has always hoped for, and she tells Ernests that the pregnancy was obviously supposed to happen. She talks about Fate and God and predestination, but Ernests is not convinced. He is taunted by things he has heard and things he has read and even things he has only imagined, and he finds himself wondering if he will be able to go on living, if she does not survive. He tries to push such thoughts from his mind, focussing only on the present.

Summer turns into autumn and then into winter. The torment in his mind begins to lessen as the doctor in Bauska assures him that both Nikolina and the baby are healthy. Ernests thinks that perhaps Nina is right about Fate and God after all. He shakes the doctor's hand as he and Nina leave the surgery, and the doctor says, yet again, that he expects the delivery to be normal. He does not expect any complications, but he wants the delivery to take place at the hospital.

Ernests begins to relax, trying to believe that everything will be all right, but then he thinks of the Germans and the Russians and all the things that are completely obliterating Latvia's future, and he is no longer so sure. Thoughts run around in his head, and he thinks how quickly things can change; he decides that there is never really a right time for anything. We only ever have the present – the past has already disappeared and the future may never eventuate. He tries to imagine himself as a father, and he wonders what it will be like. He has not had much experience of fathers; he was only eight when his own father died.

While Ernests' thoughts are focussed on the coming spring, the Russians move closer and closer to Latvia's borders. Many of the men who have been forced into the Legion are beginning to hope that the Legion might give them a way of holding back Russia and that it might eventually be a stepping-stone to a free Latvia. Most are not aware that they are thinking the same thoughts that the Latvian Rifles thought all those years ago.

XXIII

Ernests' thirty-eighth birthday fell on a very cold day in early March. It snowed most of the day and a bitter wind blew the soft snow into ever-changing drifts against the walls of the palace. As I walked along the corridors, I looked out though the tall windows, wondering, yet again, what had happened to the spring. Would there be a spring or had the earth tired of all the waste and ruin? I could understand if the earth had finally given up; at times, even I felt like giving up.

In the evening, we ate spicy cake and sang *Daudz baltu dieninu*, wishing Ernests many happy white days. Everyone was there. We were not so many, but everyone came. All the while, I wondered about the white days and the snow, and the earth finally saying *no more*. Then, as the day began to move towards its end, and those people who lived beyond the palace were pulling on coats and boots, I felt the first contractions and knew that even if the earth had given up, the baby was on its way.

Eduards and his family were about to leave when Ernests beckoned Eduards to one side. I noticed that Eduards nodded while a look of concern flickered across his face. Perhaps he was thinking about the weather; he may even have been thinking about the earth. He spoke quickly with his wife, and then he and Ernests hurried across the courtyard to the stables. I looked out the front door, watching while Ernests pulled on his coat and lit a cigarette, and while Eduards harnessed the horse to the carriage.

The snow had stopped falling, but a strong wind was blowing the fallen snow into ever-changing patterns. I shivered – from either the cold or something else – as Eduards guided the horse to the steps. One of the women came to the door with some rugs, and Ernests placed them in the carriage. Then he helped me on to the seat, and climbed in beside me. It was impossible to speak; the ice-speckled wind was too loud. Instead, he took my hand in his and held it tightly.

Eduards drove the horse as fast as he dared, but the snow-drifts were difficult to read, and there was very little visibility. The two lamps on the carriage cast strange lights that jumped erratically in front of us, drawing lines of light across mounds of snow, before quickly sketching the shapes of trees or fences near the edge of the road. I pulled a blanket around me, thinking that it was just the three of us and nothing else, and I wondered what it would be like to be the only three people left on earth. Ernests sat and smoked, still with his hand in mine. We had both pushed all our thoughts out of the present into the future; we were thinking only of arriving safely at the hospital and walking through the front door. I was also thinking of the baby, hoping that nothing would go wrong – this time.

On the line that is time, the future slowly became my present. At five the following morning, Andris was born. For all those hours, my body had not been my own; it had been taken over by something beyond my control. I felt as though I was on a long steep slide towards infinity; at times, I even relished the idea of disappearing into that infinity. The slide twisted, and it was all over. It was a boy, and we had both survived.

Then, as if the earth had decided that there was a point to life after all, the wind dropped, and later in the morning, the sun came out.

XXIV

At the end of April, Nina received a letter from Elza. The day was abnormally sunny. Next to the sun-bathed south wall of the palace, overlooking the garden, it almost felt warm. A bee, still too early for summer, flew past. Nina was watching it when Ernests brought her the letter. She had been sewing, and she put the sewing to one side on one of the stone buttresses extending from the wall. She opened the letter with her small sewing scissors as Ernests bent down to look at Andris asleep in his pram.

'My dear Nika,' she read, half-looking at the letter, half-looking at Ernests and Andris. She glanced back at the letter, skimming the first couple of paragraphs asking about Andris, telling about the children and Maksis. She was impatient. She had seen the name *Iskra,* and she wanted to know why.

She remembered how Marija and Iskra had turned up in Rīga about three years ago. They had come from somewhere east of Leningrad, much of the way on foot. They spoke of Leningrad being under siege, and how all the roads were blocked. They said that there were no trains and that there were soldiers everywhere. They had crossed the southern part of Lake Ladoga in the middle of winter by walking on the ice. Much of the time, they had walked at night. Food was the biggest problem. There was no food. Not anywhere.

When they arrived in Rīga, they had gone to the house on Kalnciema iela. It had been a long time, but Marija could still remember the street and the house. She had nowhere else to go. Most people had moved on or were dead. Having reached the outskirts of Rīga, it was not so far to walk to Kalnciema iela, not after having walked most of the way from Leningrad.

Rozalija was in her room when they arrived. She heard Elza say, "But, Marija!"

Her body tensed as she thought of the girl with the long, flowing hair. Was it possible that she was here? In Rīga? In her son's house? She opened the bedroom door while memories carried her through to the sitting room. There she stopped, facing a worn, middle-aged woman with short grey hair. Where was the beautiful long hair? The beautiful girl? Rozalija quickly looked around. Surely there had to be some mistake.

Marija moved towards her, recognition showing on her face.

Rozalija looked at the trousers and the heavy boots and the man's jacket. What had happened to *her* Marija? *Her* daughter-in-law? Who was this person with Marija's name?

"This is Iskra." Marija pointed to the girl standing behind her in the doorway.

Rozalija nodded. She could see glimpses of *her* Marija in Iskra.

The girl was not sure how she should greet her grandmother. Should she curtsey? Should she say something?

Elza was standing on the edge of something, looking in. She had never met her sister-in-law, though she had seen the old photos, and she had read the letters: a few letters that had trickled through from Leningrad.

Ilona kept close to her mother while Rozalija was still trying to make her memories fit together with the present. She thought of Jānis. What would he have said? What would he have thought? Then she burst into tears and left the room.

Nina thought of all of this as she held the letter in her hand. She could also remember how she had once thought that Marija was the most beautiful person she had ever seen. But she knew that things change. People change. After Jānis died, Marija became a mechanical engineer and worked in a large factory not far from

Leningrad. It was not practical with long hair, so she cut her hair and she learnt to smoke a pipe and swear like the men she worked with. Nina wondered whether Jānis would still agree that Bolshevism was the answer. She looked down at Elza's letter again.

'Some weeks back, Iskra decided that she wanted to be christened, and Maksis and I took her to the church to meet the vicar. When Iskra told him her name, he just stood there, looking at her, not saying anything. Finally, he shook his head and said that no Christian person could possibly be called Iskra. He did christen her eventually, but he insisted on calling her Tatjana. It didn't matter what she said or what we said. Anyway, she now calls herself Iskra Tatjana.

'Marija didn't say much; I really don't think she cared one way or the other. She says that she's moved on from religion. She frightens me at times, Nika; you know how overbearing she can be? I miss you so much. Maksis says I am being silly – about Marija, not about my missing you. I don't mind Iskra though, and Ilona gets along with her...'

Nina looked up from the letter again. She knew that it was difficult for Elza with two extra people living in the house. She sighed. She loved being in Rundāle, but perhaps she was needed elsewhere.

XXV

Summer 1944 was becoming older, and there were rumours that the war might be about to end. The Russians had again crossed Latvia's eastern border, and our days were patterned with the erratic sounds of distant gunfire and images of low-flying planes, both Russian and German, as the Germans, being pushed further and further west, counter-attacked. Buildings were being changed to rubble as places were bombed. Many people were wondering in which direction they should run; some had tired of running, others did not even get the chance to decide.

Ernests and I talked about it often. We knew what it would mean if Russia was to move back into Latvia, and we wondered if America would then insist on the Baltic countries regaining their independence. I thought of America's belief in personal freedom and liberty, and I argued with Ernests that it was only logical that she would want to come to our aid and defend our rights. After all the injustice and fighting and death, it was the only thing that made any sense. It would have all been in vain, if freedom was only to be the privilege of the powerful few.

Ernests and Andris were asleep, and I was awake. It was light outside – I could tell by the grey shadows having already caught the first wash of colour – but it was still very early. I felt anxious though I did not know why. I lay there, trying to remember. I had been dreaming, but I could not remember if my dream had been important. I closed my eyes, and I was suddenly pulled back into the dream, and then I remembered.

I was in bed, the very same bed in which I was now lying. A figure approached the bed. It was a shape that looked human, but was neither man nor woman. The features, the face and the clothes were all unimportant; it was merely a presence speaking to my mind, indicating that there was nothing to fear. Yet, I was filled with fear. I was asleep, but my eyes were open, and I could see the shapes of clothes on the chair and paintings on the wall, Ernests in the bed beside me, Andris in his cot. The presence moved closer, and I was so filled with a sense of urgency that I was almost unable to breathe. I understood that we were to leave Rundāle, and then I understood that we would even have to leave Latvia.

I could not move. The idea of leaving Latvia was too difficult to contemplate. Where could we go? How would we go? The world was at war and borders were closed. I felt as though I was suffocating with the impossibility of what I had been asked to do, and then, without anything more being said, I understood that everything would be taken care of and that all we had to do was to leave.

When I told Ernests about my dream, he wrapped me in his arms. He was silent for a moment, and then he said that we would pack immediately and return to Rīga. We left Rundāle that same day, the twenty-eighth of July, and returned to Rīga and Aunt Auguste.

XXVI

Exactly one month later, on the twenty-eighth of August, Ernests discovered that he had no cigarettes. He had meant to buy some, but he had forgotten. He hurriedly searched in his coat pockets and rummaged through the drawers of the dresser. Then he opened the cupboard, looking behind bowls and pots. Auguste frowned and said that she could assure him that there were none in the cupboard. Nikolina said that it could not be that important; he could buy them in the morning.

But he said that he needed a cigarette, and while Nikolina was asking him to wait, and Auguste was pursing her lips and shaking her head, Ernests had already pulled on his coat and was on his way out through the door.

"I won't be long," he called as the gate latched behind him with a soft click.

Later, Nina thought a lot about that evening, about things she had said and did not say, things she did and did not do. Did she kiss him when he left? She doubted it; she had not wanted him to go. Later, she regretted that she had not insisted he stay. Had she known what was to happen, she would have gone and bought the cigarettes herself. How important were they, she wondered later when she knew what had happened.

While they waited for him, they sat in the front room and sewed. After a while, Auguste put down her sewing.

"When did he leave, Nika?" She was looking at the clock on the mantelpiece.

Nina shook her head. She could not remember, but it was after she had put Andris to bed. She had not been worried, but now she could feel long strings of anxiety beginning to snake around her stomach. She tried to ignore them.

"It's not long past eight," she said. "He'll be back soon."

Auguste was worried. Once again, she picked up her sewing, but then she put it down and went to the door. She opened it and looked up and down the street. The almost empty street was clothed in the half-light of late summer; a car drove past slowly; further up the street, she could see a man leading a horse and cart. Nowhere could she see her son.

She closed the door and sat down.

"You may be right, Nika," she said. "But he left well over an hour ago, and it's not that far to go... "

Nikolina put aside her own sewing, the snakes now frantically pulling in all directions, squeezing out the anxiety and the fear. She breathed in sharply.

"Perhaps there weren't any cigarettes, or the shop was shut, and he had to go all the way into town." She reflected that the words sounded shallow and uncertain. She must remain positive. There had to be a simple explanation; soon they would be able to laugh at how worried they had been.

But the evening turned dark, and still he did not return. Night noises distracted them, and they kept hoping, but he did not come. They made tea, and Auguste prayed, and they looked out on to the dark street. Occasionally, overcome by exhaustion, they dozed for a few moments in their chairs before getting up and, once again, looking up and down the cold, deserted street.

After the sleepless night, the grey light of the early morning was cold. Nikolina stood up, pulling her shawl closely around her; opening the stove door with a metallic bang, she pushed in some thin pieces of wood and blew on the embers. She had spent the night listening: waiting to hear the gate open, waiting for a step on the path, waiting to hear his key in the door. She pulled a comb through her tousled hair and then fetched some water to make coffee. Andris was stirring in the other room, and she would have to attend to him as well. She was trying not to think, but one thought kept pushing itself into her consciousness: why had he not come home?

Auguste wrapped herself in her shawl and said that she would fetch Maksis. She took the tram. It was a Tuesday morning, but it was still early, and there were very few people on the tram or in the streets. As always, there were the grey soldiers, but she was not thinking about them now. She sat near a window, thinking only of Ernests, hoping that she might suddenly see him walking along the street.

Meanwhile, in the house on Ūnijas iela, Nina was counting the minutes until her aunt would return with Maksis. She was trying to convince herself that Maksis would know what to do. She knew that people disappeared; it had been happening for years. Perhaps Ernests would be one of these people. Perhaps she would never see him again. She thought of all the things she should have said, all the things she wanted to say, now when it was too late. She felt as though she was trapped in a box with all the dimensions except time, and then Auguste returned with Maksis, and she was released back into the present.

Maksis touched Nina gently on the shoulder as he followed Auguste into the house. "I'm sure there's a simple explanation, Nika. We'll find him. We have to."

But while he tried to comfort his sister, he was worried. Everyone was worried. Everyone knew what had happened to Ernests, but no one wanted to be the first to put it into words. Once the words were spoken, then it would be true. As long as it was possible to pretend that nothing had happened, then perhaps nothing had happened, and Ernests would return home.

They had not yet forgotten how it had felt when the Germans had entered Rīga in 1941 and liberated the city, and the sun had broken through clouds after months of darkness. They did not agree with Hitler, no more than they agreed with Stalin, but many had felt that the Germans might move them closer to a free Latvia. Some even volunteered to fight with the Germans. Then the Nazis began extermination programmes, and the Latvians realized that they were being herded back into the tunnel. And they stopped volunteering.

But that was in 1941. Now it was 1944, and the Germans were becoming desperate. Everyone knew about the Latvian SS Legion and the conscripts; they also knew that the Germans needed more men on the Eastern front in order to stop the Russians. In 1944, the Germans began conscripting much older men and even young boys. Maksis did not have to wonder what had happened to Ernests. He already knew.

Not long after he had arrived at Ūnijas iela, Maksis left again. As he was leaving, he held my hand tightly, promising that he would do his best to find Ernests. I remember that I nodded. There was nothing that I could say; everything was now up to Maksis.

But when he returned some hours later, without Ernests, I understood that sometimes one's best is just not good enough.

"Well, at least we know where he is." Maksis sat down and pulled out a cigarette.

My brother's face gave me no reason to begin hoping, and I watched him light the cigarette before drawing on it deeply, almost as though it was a necessity if he was to keep talking.

He told us that he had gone to the German camp headquarters. He knew that he would not be conscripted – 1906 was the new cut-off point. He also knew how to get what he wanted. People rarely said no to Maksis, but the officer-in-charge did complain that it was against camp policy. He flicked through a pile of papers and then said that Maksis could see his cousin for a few minutes. The officer hoped that Herr Kindahls realized that this was a special favour. Maksis, standing in the makeshift office, nodded.

When Ernests finally entered the room alongside a German soldier, Maksis noted how grey and tired he looked. He would not have slept; he would have been reliving everything over and over again in his head, trying to push it all back to that moment before he left the house. He would have been wondering about the worth of a single cigarette.

The German soldier had a sub-machine-gun slung over his

shoulder. He moved a few steps to one side. The man at the desk was typing. There were a couple of officers talking at the other end of the room. Ernests said that he had been picked up soon after he had left the house the evening before. He had not even reached the tobacconist; he had not bought cigarettes.

It was a German truck with a canopy over the back part. It was picking up men, but Ernests did not notice the truck at first; he had been looking down at the ground, thinking about other things. When they stopped him, they looked at his identity card. If he had been born a year earlier, he would have been able to continue. Perhaps he would have even bought his cigarettes.

The German soldier was getting restless. Maksis pushed a few cigarettes into Ernests' hand. Ernests smiled wryly and said that obviously life was not to be enjoyed, but to be overcome. He said that he had no idea what would happen next though he suspected that they would soon be moved south. He took off his glasses and wiped them on his sleeve. Maksis put his hand on his shoulder. He wanted to tell Ernests that he *would* overcome, but it sounded empty and false. He also wanted to tell him that he would get him out of the camp and back home to his family, but he knew that there was nothing he could do. Not now. Not any longer.

The soldier straightened up and moved closer to Ernests. Maksis shook Ernests' hand, holding it longer and more firmly than usual. Ernests asked him to take care of his family; he also asked Maksis to tell me that he was sorry – there were really no words to explain what he felt.

Then the soldier motioned to Ernests to follow him, and Maksis turned and left the building.

When Maksis told me all this, I dropped through infinite levels of darkness. As I was falling, I tried to grab on to words that might have described what I was feeling.

"Maksis, why did he go? We told him not to. We told him to wait." I looked around the room, at Auguste sitting in her chair and at Andris in his pram. Then I thought how this was bigger than any of us. It was bigger than Ernests; it had always been there, waiting to happen.

Maksis put his arms around me and held me tightly. I had always felt safe with his arms around me, and even more so now. The falling stopped abruptly.

I closed my eyes, trying to compose myself. After a moment, I reluctantly disengaged myself from my brother's arms and sat down on a nearby chair. "It probably would have happened anyway, wouldn't it?" The tears were welling.

"Possibly..." said Maksis, lighting a cigarette. He walked across across the room and stood in front of the window. "Who knows?" He shrugged and drew on the cigarette. "He was born at the wrong time." He attempted a smile, but there was not much to smile about.

The smoke from Maksis' cigarette wound around the images racing through my head. I had heard what it was like in both Germany and Russia. I wondered whether I would ever see Ernests again. I knew that I had to keep him safe by not thinking such thoughts, but, even as I tried not to think, my mind insisted on sorting through all the possibilities, picking them up one by one and turning them over. None of them had a happy ending. What was it I said to him before he left? I remembered my irritation when he said that he was going out. If only I could see him now and tell him what I should have told him. I felt so powerless. I wanted him back.

Maksis had finished his cigarette and had begun to make tea. I got up and went to find Auguste.

XXVII

Valdemārs Ginters had been extremely worried about the Germans. Like everyone else, he knew that the dates for conscription had been changed. Most of the men at the State Historical Museum had already been conscripted, and Ginters could not afford to lose Ernests as well. Like Ginters, Ernests *was* the museum. Ginters wrote a letter with the official letterhead, explaining the situation. They needed Ernests. He wrote about Rundāle and the work that had been carried out there. He finished by saying that Āboliņš was irreplaceable. He signed the letter and gave it to Ernests on the twenty-sixth of August, two days before Ernests was captured. Ernests had shown the letter to the Germans, but they were not interested in museums. They were interested only in winning a war that was very quickly sliding away from them. The officer at the camp shook his head and returned the letter to Ernests. He understood the situation, but this was war, and there was nothing he could do.

The day after Ernests was captured, a truck pulled up outside the museum, and a German officer and three soldiers walked in through the front door. There was no one on the ground floor, so they took the stairs to the next level. Ginters was there boxing up some of the exhibits. The officer asked him where they could find Valdemārs Ginters. It was important, and they did not have time to waste. Ginters left the box in the middle of the room and said that he would fetch Ginters. He left the Germans in the room while he disappeared down the back steps and out a side entrance.

The Germans waited in the room. The officer walked around,

looking at the exhibits that were still on show. The soldiers stood partly at ease. The officer looked at his watch. He wondered how far the man had had to go. The minutes passed. It was very quiet in the large room. No one came. More minutes passed. Then the officer realized that no one would be coming. He shouted at his soldiers to search the museum, but it was too late. Ginters had gone.

The officer and his men searched the whole area in their truck. Eventually, they had to give up. Valdemārs Ginters had disappeared.

XXVIII

He lives about fourteen kilometres outside of town. Having left his mother's street, he turns on to the road that runs between Lidköping and Skara. It is a wide, straight road, running through large stands of pine and past small farms where combine harvesters can already be seen moving across the fields. He remembers hearing that the road had been built to act as a runway in the event of war, and then he wonders why he should think of something so unnecessary when everything around him is slowly collapsing.

He has driven this road so many times that it almost feels as though the car knows its own way and that he is merely a passenger. He overtakes a tractor and waves automatically to the driver. The driver, an elderly weather-beaten man, waves back. Andris reflects on the fact that he knows nothing about the man: what may have happened to him yesterday or today. Or what is likely to happen to him tomorrow. Perhaps he has just lost a wife, a child. Perhaps there is a foreclosure on his farm, or some silent, creeping illness invading his body, which means that he will have to sell up and move elsewhere.

The tractor has disappeared into the distance behind him, and with difficulty he puts the man out of his mind. We think we know other people, but we can only ever know what they want us to know. The smile and the firm handshake can be saying: This far, but no further! He overtakes a car and then pulls back into the right lane.

It is still his pain, his sorrow and his loss. He has not yet had to share it with anyone. Soon it will lose the form it now has, and *it will run in many different directions; he will be unable to contain it. It will no longer be only his. He will be faced with his own shock and his own pain, but the shock and the pain will be embodied by other people, and he will need to be there to console, to explain and to try to understand.*

To explain. He shakes his head slowly. There just was no explanation. He passes the huge bunkers on his right – large enough to house small aircraft in the event of that war which will most probably never happen. He turns off the main road to his right and drives through a small hamlet. Beyond the last house, the road crosses a hill, and then, suddenly, there is only flatness. He can see a few houses dotted between the fields and even scattered bits of forest, the trees that were permitted to remain and mourn those that had been felled.

He can see his house. He is already wondering what he will say and whether he will be able to restrain the shock and the pain, or whether they will burst forth like something from some old bottle from which the cork has been removed. And whether, after they have filled the room, they will rush out through all the windows and will eventually fill the entire earth.

XXIX

At the end of September, they left Rīga, and they travelled by train to Ventspils on the west coast. The train was packed with the crowds of people who were trying to leave before it was too late. Nina had begged Auguste to come with them, but she had refused. Someone had to look after the house and keep it safe until everyone returned. That is what she had said, but Nina suspected that she was staying because she wanted to be there when Ernests came home. Auguste was so sure that her son would return, and she did not want him to come home to an empty house and realize that everyone had left.

Like so many others, Auguste firmly believed that everyone would return very soon and that things would be the same as they had been before the war. The Western Powers would step in and insist on Latvia and the other Baltic countries resuming their former independence. Russia would then admit a tactical defeat. It was only a matter of months at the most. In the meantime, she would stay and look after the house.

It was impossible to change Auguste's mind. Late summer turned deep yellow, and Nina was still undecided, pulled in two directions, not knowing what she should do, only knowing that she had to save her son. She was not as optimistic as Auguste about the Russians backing down. She had seen the tunnel of 1940, and she could again glimpse the opening. She knew that the gaping mouth would devour both adults and children. She knew that she could not stay, not now that she had Andris. But she understood Auguste. If she had been able to stay, she would have done so in spite of the tunnel. Then she wondered if Ernests would ever be coming home, and whether he would expect her to stay when everything around her was once again disintegrating into terror.

She hugged Auguste without speaking and walked away from the house, holding Andris on her arm. At the gate, she turned around one last time, and the image of her aunt, as well as all those things that she had wanted to say but could not, collected together into one unforgettable memory.

Many had decided to stay because, like Auguste, they argued that not only could nothing be as bad as 1940, but now the rest of the world was watching and would certainly act; others felt that the uncertainty of exile was more terrifying than staying where they were. Marija and Iskra remained in Rozalija's house on Kalnciema iela; they had lived in a Soviet system for so many years that they could not understand why people wanted to leave. Maksis only shook his head, thinking about the Year of Terror.

Hermine and her family were staying. Lucija had already left. She hoped to reach Germany, and from Germany she intended to continue on to America. It sounded simple, but Nina knew that, even if Lucija reached Germany, there was no guarantee that America would accept her as a refugee. There were tears and goodbyes, but everyone expected to be returning soon. No one expected to be gone for ever.

Nina stepped off the tram at the central station, thinking of all the other times she had been at the station. She remembered that very first time when she was only eight or nine. There were lots of people then as well; things had not changed that much. Like then, most of the people around her were being funnelled into the gaping mouth of the station. Holding Andris tightly, she thought of Ernests and 1941 when they had travelled to Rundāle. Now the soldiers were grey, and the flags and the picture of Stalin had disappeared. She wondered how long it would be before the grey was once again replaced by brown and Stalin, dusted off, would be lifted back on to the wall in the entrance hall.

She caught sight of Maksis and Elza. They were standing near the entrance as Maksis had promised they would be.

Rozalija was holding on to Jānis's hand, and Ilona was carrying a small bag. Nina looked at Ilona, thinking that she was only a little older than she had been all those years ago.

They travelled first to Jelgava, where they had to change trains, and then via Tukums and Kandava to Ventspils. It was a long trip, and no one really knew what would happen when they finally arrived in Ventspils. Places had already been bombed – they could see that from the train – and the irregular sound of gunfire was part of everything around them. Several times, the train stopped, like some long caterpillar frozen into inactivity in a space it did not completely understand, and everyone fell out into the ditches or the forest where they hid until the plane overhead had moved further south, and they were able to re-board the train.

There was very little room to move on the train, people and baggage falling out of over-filled compartments and occupying even the corridors, everyone squashed together while focussing on points beyond the immediate present, willing themselves into a future that had to be different. Most were hoping to find places on boats going from Ventspils to Germany or Sweden. Elza was concerned – there were so many people – but Maksis said that he had taken care of everything. He knew what he was doing. Nina wondered quietly how long it would take before the Russians stopped people from leaving.

The evening before they left Rīga, Nina had sat on her bed, her mind filled with all the people she had known and loved. While many of the memories were only vague, some of them disappeared to become part of other memories, reappearing all the more stronger and confident. She knew that she should be packing, and several times she had glanced at the small case still lying empty on her bed. She got up and walked across the room to the window, thinking that there was not space for a whole life in one small cardboard suitcase. From the window she had looked out on the fading garden. It was telling her that it would soon be autumn, while she desperately wanted to remember everything as a sunshine-filled, summer garden. Summer and flowers and Ernests lying on the grass reading to her... She closed her eyes tightly. She had been trying so hard not to think of Ernests. She must not think of him, not now. Not when she had no idea where he was and whether he would ever be coming back. To Latvia. To anywhere.

The hot, burning sensation behind her eyes and the churning anxiety inside of her were not new: both feelings had plagued her for weeks. She breathed in deeply, and, opening her eyes, she returned to the case lying on the bed. She packed a few pieces of clothing for herself and Andris; between the clothing she placed some jewellery, her passport and a few photos. The photo of Ernests she slipped into her coat pocket, knowing that even small cardboard cases could become superfluous. She closed the case, still trying not to think of Ernests, wondering whether there was a possibility that they would never return. The thought was frightening. She ran down the stairs and into the front room, where her aunt was sewing. For a moment, she stood at the door, her mind full of all the things that might or might not happen, then Auguste dropped her sewing and stretched out her arms to her.

People knew what was likely to happen when the Germans were defeated; they had already experienced 1940, and they did not want to relive the nightmare. The optimists still believed that the West would step in, and that everything would revert to what it was like before the war. The realists knew that Russia would never relinquish her hold on the Baltic countries; she was merely resuming what she regarded as her right. Those who had read more and observed more knew that the Baltic countries were just the beginning: Russia wanted all of Eastern Europe. Possibly all of Europe.

People remained where they were, or else, like Maksis and his family, they tried to get away before it was too late. In August, the small dribble of people leaving was already turning into a river which, by October, would develop into a flood. The push of the Red Army from the east meant that escape routes were mainly limited to the west of the country. Some people fled westwards to Sweden, and from Sweden to America, England or Australia; most fled south-west into Northern Germany. Some stayed in Germany, others moved on. In September, it was still possible to flee while the Soviets were concentrated on vanquishing the Germans, and the Germans were holding on, hoping that in spite of everything they could still win the war.

There were crowds of people in Ventspils, and it was noisy and jarring. Nina saw many German soldiers, and she thought that the Germans would also be wanting to leave, but Hitler was clinging to the belief that he could still win the war, and the fate of the German soldiers in the Baltic States was probably of little importance.

The group from Rīga was met by Alberts, a friend of Maksis'. He lived on the coast at Saunaga, near the north-western tip of Latvia. An idealist, he had joined the Communist Party a decade earlier. When he later became disillusioned, he was already trapped within the mechanism of the Party, occasionally wondering about things like idealogical blindness. His large farm had been swallowed up by Soviet collectives in 1940, and now he only had his house and a small plot of land left. He was hoping to be able to help Maksis; it would not remove all the mistakes, but it might it easier to live with them.

He owned an old, battered green truck, which he had parked a few streets beyond the railway station. When they all reached the truck, after having extricated themselves from the crowds and the noise, he lifted their few bags into the back, and then helped Rozalija into the cabin. Nina passed Andris up to her mother, knowing that it would be warmer there than in the open area at the back, and Rozalija made room for Jānis to sit between herself and Alberts. Maksis stubbed out his cigarette on the sandy ground and helped Elza and Nina clamber over the mudguard. He lifted up Ilona and then swung himself over the edge. There were piles of rough woven bags to sit on, but nothing was very clean.

Alberts cranked the engine, climbed into the driver's seat and, slamming his door, released the brake. Slowly, the truck pulled out on to the road and began the long trek up the coast.

It was already late afternoon, and shadows were lengthening across the road. Nikolina noticed that it had become colder and that rain was threatening. She was worried about the prospect of rain, but she was pleased to be leaving Ventspils and all the crowds of people. They passed several stork nests high up on posts and house tops. Soon the storks would be moving south. To Africa. She thought how everyone was moving somewhere. Then she wondered whether, like the storks, they would also be coming back.

It was very late when they finally reached their destination. The stone farmhouse was hidden behind a clump of white birch trees; beyond the house Nikolina could sense the beach. It was too dark to see anything, but she could hear the waves breaking on the sand.

Alberts' wife had died some years earlier, his younger son was in the army, and his daughter had long since married and was living in Daugavpils. Now he and his elder son, Emīls, worked what was left of the original farm.

For a whole month, they lived in the house by the ocean. The women did everyday things, like cooking and cleaning, in an attempt to push away thoughts of the future while tying themselves firmly to the present. Then the Red Army marched on Rīga, and it became even more imperative that they leave. Maksis said there was a right time and a wrong time; they had to choose the right time.

The news coming through to the house in Saunaga was erratic, but with the Russians now controlling Rīga, they were sure that the concentration of military strength around Courland would be increasing. Stalin was hoping to wipe out the Germans in the area, no matter the cost to his own troops; Hitler was hanging on, hoping for the miracle that might give him victory.

While everyone waited for a miracle or something else, Latvian Communists fighting on the side of the Soviets came face to face with Latvians conscripted into the German SS Legion.

Alberts and Maksis spent most days away from the house; on their return, they would often discuss boats and departure points. While the adults were mainly concerned with boats, Ilona and Jānis were happy helping Emīls feed his chickens and pigs, or watching Alberts stacking wood and cleaning machinery.

In October, Maksis said that there would be a few nights without a moon. This would probably be their only chance. He had walked along the beach – so many times – and he had checked the points from where they might be able to leave. He was most concerned about the guard towers. They were spaced out, but they seemed to be manned all the time.

He walked up and down the cold beach, smoking while looking out across the dark water. Thinking. Then he and Alberts disappeared with the truck one morning and did not return until the evening. When they returned, Nina knew that something was different: Maksis appeared more relaxed.

The following evening, they took farewell of Emīls and walked down to the beach. It was completely dark. The waves were breaking on the shore, but it was too dark to see them as waves. They appeared only as glistening tops and, occasionally, as a long run of water against the sand. Nina wondered about the guard tower further up the coast. Its light was not sweeping the water or the beach. The tower itself was in darkness.

She looked at Maksis, and he put his finger next to his nose.

"All sorted," he whispered.

Where the sand ran into the forest, a small rowing boat had been hidden behind some bushes; after pulling it down to the water, Alberts rowed them all out beyond the breakers to where a large, open fishing boat was waiting. There was very little cloud, and it was cold.

On his first trip, Alberts took Rozalija, Nikolina, Andris and Ilona. Rozalija said nothing, holding on to the side of the little rowing boat with one hand – her knuckles white against the wet timber – and on to Ilona with her other. Cradling Andris in her arms while listening to the sound of the oars cutting through the black water, Nina knew that her mother was frightened, but she was also frightened. She could see the fishing boat ahead of them, an indistinct shadow bobbing on the dark water, and she focussed on it while her mind grappled with words from prayers not completely forgotten.

Men already in the fishing boat pulled them all on board, Alberts pushing off again immediately. Everyone huddled in the darkness, listening to distant, muted sounds and the water lapping the sides of the boat while they waited for Alberts to return. Now he would have reached the shore; now the others would be in the boat; now they were back alongside the fishing boat.

As the last person pulled himself on board, the owner of the fishing boat lifted the anchor, and the boat quickly headed for deeper water. Alberts disappeared into the darkness. No one spoke; everyone was desperately clinging to a point in the future, well beyond the present moment, while trying to ignore thoughts of watery, unmarked graves.

After some minutes, they looked up. They could hear a plane coming towards them. It circled and then flew over them with both guns firing.

Had there been room, the people on the little boat would have thrown themselves on to the floor, but it was impossible. Instead, they hid their faces under shawls and blankets, wrapping their bodies around small children while praying to whatever god they believed in. The man who owned the boat shook his head. They would not be able to continue; the plane would be waiting for them further out. They could not see the plane. It was too dark, but they could hear it far off in the distance above their heads. It was wheeling around, and it would soon be back.

The man cut the engine. There were no lights on the boat. Everyone sat very still. The plane flew over, and the people in the boat froze as the guns fired a second time. The gunners were using tracer ammunition: the tracer and then four shots. Water sprayed along the side of the boat as the shots came very close.

Everyone wanted to scream, but dared not, while mothers held hands over the mouths of small alarmed children.

They heard the plane wheel around to the south before disappearing. Would it return? The boat owner was certain that it would. He guessed that the machine-gun was being reloaded and that they had a very small pocket of time in which they might be able to return to the shore. The pilot knew that they were there, and he was not likely to give up until he had sunk the boat.

The little fishing boat swung around and moved quickly back towards the shore. In the distance, they could hear the plane returning, but now they could see the shore, were within swimming distance, were within wading distance, were on the shore, holding each other, looking westwards, letting the tears flow that had been held back before. Before, when they knew that they had to return, when all their plans had been overturned, when all their hopes and dreams had been crushed.

Would there be a new attempt? Would it be possible? Maksis and his little band returned to the farm. The other people who had been in the boat disappeared as quickly and as quietly as they had appeared. The fisherman and his boat had also disappeared. Now there was only the darkness.

Nikolina held on to her baby and the little case containing her past life. She had made up her mind. She would stay in Latvia. As soon as it was possible, she would return to Rīga.

XXX

In the chess game of war, the Baltic States had become pawns, which everyone knew could be easily discarded to achieve victories for others. Neither the United States nor the United Kingdom wanted to upset Stalin – he was providing millions of troops – and the Western Alliance preferred him as an ally and not as an enemy.

Already in 1941, Britain, with the backing of the United States, was negotiating with Stalin the restoration of the 1940 map of the Soviet Union in return for military co-operation against Germany. By 1943, Roosevelt was arguing that countries impacted by the negotiations would eventually learn to live with Russia in both understanding and harmony. He was prepared to trust Stalin, and he believed that if the Western Powers met the Russian leader's demands, Stalin would decide to work with them for world peace. By early 1944, Roosevelt had given the Russians permission to take over the Baltic States and a section of Eastern Europe.

But it was Churchill's meeting with Stalin in October, 1944, that finally added the stamp of approval when Britain agreed to return to the Soviet Union all former Soviet Union citizens who had been liberated from the Germans. It was not strange that no one was doing anything to save the Baltic peoples. People who have been given away cannot be saved.

XXXI

The following day, Maksis decided to try again. He was doing his best to remain optimistic, but we had seen how difficult it was to escape in a little boat. Many boats had already sunk after being shot at, while others had gone to the bottom of their own accord in rough seas. I was now reluctant to take the risk. Thinking of Andris, I was overwhelmed by responsibility. No matter what I decided, it would be the wrong decision, and I wanted Ernests to be there to help me make the right decision. But what was the right decision? I thought of what might happen. If we stayed. If we left. Both Maksis and Elza talked at length with me, and I heard what they said, but I was no longer prepared to take such a step. I kept seeing Andris at the bottom of the sea, and I decided that anything was better than drowning. After everyone had left, I would return to Rīga and Auguste.

Would I see Maksis and Elza and the children again? Would I ever see my mother again? My decision to remain faltered as my family dressed in their warmest clothes and prepared to leave the house. I was unable to say anything to my mother or to Maksis; I held their hands tightly. Could I possibly keep them with me a little longer? I bit my lip to hold back tears. Then I pulled on my coat, and, wrapping a blanket around Andris, I said that I would follow them to the shore.

They left in the early afternoon, when heavy cloud cover and light rain were whispering about evening, and I stood on the beach until the little boat, sucked up by the clouds and the rain, finally disappeared. While I remained standing, surrounded by the cold wetness and my own thoughts, Alberts pulled the rowing boat up into the undergrowth; then he stood next to me for some time, smoking the end of his cigarette. I think he understood my need to remain on the beach while I followed them all in my mind, trying to keep them safe. Eventually, he took Andris, wrapped up in his blanket, and returned to the house. I did not object; the rain was heavier, and it was very cold.

After Alberts left, I moved back into the forest behind the beach, still looking out across the water but protected now by the trees. Beyond the quietness, I could hear only the rain and the sound of the waves against the shore. I felt anxious and uncomfortable, trying to imagine them all on the boat now well out to sea. Then my thoughts suddenly scattered like water in a pond, its surface broken by a falling stone. I was no longer in a forest somewhere on the edge of the Baltic Sea; I was in Rīga. And everywhere there were Soviet soldiers and tanks and trucks. And red flags hurriedly stretched across statues and buildings. The noise was what frightened me: the noise of sub-machine-guns, tanks rolling over cobbled streets, people running and shouting. I could see boots marching over streets where I had once walked with Ernests, and where I had run as a child.

I woke with a start. Had I actually been asleep? Here among the cold, water-dripping trees? Was it a dream, or was it something else? I looked out across the water, seeing nothing through the sheets of rain, and I started to walk towards the house, and it was then that I heard shooting and saw a plane wheeling in towards the shore. Then I saw the figures in the water, wading towards the beach.

As I ran back down towards the beach, I saw Maksis carrying Jānis, and Elza in tears, holding Ilona's hand. They had been shot at when they were in the boat, and the plane had followed them almost all the way back to shore. I looked around and saw other people in the water and on the beach, their faces already showing the horror of what they had experienced and the disbelief that they were actually still alive. I hugged my family, not knowing whether I should be overjoyed that we were all together again, or whether I should be devastated that they had not succeeded. Their exhaustion and disappointment were so obvious, but I had been given a sign. I knew now that I also had to leave and that someone was still watching over me. I was not supposed to be part of the devastation that was already sweeping through Latvia.

Later, when we had returned to the house, Alberts fetched some vodka and sat down at the well-scrubbed table with Maksis. He shook his head wearily. He pushed one of the glasses towards Maksis.

"There has to be a next time," he said, looking into his own glass before quickly emptying it in one mouthful.

Maksis sat looking at nothing in particular. He was totally spent. His face was grey, and the hand holding the glass was trembling.

"Perhaps we have used all our next times." A slight flicker of a smile crossed his face. "It was far too close today." He reached over and poured himself a second glass. "I still don't understand how they could have missed. We could see the shots in the water, all around us." He drank quickly.

Like Alberts, I knew that it was going to be difficult for Maksis to try a third time.

Having made tea while Elza put her two children to bed, I sat quietly in the small kitchen, absorbing the wonderful presence of my brother. The brother I thought I may have lost for ever. While everyone else was shattered, I felt that my life had been returned to me, not only my life but the lives of all those dear to me. I wondered how I could have considered separating myself from them. They were returned for one purpose only, so that Andris and I could make the crossing with them.

I placed her hand over my mother's. We had never had an emotional relationship, and the physical contact felt strange. I could understand my mother's disappointment, but understanding was mixed up with my own happiness at having been given another chance. Should I weep with them over their failed attempt or should I rejoice over their return? I was still not sure. Had they succeeded, I would never have known.

My mother drank the hot tea and, after a long silence, turned to me and said: "I'm actually glad that we had to return." She was quiet for a moment, searching for words. "I'm not sure that I could have gone on living without you, Nika."

I kept my hand on her hand, holding on to the words, not wanting them to break up and become part of the silence around us. They were the most beautiful words I had ever heard my mother say to me.

XXXII

I asked him, "But, Maksis, the guards. Why were there no guards in the tower?" I remembered the look he had given me the first time we had tried to leave. But there had been no guards in the tower the second time either. "What happened to them, Maksis?"

Maksis looked at me for a moment, and then he picked out a cigarette from the small silver case in his coat pocket. He tapped the cigarette lightly on the table with one hand while he searched in his pocket for his lighter.

"They were bought, Nika." Finding the lighter. Lighting the cigarette. Leaning back, drawing in the nicotine.

"Bought?" I looked at my brother, the soft trail of smoke winding around his head.

He laughed, removing the cigarette from his mouth. "I bought them."

I looked at him. Perplexed.

"Do you remember the day Alberts and I disappeared?"

I thought back, trying to remember. Things were all so hazy. So much had happened in such a short time. I nodded.

"We were fetching vodka." He ashed the cigarette. "Three whole demijohns."

I wondered where they had found so much vodka. Grain went to food now when there was so much hunger everywhere. Vodka was hard to come by. There was much I wanted to ask, but I said nothing.

"Then I talked to the guards in the guard tower. They became very friendly when I said that I had vodka." He laughed again.

"And when I said that I could give it to them, they were suddenly extremely helpful. They told me that there would be no one in the tower for a couple of days."

Maksis looked at me. "Two demijohns of vodka." He returned the cigarette to his mouth.

"But we are still here. We haven't left." I wondered what would happen now when the vodka was all gone, and the guards had returned to the tower.

My brother quickly looked across the room at Alberts as he removed the cigarette from his mouth. "I'm hoping that the deal still stands." He got up and pulled on his overcoat. The rain of the previous day had all but disappeared, and there was a weak sun pushing through the clouds. "I'll be back," he said as the door closed behind him.

The autumn storms are gathering on the horizon, and the Russians are quickly spreading out over Latvia. Soon no one will be able to leave. But as Maksis walks away from the house, he reflects that without a moon the nights are still dark. There is still a chance that they will escape, but it is becoming smaller. Ventspils has already been bombed several times. He walks through the wet forest, breathing in the freshness of the rain and the general smell of decay and mushrooms. When he reaches the shore, he stands for a few moments, lighting a cigarette, looking out to sea. He listens to the waves beating against the beach and wonders what it is like across the water in Sweden. He wonders if they will ever get there; it is not much further than than one hundred nautical miles, but everything seems to be against them. He is not sure if he has the strength to try one more time.

He pulls his coat tighter around him. He looks in the direction of the guard tower. He can see that the guards are there. He crushes the cigarette under his boot and walks in the direction of the tower. It worked before; it has to work again. They have to leave that evening. It is the twenty-first of October, and now the moon will begin waxing.

He keeps behind the trees and looks up into the tower. It is only metres away. A timber hut held aloft on a timber construction; one of the more basic towers that had appeared along the coast in the last few months. He can see the wooden stairs winding around the outside of the support construction. The hut itself would probably not hold more than than five people at the most. He knows that there is a window on the sea side, the side that is looking away from him. One of the guards opens the door at the top of the stairs and stands for a moment, looking over the railing. It is a different guard. Maksis realizes that there has been a change of guard. He wonders whether someone had become suspicious or whether it would have happened anyway. He remains standing there for a long time, trying to make up his mind, changing plans. Making new ones. Then he returns to the house.

We leave the house in the early evening and walk quietly down to the beach. No one speaks; everyone is wondering whether or not we will succeed – this time. Maksis has said that he will meet us on the beach, but he is nowhere to be seen. Alberts and Emīls pull the rowing boat down to the edge of the water. Further out, just beyond the breakers, I can see the shape of the fishing boat; it is too dangerous for it to come in any closer. The fisherman has come as close as he dares. The sea is not rough, but it is not calm either. He waves to us, wanting us to hurry up; there are already people on board.

Alberts rows back and forth between the shore and the fishing boat. Maksis is still nowhere to be seen. I begin to be anxious, and I wonder what will happen when everyone is on the boat. Will it leave without Maksis? I am already in the fishing boat, and I look up at the tower, and I notice that there is a light on in the room, but the circling light has stopped.

The man who owns the fishing boat is blowing on his fingers, looking at the waves, gauging the wind. He is impatient. He wants to get away as quickly as possible. He is ready to pull up the anchor when I see Maksis running along the beach. Alberts is waiting for him; he knew that he would come.

When Maksis finally pulls himself up into the fishing boat, he holds Alberts' hand a moment, neither man saying anything. Then Alberts pushes the rowing boat away from the edge of the bigger boat and heads back over the breakers towards the shore.

The anchor has been raised, and the boat heads west out into the sea. It is an open boat; there is no upper deck and no protection. Just a small engine, a rudder for steering and a greasy tarpaulin in case of rain.

It is cold and dark. I cannot see the other people huddled under coats and rugs, but I know that they are there. A child cries, and its mother comforts it. There is still no movement from the guard tower. No spotlight. The boat moves silently in the darkness into deeper water, heading west.

I see that the owner of the boat nods at Maksis and smiles. Perhaps he knows more than I do. I hold Andris in my arms. The boat is sitting low in the water, and the waves seem very close. I am already feeling cold, and we still have hours ahead of us. The shoreline disappears. I know that it is there, but everything is dark, and we are moving further and further away from everything we have ever known. I think only of Ernests, wondering where he is and whether he is still alive. I wonder if I will ever see him again.

We are completely immersed in cold, wet blackness. It is around us and above us and under us. I sit near the back of the boat with Andris in my arms. I have wrapped him in several shawls, but the cold is seeping through everything.

We are almost fifty people pressed up against each other in our coats and shawls and rugs, hugging our small bags of possessions, all we now have to connect us to our homeland. As the dark shore becomes even darker and finally disappears, we wonder silently if we will ever return.

There is no room to move on the boat. We have to keep still, knowing how easily the boat could sink. It has already happened, many times. Some boats have sunk with too many people on board, while others have been fired on by Russian planes. I close my eyes, not wanting to think about such boats, cramped with people, losing their way in the middle of a cold, dark space. They may have spun quickly out of control, taunted by angry winds and enormous seas, or they may have sunk slowly, no longer able to keep afloat. I know that, if we were to sink, no one would ever know because no one knew that we had left. I bury my face in Andris' shawls and breathe in his peaceful baby smell. For his sake, we must keep afloat. We have to reach Sweden.

I think again of Ernests. I wonder where he is. Will he find us when he returns? If he returns. Should I have stayed in case he returns?

Maksis is sitting next to me; I know that he understands. We have passed through such places before. He stretches out his hand and places it on my knee. "Everything will work out," he whispers.

I nod, hanging on to his words. Yes, everything will be all right; it has to be.

XXXIII

Nina looks at her brother. Her eyes ask: Tell me what happened?

Something, almost like a smile, runs across his face. He looks tired. His arm is around Jānis. Latvia is disappearing to the east. Around them is only darkness.

He looks back at her. "Later," he says, touching her hand. "When it is all over."

She nods slowly.

More than an hour has passed when they hear a sound. Everyone strains their ears against the solid wall of blackness. From the sound, it has to be a boat, and it is coming towards them. As it gets closer, they can almost make out a very small light on the deck. They see that it is a German patrol boat, and a ripple of panic moves through the little fishing vessel. Some, but not all, of the German patrol boats pretend not to see people fleeing across the Baltic Sea.

As the patrol boat pulls alongside the fishing boat, Maksis greets the captain in German. He says that they are on their way to Estonia, but he is worried about the compass. He would be grateful if the captain could tell them if they should change their course.

The captain shakes his head in exasperation. Yes, they are definitely well off course. He takes the compass and alters it, before handing it back to Maksis. The wind is rising, and the salt spray is in everyone's face and hair. The little boat rocks on the water. Having thanked the German captain, Maksis sits back down while the owner of the fishing boat changes the direction north-north-east.

The German boat disappears quickly, leaving them once again alone in the middle of the very dark and restless ocean. They dare not change their course back to what it was. They know that they will miss Gotland. They will swing around to the west in another hour or so.

Maksis sits and ponders over their meeting with the Germans. He lights a cigarette, thinking about things that do not make much sense. He knows that Germany has been allowing the movement of boats between the three Baltic countries, but now Germany herself is on the run. Perhaps the answer was hidden somewhere there. The biggest worry is the Russian navy. Since Finland pulled out of the war, Russia has had unhindered access to the Baltic Sea. He draws on his cigarette and tries not to think about things that might not even happen.

Nina remembers her dream and how she had been told not to worry, because everything would be taken care of.

The night is long and cold. The wind increases, but the boat remains steady in the water. Small children cry occasionally and eventually fall asleep exhausted.

The man on the tiller does not talk much. He guides his boat over the waves, looking at the few stars visible in the cloudy sky. Soon it will be impossible to get across the Baltic Sea; the Russians have already put roadblocks on the roads leading towards the coast. Soon they will increase the guards on the coast. Today, tomorrow, next week. He does not know for sure, but he knows that it will happen.

No one can move in the boat. There is so little room. It is a strange feeling, being cramped in the darkness, not being able to see anything and hearing the roll of the water and feeling the lurching of the boat.

Then, towards dawn, the shape of a ship appears on the horizon ahead of them.

XXXIV

It is morning in a guard tower just a few kilometres south of Kolka on the Latvian west coast, and three Russians are slowly waking. They cannot remember much from the previous evening, but they know that someone else has been there. They look around the room, but they are the only ones there. One of them is holding his head in his hands. They become aware of the grey chill that has seeped into the room. The stove is dead and cold. The older man opens the metal door and pushes in some wood and some kindling; he watches as the small flame takes hold, and then he shuts the stove door. The youngest of the three steps out on to the platform, letting the cold morning air cut through his body. There are so many pieces that have to be remembered and then joined together. He shivers, but at the same time he feels that the sudden rush of crisp, cutting air is doing him good. He swings himself down the stairs and runs up and down a few times beneath the tower. Then he relieves himself while he looks out to sea. The chill is getting worse. He buttons his trousers and returns to the tower. He is pleased to get back to the room which has begun to feel slightly warmer.

The other two men have noticed that the signal light has been switched off. They talk about it for a moment, but no one can remember when they would have done such a thing. The young soldier sits down at the table and lights a cigarette. The older man opens the journal and sits tapping his fingers on the table. Then he looks at the other two and asks, "Nothing to report?"

They both shake their heads, and he writes the same in the journal: Nothing to report. His handwriting is neat. The ink glistens for a moment on the page, but it dries quickly. He closes the journal, and he moves a pot of water on to the stove that is now well alight. Whatever happened, it will remain their secret.

Alberts and Emīls are not so lucky. It is difficult to have secrets when there are other people taking notes and making observations. Several months later, when the Soviets have moved in and all the exits have been closed, someone begins to question why the people staying with Alberts and Emīls are no longer there. Alberts and Emīls are both shot.

XXXV

The dark shape looming in front of them is coming closer. Some of the people are wondering whether or not they should panic. So close and yet still so far away. The man on the tiller says that they should try to remain calm. Maksis believes that it is a Swedish ship. Another man fears that it could be a Russian ship flying a Swedish flag.

There is more light in the sky. It is possible now to see that the sky and the water are two separate elements. The ship, a destroyer, is grey, and the flag is blue and yellow. Soon it is possible to see figures on the upper deck; they are all in uniform, and they are standing near the railing.

The people who could not decide whether or not they should panic quickly decide on a compromise and throw all their papers overboard. Now they are nobodies, unconnected with any country or any government. They feel safer and, yet, at the same time, more vulnerable, more lost. Nina holds her baby and her small cardboard suitcase. She has lost almost everything; she cannot afford to lose her identity as well.

The men on the ship have thrown some ropes over the side, and one of them lowers himself over the edge. Nina is impressed by his agility – a figure in white against the grey hull. A man near the railing has a megaphone. He tells the people not to be afraid. He speaks German and Swedish. He tells them that they are safe. The people who panicked look into the water, but their papers have all gone.

The man from the ship secures the boat to the side of the larger vessel. Maksis and two of the other men help him. A rope ladder is thrown over the side, and the Swedish sailors help the people from the little boat on board. Children, bags and small suitcases are passed from hand to hand, up the ladder and over the railing. The men climb up the ladder themselves, holding on to nervous women or old parents. The man with the tiller sits patiently, keeping the boat steady, offering words of encouragement. When everyone is on board the destroyer, he ties the tiller in place, and taking hold of the rope ladder he climbs up on to the ship.

The destroyer sets course for Nynäshamn on the Swedish mainland, north of the island of Gotland. The little boat, now released from all its ropes but one, is towed behind the destroyer – a large whale and its calf.

They had thought that they were closer to Sweden than they actually were, and the fact that they had to change direction has taxed everyone's navigational skills. It takes the ship almost all of that day to reach Nynäshamn. During the trip, the refugees are well taken care of below decks. Food and dry blankets are handed around. Babies are given warm milk, and children, happy to be able to stretch cramped legs, shyly accept sweets from the attentive sailors. Mothers drink hot coffee and wonder how they survived the trip. The men look in admiration at the ship and its cannons.

Nina notices that the ship is called *Gävle*. A strange name that she cannot pronounce. She puts it away inside of herself; her first Swedish word. It is the twenty-second of October 1944.

At some point, the little boat breaks loose and disappears, an empty rope left hanging over the destroyer's stern.

The man who owned the little boat shrugs. "It has done its work," he says.

Three

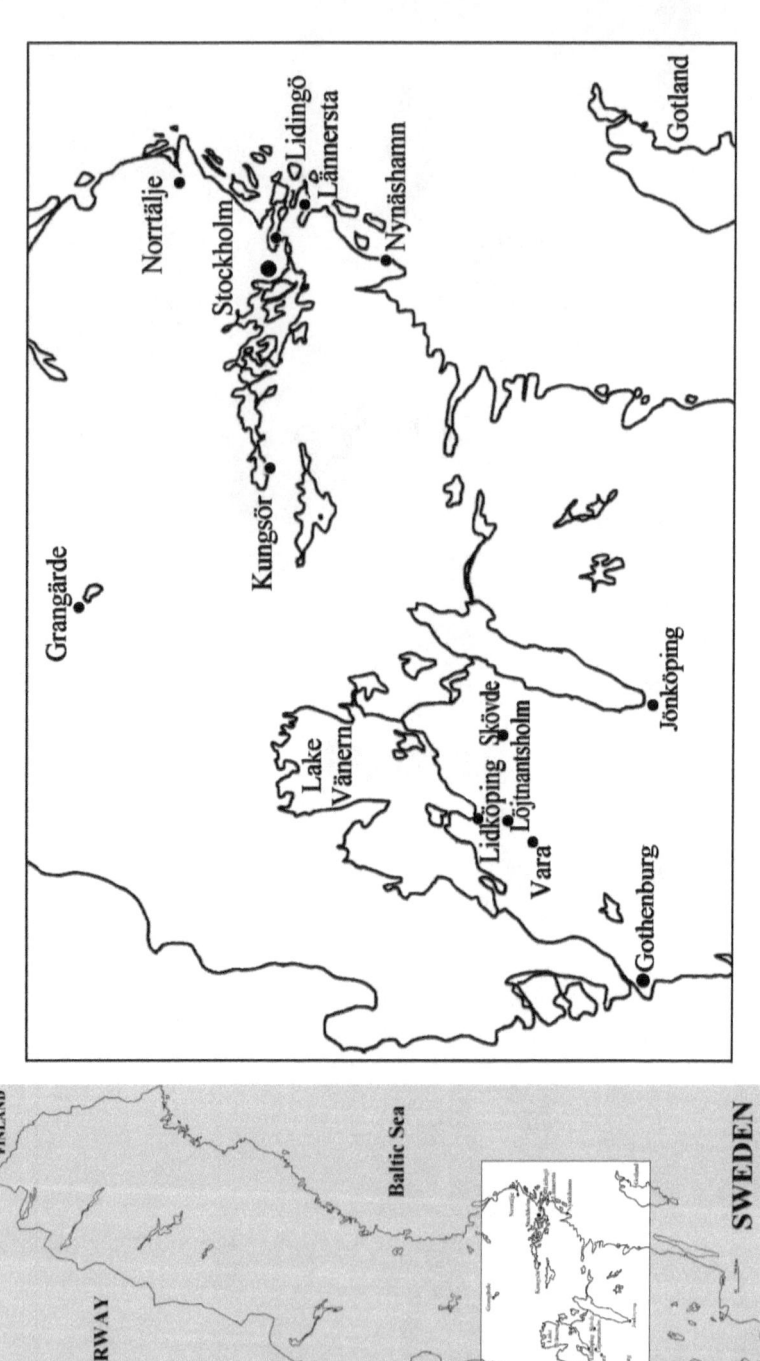

I

His pain is no longer his own; everyone now shares it. It has spread throughout the entire house, pushing against the afternoon light and replacing it with a grey emptiness. Questions slip out from behind furniture and long flimsy curtains, but remain unanswered. Eventually, they return to their hiding places, to wonder and to brood.

The children say it cannot possibly be true. There has to be a mistake; perhaps she was merely sleeping. He shakes his head, knowing better. He closes his eyes and watches the past few hours passing again before his mind, in slow motion. No, there was no mistake: this is what life is. If there is a beginning, then there also has to be an end. We spend all our time huddled in the middle, wondering about the beginning while refusing to accept that there must be an end. Everything has to end. Everyone has to end. This day would also end.

He thinks of her white hair neatly pulled back in a small bun on the back of her neck. He also thinks of the dark woollen hat she always wore when the weather was colder. He hugs the child crying quietly, and then he walks across to his workshop and sits looking out of the window, seeing nothing.

II

In her diary, she wrote: 'On the thirty-first of October, we left Nynäshamn to travel further north. We had been given very little information: we were not told how far we would be going or even where we were going. When we reached the train station, after the bus ride from the camp, we were directed to a second-class carriage, and we became a little anxious as to what might lie ahead. But the carriage was surprisingly comfortable, and our fears, as it turned out, were completely unfounded.

'The train headed north and passed through many stations, both large and small, all with strange unpronounceable names: Segersäng, Hemfosa, Tungelsta, Västerhaninge, Älvsjö... Then, at midday, we reached Stockholm's South City Station. I was completely overwhelmed, unable to believe that I was actually in Stockholm. I looked around me, at the islands and the bridges and the buildings, wondering if I was in the middle of a dream, or even a nightmare, and that I would soon wake up and find myself somewhere else and nowhere near Stockholm.

'But we did not leave the train in Stockholm. The train did not even stop but continued north and then west, past Karlsberga, Spånga, Backeby, Enköping, Gillberga, Västerås, Dingtuna, Kolbäck, Köping. Many more strange, unpronounceable names. From my window, I watched as the train rushed past large forests and innumerable lakes. Wherever I looked, there were birch trees – some with yellow autumn leaves still clinging to branches – and dark green-blue spruce. There were also lots of rocky cliffs, many of which were completely overgrown with green and grey moss. Eventually, I became quite dizzy with the movement of the train and the never-ending stream of new sights, and I was forced to close my eyes.

'It was already quite dark when we finally arrived at our destination: a place called Kungsör. From the train window, I could see trucks and buses lined up outside the station. As we got off the train, we discovered that they were there to take us to our next home – a school's gymnasium.'

The people washed up on Gotland or pulled out of the water at Nynäshamn were later moved to one of the many quarantine camps, all part of the hastily planned refugee process, and many, like Nina and her family, were sent to Kungsör. After they had gone, and after a strange, empty silence had settled over the town, Nynäshamn continued to look out across the water as though nothing had happened. But something had happened, and the buildings, and even the people living there, knew that things would never be exactly the same again. Everything and everyone had absorbed the pain and the disbelief of the people who had stepped on to the rain-swept wharves, people who had clutched small bags filled with the few disparate things remaining from their past.

After Nynäshamn and Gotland, news of what had happened combined like rivulets into something wider and faster, running through the country, turning people's attention eastwards and beyond. Newspapers published long articles, and many Swedes shook their heads and wondered how such things could have been happening, only one hundred and fifty kilometres beyond the safety of their own borders.

Boats had been sunk. Many people had drowned, while many others had been shot or captured. Those who had stepped on to the wharf in Nynäshamn wondered why they had been saved. They looked around and saw no destruction, no yawning holes after bombs, no homeless people, no orphaned children. They wondered how it was possible that the world could be so different on the two sides of such a small space.

Outside the camp where they sat in disbelief, they were able to glimpse neat red cottages and clean stone buildings while their souls remained caught up in a nightmare that refused to go away. They did not know whether they should feel relieved or guilty. They had dragged themselves across dark, cold waters, while behind them there were many who now slept somewhere in that vacuum between fear and freedom. There were also many who had not dared enter that space, who had decided that the cost of uncertain freedom far outweighed the fear that they had had flung upon them.

After all the fragments of disbelief and uncertainty and guilt and thankfulness had become fused together in the name *Nynäshamn*, Nikolina and her family spent six weeks in quarantine in Kungsör, hidden behind barbed-wire fences erected to enclose the threat of tuberculosis, typhoid and cholera. It was during these weeks that the fragments began to unravel, and the enormity of their flight, their rescue and everything that happened both before and since finally assumed shapes – many still wrapped in question marks – which could be dealt with only in small pieces or could be locked away in some part of the mind marked *never to open*. Keys were then purposely lost or thrown away. Now the focus was entirely on survival.

They did not know why they were safely behind friendly barbed wire in Sweden, while others were lying at the bottom of the Baltic Sea, or, even worse, were imprisoned within the boundaries of that which had always been their home. Nothing made sense any longer. The concept *home* had been distorted. They had no home. Other people had opened their own home to them; they were thankful, but they did not have the words to express their thanks. Some of them tried to say what they felt in German, but the borrowed language did not always describe what they really felt. It had been easier to have said everything in the language they spoke with each other, but those who passed in and out of the barbed wire, trying to help, understood without really knowing why.

In the darkness of the long winter nights, Nina's thoughts

attempted to make sense of all that had happened since they had left Rīga, even since they had left Rundāle. She could still not understand why they had been spared, when so many others had died. She knew that she had to keep going for the sake of those who had perished. But she was no longer sure of where she was going. She missed Ernests, and she missed Auguste. All she wanted was for things to be as they used to be.

It was while they were still in Nynäshamn that Maksis remembered the look Nina had given him in the boat. They were sitting on their own at a table near a window, in a large common room. Through the window, past the houses, it was possible to see the water, cold and ammunition-grey.

"After I left you," he began, his cigarette-case on the table, his lighter in his hand, "I walked to the guard tower." He opened the case and took out a cigarette.

Nina nodded. She had known that he must have gone to the tower.

Maksis put the cigarette between his lips, and Nina watched while the small flame from the lighter enveloped the tip of the cigarette. Then he breathed deeply, putting the lighter back in his pocket. For a moment, they both sat looking beyond the buildings at the water while the nicotine surged into his lungs, and the tip of the cigarette continued to glow. No one said anything; Nina followed a bird with her eyes as it flew across the water and then wheeled around towards the houses. When she lost sight of the bird and looked back at her brother, the cigarette was between his fingers.

He said, "They had changed the guards, you know."

No, she did not know. She looked at him, waiting for him to continue.

He shrugged. "Those bloody guards!" he said, wondering, yet again, as to why they had been changed, suddenly, without any warning. "Anyway..."

He looked out at the water beyond the houses. "We were running out of time. You know all of that; we had to leave that evening." He drew on the cigarette. Quickly.

She nodded.

"I still had some vodka left."

Nina thought how he had already used two of the three timber-encased demijohns that, for a few days, had stood in a corner of Alberts' kitchen. Maksis had covered them all with a large, maroon-coloured, knitted rug, but then two had suddenly disappeared, and the rug, folded in half, more than covered the remaining bottle.

"I had wanted to leave it with Alberts." he said, thinking how life insists on forging its own strange, unexpected paths. "Twenty litres." Maksis ashed the cigarette. "Our lives in the balance against twenty litres of vodka."

She looked at him and thought: Tell me what happened.

"I took the vodka and walked to the tower." He remembered how nervous he had been, the perspiration nudging and pushing through his clothes in spite of the cold. He had known that things could easily go wrong, just like when life cuts new paths and forgets about the precipice. While he walked, many images had rushed through his mind, including one of him lying dead on the beach. He had tried to obliterate the image; he knew that he had to stay alive. Everything depended on him.

While he was still looking at his sister, he drew on his cigarette one last time, and then he stubbed out the end in the glass ashtray. He massaged his forehead with his fingers and leant back in his chair. Then he told Nina what had happened after he had left the forest and had walked up to the tower.

III

The tower straddles both the edge of the forest and the edge of the beach, and, as Maksis reaches its foot, the door at the top is flung open, and a sub-machine-gun is aimed at him. He puts down the vodka, carefully. All the time his eyes never leave the gun. He raises his hands above his head.

"Don't shoot!" he calls out in Russian. "I'm a friend!" But his body tenses, waiting for the shots – the sharp sounds and the burning pain – that do not come. He thinks how easy it would be to shoot him where he is standing. There is no reason for the guard not to shoot him.

The soldier with the gun laughs quickly, the sound cutting the still, grey afternoon with a harsh, sharp line. "Friend?" he asks, still pointing the gun.

"Yes, a friend. A friend celebrating the end of the Germans." Maksis does not want to lower his hands, but he nods towards the vodka near his feet. "Perhaps we can celebrate together?"

The Russian has not yet let go of his suspicions, but he lowers the gun. "You have vodka? Real vodka?"

Maksis still has his hands in the air. "Lots of it. Good quality vodka – not the usual rubbish," he says, still thinking that this man could so easily shoot him. "Long live Stalin! Shall we drink to Stalin, to Russia, to the end of the Germans?

The young Russian is bored and cold. Perhaps the dull evening stretching out before him might not be so dull after all. He has already lowered the sub-machine-gun. Another man appears at the door. Curious. Suspicious.

Maksis nods to him. "Long Live Soviet Russia!" His mind is

racing around so many other things. Will they let him live? And if they do not let him live, will his family still be able to escape?

Without him?

He wants to keep living; he does not want to die.

The second man repeats, "Long Live Soviet Russia!"

The two men on the platform talk hurriedly between themselves. Someone calls out from inside the room, and the second man returns inside. The first man beckons to Maksis, who cautiously lowers his hands and picks up the large bottle in its wooden cage. It is heavy, and he needs both hands to carry it. He walks up the stairs slowly, knowing that the man above him still has his weapon in his hand. But the man does not shoot him, and, as Maksis reaches the top, the soldier slings the gun on to his shoulder and helps Maksis carry the vodka into the room.

As Maksis is straightening up after placing the heavy bottle on the floor, he is aware of someone standing next to him, and he feels something hard and cold against the side of his head. He stops breathing. He knows that the hard, cold thing is the barrel of a revolver. He imagines the man's finger tightening around the trigger. He knows that the tightening will be the line between light and darkness. There is now, and then there will be nothing. He waits for the nothing. The room is completely quiet. It is as though time itself has stopped, and everyone is waiting for the nothing. Seconds rush past while his mind explodes with memories of what has been, and he tries not to think of what is about to happen.

There is no shot, no quick line drawn between now and then. The man with the revolver returns it to its holster and stretches out his hand. He is smiling. "Lieutenant Alexsey Nikolayevich Denikin."

Maksis feels as though he died, and is now being dragged back into life. He cannot find his voice; it must have been left behind in that other place. He takes Aleksey's hand and nods. He can still feel the sweat on the back of his neck. Cold sweat.

The third man in the room, an older man, has been standing near the window. Now he crosses the room. "Captain Boris

Mikhailovich Malikov." He stretches out his hand while looking at his lieutenant without expression. "You must try to forgive Nikolaich."

Maksis nods again, feeling life trickling back into his body, finding its voice. "Maksim." He does not want to give them his name. He thinks of Jānis. "Ivanovich."

The captain has worn features. He looks at Maksis. "A friend of Stalin?"

Maksis can still not believe that he has moved from his past to his future. His left hand is still by his side; he tightens it into a fist. "Our dear father! May his life be long and fortunate!"

He thinks of the man who instigated the Year of Terror, the man who sent thousands to their graves and thousands more to hell. He knows that he must remain focussed; there is too much to lose.

He continues, "A great man! A really great man!" He waits to be struck down by some unexpected thunderbolt, but nothing happens.

Boris Mikhailovich smiles. "Welcome, my friend. Please, sit down." He turns to the youngest of the three men. "Sanych, get some glasses!"

Maksis looks at the man who first appeared on the platform, the man with the sub-machine-gun.

"Junior Lieutenant Yuri Aleksandrovich Samarin," says the captain, following the direction of Maksis' gaze.

Maksis nods and sits down on one of the two benches at the table. He looks around the room; it is not very big. Besides the crude table in the centre of the room and the benches on either side, there is a stove in the corner near the door, and Maksis can feel the heat from it pushing its way across the cold of the room. Near the stove, there is a pile of wood. There are a couple of roughly-hewn shelves on the wall furthest from the stove, with a collection of papers, books, glasses, pots and a tin of tea. Opposite the door, there is the large window looking out over the ocean.

His eyes rest on the large spotlight at the window. There is some kind of mechanism under it to allow it to move in a half circle, but it has not yet been switched on. There are some binoculars hanging from a nail on the wall; next to the spotlight, there is a machine-gun mounted on a stand, looking out over the water. Ready to shoot.

Yuri has found some glasses; Maksis removes the lid from the bottle.

"*Budem zdorovy!*" (Let's stay healthy!) Maksis says, as he measures out the liquid carefully. "Come, comrades – let's drink to victory!"

The afternoon has only moved half an hour since he left the house; the sky is metal grey, and there is a threat of rain. He is still alive, but he knows how quickly things can change.

They down the first glass.

"*Chtob vse byli zdorovy!*" they all say.

Maksis refills the glasses.

They drink a second glass. "Let everybody be healthy!"

The captain pours another round. He nods at Maksis before he drinks. "Your health!"

Maksis nods back and lifts his own glass.

The glasses are filled again, and any tension that may have been in the room is quickly disappearing. They are now all sitting around the table. After some minutes, Yuri gets up and walks to the window. He removes the binoculars from the nail and stands, looking out over the water, his back towards the room. Then he replaces the binoculars, and smiling, turns and walks back to the table. "Victory to Russia!" he says, sitting back down at the table.

"To Russia!" says Maksis, and then, "Another round?"

The guards relax. Both of the lieutenants are quite young, and the man called Yuri would be considered handsome. When Boris Mikhailovich gets up to refill the glasses, Maksis notices that he moves with a limp, possibly a war injury.

Soon they lose count of the number of glasses. Some of the vodka has spilt on to the floor. The afternoon wears on. They talk about Russia and her victories in Latvia and other places.

Everyone becomes friendlier. Aleksey, known as Nikolaich, puts his arm around Maksis and tells him what a good friend he is, and that he had never intended to shoot him. That it was just a joke. Maksis smiles. Someone says something derogatory about Germans. They all laugh. Another toast for the Russians, Stalin, the end of the war.

It is becoming greyer and darker. Someone gets up and switches on the light. Slowly it begins to swing from side to side, lighting a path across the water.

There is no end to the vodka. The men become even more friendly. They talk about their families, their girlfriends, Russia. Boris Mikhailovich is from Leningrad. Maksis says that he has also lived there. Once, a long time ago. The man looks at him as he would at a long-lost brother, and they both toast Leningrad. Then they toast Moscow and Stalin and Russia.

The light continues across the water. The afternoon merges into evening. It is dark. Maksis thinks of the people in the little house beyond the forest; they will soon be getting ready to leave. Yuri already has his head on the table. He is sound asleep. Aleksey says yet again that Maksis is a true comrade, a great friend. The captain thinks of his home and his wife and his two grown children. He offers a toast to all of them and then to Maksis. Maksis pours another round.

Boris says something about people escaping in small boats. Maksis shakes his head and asks why anyone would want to leave, now when the Germans are being annihilated.

Nikolaich starts singing; then the singing stops, without warning, and the lieutenant slides off the bench on to the floor. Now only Maksis and the older man remain at the table. They continue drinking glass for glass. There is very little vodka remaining in the bottle when Boris Mikhailovich finally leans back on the bench with a sigh and falls into a deep sleep.

Maksis listens to the mechanism driving the light. Backwards and forwards. He sits for a short moment. Then, having checked that all the men are sleeping, he turns off the spotlight and leaves the tower, quietly closing the door behind him.

The cold air rushes at him when he opens the door. For a moment, he feels dizzy. He closes his eyes tightly, holding on to the rail, regaining his balance. Then he breathes in the moist night air and, opening his eyes, carefully climbs down the stairs. Now he must hurry. They will already be on the beach. They could even be in the boat. He prays that the guards remain asleep, at least until the boat is beyond the range of the tower.

IV

Sweden had been one of the few countries able to retain a semblance of neutrality during the war. Although affected by shortages and the general anxiety of war, she did not have to watch in terror as centuries of culture were reduced to blackened rubble. No one marched in and demanded that she accept a Pact of Defence and Mutual Assistance. No one sent her citizens to Siberian labour camps, or had them shot on trumped-up charges. No one pulled down signs in Swedish and replaced them with signs in a foreign language.

The Allies, concerned about Germany's access to northern Sweden's rich iron ore deposits, eventually decided to seize the mines together with the harbours in both Sweden and Norway, through which the ore was shipped. But Germany became aware of the plans and, taking the initiative, invaded and occupied both Norway and Denmark, thereby securing the waters off the Norwegian coast. Sweden, still supplying Germany with iron ore, was spared, though, with her neighbours to the west already occupied by Germany and those to the east under assault by the Soviet Union, her position by the early 1940s had become extremely precarious.

Being neutral may have given Sweden certain advantages, but it demanded agile footwork among a barrage of unpredictable expectations and requests. When the path took a sudden turn or ran along the edge of perpendicular drops, she had to retain her balance, knowing what would happen to her if she were to fall. She gave certain concessions to Germany and other concessions to the Allies. Journalists were reminded not to lean too much towards either one side or the other. They were told to offer unemotional reportage, without any personal evaluations – even if their own personal evaluations may have been correct. Objectivity was the keyword. As the war accelerated, it became obvious that this was not always easy. It was impossible to remain completely impartial: thousands of Finnish children and Jews were given sanctuary; then, in 1944, Sweden opened her doors to the Baltic refugees.

V

The refugees remained in quarantine at Kungsör until the eleventh of December, when it was decided that none of them were contagious, and they were moved again. This time they were sent to Grangärde in Dalarna, in central Sweden, where they were surrounded by frozen lakes and forests already dusted white. They knew that the beauty was there – clean and crisply cold – but it remained outside the camp while, on the inside, immigration officials and social workers interviewed them from behind large desks covered with piles of papers. The officials then wrote things on other papers and put the new papers on the piles already on the desks. Most of the interviews were carried out in German.

Maksis spoke with employment officers who studied his qualifications and told him that they would see what they could. There were many professional people in the camp, but none of them spoke Swedish, and the people behind the desks had to decide what to do with them. By the spring of 1945, they had worked their way through some of the piles, and then they told Maksis that he had been offered a position with a chemical technical company in Saltsjöbaden. The owner, a German called Fischer, was happy for Maksimiljāns and his family to live with him until other accommodation could be organized. Family did not include Rozalija, Nikolina and Andris.

Maksis and Elza and the children would be leaving the camp, and they would be starting a new life. Nina tried to convince herself that she was happy for Maksis while other emotions rapidly expanded within her, making her aware of her devastation. In all the months that had passed since they fled, and even before, she had never once thought that they could be separated, and the enormity of what she had done took on the form of an immense black cliff that was moving closer and closer to her, threatening to enclose her in total darkness. Threatening to suffocate her. If only she could turn off her mind and stop thinking. She tried to imagine herself back in Rīga, in Auguste's house, Ernests sitting in the kitchen talking to Maksis. This is the way it was supposed to be. But, while she was forcing herself back into the past, pushed-down feelings of bewilderment and uncertainty were being squeezed to the surface. The cliff was closing in, and she could see no way past it; she wondered how she was going to be able to survive, without Ernests and now without Maksis.

She needed to find a balance within herself, but she did not know where to find the point of equilibrium. Her thoughts persisted in swirling in all directions, collecting memories. She found herself in Petrograd, enveloped by a thought that had stopped in its flight and had come closer, solidifying as it did so. It was a thought made up of lines of red and purple on black; as she concentrated on it more intensely, she could see the soft folds of cloth, and then she remembered.

The scarf. Packed away among all the thoughts and all the memories, hiding somewhere in the background while everything else surged past. It had beckoned to her, wrapping itself around her, pulling her back through all those memories and all that time.

She was in Petrograd. She peered at the memory as everything became brighter, clearer. She could see her own shadowy shape, and next to herself she could see another shape. As she moved closer, she could see that it was Maksis. She recognized buildings, and she wondered if everything looked the same now as it did then. She doubted it. So much had happened since Petrograd. It was not even called Petrograd any longer. Would she ever be able to find her way back to those memories? She peered into the darkness and followed the shapes. Her mind had become the streets of Petrograd. As she stepped into her own mind, she stepped into the past. The figures and shadows came to life, and she was no longer in Sweden, but she was twelve years old, holding Maksis' hand somewhere on a street in Petrograd.

She thought that it may have been summer; they were out walking, and they stopped before a street stall. There were many people in the street, pushing and shouting, looking at merchandise. She could see the old woman, with the embroidered headscarf, sitting on an upturned box, reading her cards. Further away, Nina could see some brown-grey soldiers smoking, part of the crowd, yet disconnected. Then her mind propelled her further along, and she saw that she was trying to keep up with her brother while people pushed all around her. Suddenly, she darted to one side as a horse and cart hurried past, and she saw Maksis laughing as he pulled her closer to him, telling her to watch where she was walking. That was when they stopped in front of the street-stall with all the scarves.

Several lines, strung between grey poles quickly hammered into the soft earth, were covered with scarves of all colours and patterns.

"Would you like one, Nika?" he had asked, pointing at a scarf, the cigarette between his fingers, his other hand still holding hers. "Perhaps this one?"

She had barely caught her breath after the horse and the cart. She looked up at the beautiful pieces of fabric hanging above her head. She was both confused and delighted. She imagined herself touching one of the squares of fabric, holding it against her face, running her fingers over the intricate patterns.

The cigarette was still in his hand. She noticed the glowing red tip.

"Come on, Nika. Which one do you want?" He smiled at her. The red tip moved in an arc as he pointed to the scarf that was closest to them. "This one?"

The stall-owner, a dark-haired woman in a long, red skirt and a man's overcoat unbuttoned over a black and yellow blouse, watched them hopefully but not too hopefully. She touched a couple of the scarves, opening out the folds, showing the patterns, indicating the colours.

Nina noticed the woman's worn boots, and then she looked back at the colours, the colours that were moving and disappearing. Some of the shawls were bunched up together, forming bundles of colour.

Nikolina pointed to a scarf near the end of one of the lines. It was a black scarf edged with three wide bands of flowers in red and purple. There were other colours there as well, but it was the red and purple that caught her eye.

"This one," she said softly.

Later, as she walked back home with Maksis' hand in hers, holding the scarf against her face, feeling the soft, smooth woollen texture of the cloth, sensing its comforting, warm smell, she remembered feeling happy and content and safe. She no longer had the scarf, but she wished that she could still feel Maksis' hand in hers and that nothing would make him let go.

But, on a light-filled early spring day when new leaves were appearing as small pale-green mouse ears on dark branches, Nina felt her brother's hand slip from her grasp as Maksis and his family were collected in a black car and taken from the camp to the station. Nina followed them out into the yard. Then, after the car doors had slammed shut, and the car had moved off, she remained standing, waving until she could see them no more. Eventually, she went back inside, trying to hide her red eyes and wet face behind her hand, hoping she would not meet anyone. She wondered if it was possible for things to get any worse. She did not think so.

Finally, she ran out of tears, and all that was left was a stomach-twisting sense of indescribable loss and the razor-sharp pain of separation. If there had not been other people around her, she would have shouted out her pain to the God who had quietly watched while her country had been violated, while her husband had been taken from her and, now, while her brother – the only remaining rock in all the uncertainty that surged around her – had also been taken away, leaving her on her own.

But she knew that she was not completely on her own; she had her mother and Andris. As the tears dried, she knew that someone – was it that same God? – had been watching over her. She thought of Saunaga and the planes and the guns and of everything that could have happened and did not happen. Was it that God who had stood next to Maksis in the tower and who, later, had stayed with them in the boat? Did He keep them afloat until help had appeared from nowhere?

She shamefully regretted all her negative thoughts. She had been ungrateful. She hoped that God would understand. She was, after all, only human. She washed her face, wiping away the marks of tears, then later, she wrote long letters to Maksis and Elza. Perhaps, eventually, they would all be reunited in Stockholm. If she believed strongly enough, then it might happen.

And while she was still clinging to that belief, the war ended, and Peace was proclaimed. People looked around at themselves and each other. They saw the devastation that had been wrought, and they despaired of moving on while they knew that it would be impossible to return to what once might have been considered normal. Nina read newspapers in German and Latvian, and she picked through words in Swedish articles, where black and white photos said more than the text she could barely understand. She learnt of the chaos in Germany and of the thousands of displaced people without proper accommodation and without sufficient food. She looked at the photos, and she thought of Ernests. In Grangärde, they had shelter and food. She thought again of her ingratitude, and she hoped that God understood. She was, after all, only one insignificant person among all those millions of people, all crying out for help. God need not have helped her but He had.

On the eighth of May 1945, the world celebrated with such an outpouring of joy and relief that people wondered how it had been possible for the war to have continued for so long. It was obvious that so many, on both sides, had only ever wanted a peaceful resolution. Nikolina read about the suicides of Hitler and Goebbels, and she thought back to Rundāle in 1941 when Goebbels had told her that some mistakes can have disastrous consequences. She knew that the last six years had been a dreadful mistake; she wondered if anyone would now have the energy to deal with the consequences.

There were many other Latvians in the camp, and she felt as though she were on a small, but vaguely familiar, island. She did not know these other people, but their stories were similar, and they were able to communicate with each other using words that reached back across the Baltic Sea, into a time that had now disappeared. Beyond the island there was still darkness, but it was beginning to lighten somewhat as her tongue learnt the strange Swedish sounds, and her mind grappled with the different customs and the generosity of a people who had only heard about the darkness but had not experienced it. Perhaps all the broken, jagged, blackened pieces would suddenly revert to what they had been. Treaties and documents would be torn up, and then, perhaps, they would all be able to go home.

Most Latvians believed that international pressure on the Soviet Union would make Stalin release the Baltic countries, but, as the game being played between the Western Powers and the Soviet Union became more apparent, it was realized that such hopes were nothing more than the stuff of dreams. For many, though, dreams are the thin line between survival and oblivion.

While the world rejoiced, Baltic refugees anxiously began to await deportation back to their home countries. The Baltic States were now considered to be part of the Soviet Union, and it was difficult to know how other countries would deal with the thousands of refugees from Latvia, Lithuania and Estonia. The United States and Britain had agreed to recognize the 1940 borders of Soviet occupation in return for Stalin's continuing support, while, in other forums, they declared the annexation of the Baltic countries to be illegal. All the most powerful countries were still playing games, and the less powerful, easily dispensable countries had become a form of insurance that could be easily negotiated.

While Britain and the United States moved cautiously around the issue, Sweden gave diplomatic recognition to the Soviet Union's incorporation of Estonia, Latvia and Lithuania, implying that the Baltic refugees were, in fact, Soviet citizens. Thousands of war-weary people in Sweden who had believed that they found a haven from both the past and the future waited in suspense to hear that they were no longer welcome.

Each day, Nikolina and Rozalija expected to be sent home, to a home that no longer was a home. Nikolina thought a lot about ingratitude and retribution. If she had been able to disappear into some bottomless hole, she may have done so, but she had Andris to think of, so she concentrated on positive thoughts and hoped that the Swedes would let them stay.

Then the Swedes announced that there was actually a distinction between civilian Balts and those who had served with the Wehrmacht. It was decided that the refugees would be allowed to remain where they were.

VI

She writes with black ink on a thin sheet of lined paper. When she looks up, she can see the yellow and green plains of southern Sweden stretching out beyond the window. She thinks: Don't worry. She writes: '*Please* don't worry about us.' Were she Elza, she probably would worry. Thinking of the isolation and the distance.

After all those months in the camp, they were not sent to Stockholm to join Maksis and Elza, but to Västergötland on the opposite side of Sweden. Some families needed extra hands on farms; others had seen all the images and read all the words. This was a family who was trying to come to terms with all the black and white pictures – and the words.

The camp had been slowly emptying for some time; faces that had become familiar had disappeared, chairs remaining forlornly empty around the dinner tables. Those who remained had then wondered how long it would be until they also would be moved elsewhere.

It was a warm Sunday morning in July, shortly after breakfast. Nikolina was in the kitchen stacking dishes when Per, a somewhat stressed middle-aged man who worked in the office, put his head around the door and said that he needed to talk to her. She wiped her hands on a towel hanging near the large deep sink and straightened her hair. She was almost sure that she already knew what he wanted to talk to her about, but she was trying not to imagine what he might, or might not, be going to say. She needed to hear him say that they would be moved to Stockholm, somewhere near her brother, and she did not want to jeopardize her chances by thinking about what she wanted him to say. Or what he might not say. She knew that she had to clear her mind of all such thoughts, both positive and negative; only then was there a chance that he might have something positive to tell her. A small whirlwind of excitement rushed through her. In spite of her resolution to keep her mind completely blank, she could not help wondering if they might be about to be moved somewhere, and if there actually was a chance that she might see her brother and his family again.

Per opened a map of Sweden across his large, but very cluttered, oak desk – the creases in the map forming long straight lines of hills, cutting the map into sections – and pointed to a small dot in the south-west, not far from a large lake.

"This is Vara," he said in perfect German. "Jan and Svea Swantesson." He looked at her then, needing to explain. "They are the people who have offered..." He looked back down at the letter he was holding in his hand. Should he say: to take you? It sounded wrong. He decided to let the sentence hang there somewhere above the map, with his finger above the small dot.

When Nina did not say anything, he continued, his eyes running quickly over the letter. "It says here that they own a large dairy." He placed the letter on the table and began to fold up the map. The lines of hills disappeared as the map became smaller and more compact. "It will mean that you can leave the camp." He was quiet for a moment; when Nikolina still said nothing, he added, "I understand that there is a house, a separate house."

After all the months of living with other people, Nikolina's eyes lit up momentarily. She imagined being in a house of her own without lots of strangers. Without Maksis and Elza and the children.

She took a deep breath. "We had so much hoped to be sent somewhere near Stockholm." She faltered, "My brother and his family were sent there." She was wondering about positive and negative thoughts and the extent to which they can influence anyone's future. Perhaps she had thought all the wrong thoughts?

Per looked at her, almost sympathetically. The letter was

lying on the table, next to the map now without any hills. "Yes, Frau Abolins. We are aware of that." He sighed, "We do what we can to keep families together, but it is not always possible. And Frau Abolins' situation is somewhat difficult. Two women and a baby." He looked apologetic.

Nikolina nodded. She understood what he was trying to say, what he did not want to say. She was worried that she may have seemed ungrateful.

She said, "I do understand. I really do." She suddenly felt a need to make him feel at ease with the decision. After all, it was not his fault that she was going to be sent to the other side of Sweden, away from her brother. He needed to know that she appreciated his efforts and the kindness of the family.

"We are very grateful." She was going to just say *grateful*, but she felt that it was necessary to emphasize her gratitude, especially now when she had seemed so ungrateful. She looked down at the very clean polished floor. "When do we leave?" Positive thoughts. No thoughts. There were other forces that seemed to be stronger.

"The day after tomorrow," said Per, leaving the safety of his desk, opening the door for her. He pointed to the calendar on the wall. "The twenty-third." He no longer knew what to say or do, not now when he had done everything that he could do. He would have liked to have been able to have done something else, but he did not know what that would have been.

Once again, she picks up the pen and continues writing: 'Löjtnantsholm: a general store and a few farms scattered along the road between Jung and Vara.'

She has not yet been to Jung, but she was recently in Vara with Janne Swantesson, registering with the Police Authority and collecting a furniture voucher from the Social Welfare Office. While the horse, tethered to a tree near the town square, had waited patiently, she and Janne had walked first to the Welfare Office and then to the Police Station. The day had been cool but sunny, and, with the yellow-orange splash of early autumn colouring the bustle of people and carts and cars, Nina had almost forgotten that she was a refugee, without a husband and without a country. But, at the Welfare Office, the colour had quickly became muted as the officer, looking at her from behind heavy-rimmed glasses, wrote *Stateless* in the section marked *Citizenship*. Later, at the Police Station, even the very pleasant police officer had hesitated and, in the same section, wrote *not known*.

She continues writing: 'There is a river about one kilometre south of our house. Well before you reach the river, you pass the Swantessons' house – a big white house on our side of the road. Opposite, is the general store.'

Nina thinks of Gerda standing behind the dark-brown timber counter at the back of the shop. She can see the wooden boxes and bins filled with apples, carrots, potatoes and swedes; the dried fish and the pots and lanterns, all hanging from the ceiling beam; the motley array of different-sized tins on the many shelves behind the counter – tins containing coffee, tea, flour, rock-sugar, spices, preserved meats, salt, biscuits – and, on the floor, cans of kerosene and sacks of grain. She can see the large round yellow cheeses, covered with a cloth, at one end of the counter, and, at the opposite end, the jars filled with coloured sweets, the scales and the coffee-grinder standing heavily in the centre. As she continues to run her eyes around all the images, she notices the two barrels of brine – one with fish and the other with gherkins – the stove to the right of the door and the beige-coloured poster advertising soap. Her mind is filled with Gerda's shop, and her nostrils are filled with a smell made up of the shop and everything in it. Nina thinks of Gerda's big smile and the sweet or the apple Gerda pushes into her hand – 'For Anders!' – and of Kalle holding the door open for her as she leaves the shop. She also thinks of the times Kalle has taken her basket saying: 'I'll be going up your way soon, Fru Abolins. Just leave this here with me, and I'll drop it by to you.'

Her thoughts have begun to wander; she tries to bring herself back to her letter. 'Our cottage is next to a very large pigsty' – thinking of the smell and the flies – 'and, on the opposite side of the road, but further back towards the river, there is a dairy farm. It is a large farm, and there are lots of cows.'

She thinks that she should say something about the cottage. Elza will be wondering.

'The cottage is quite small. There is a kitchen, a living area and two very tiny bedrooms. There is also an attic, but I think it has only ever been used for storage. No one would be able to live there in the winter, except mice. When we first arrived, there was something wrong with the stove, and the whole house was filled with smoke.'

Nina thinks of the sticky, grey-black smoke that had stung their eyes and had made breathing so difficult, and the film of grime that had settled on everything in the house.

'Fru Swantesson was very apologetic. Of course, she had no idea, the cottage had not been used for several years. Anyway, now we have a new stove, so really Ezīti, we have nothing to complain about.'

She thinks about what she has written. They are safe; they have somewhere to live, and they have food. There are even people who care about them. Then she thinks of Ernests.

VII

During that first year in Sweden, the name Maksis was filtered through the Swedish language and eventually became Max, and Jānis became Janis. With time, even the *h* and the *s* from Kindahls disappeared. The surname that had once belonged to a Swede in Sweden reclaimed its place as a Swedish name.

When Maksis and his family left Grangärde that morning in the black car, yet another tie with home snapped. While Nina had tried to hide her devastation behind her hands, her brother had looked stoically out of the car window, inwardly hoping for all those things that just then seemed impossible. Jānis had cried because he wanted Grosīte and Aunt Nika – most of all he wanted Grosīte. Ilona had sat looking straight in front of her. She had already accepted that nothing in life could be trusted: nothing was for ever. They would move, and then they would move again. That is what life was all about. It was just a matter of being prepared. Elza had wiped her eyes with a white handkerchief. Like Nina, she had not expected that they would be separated. Maksis had turned away from the window and had put his hand on Elza's knee. There was nothing he could say. He had always told Nina that he would be there for her, and now he would not be there.

"It will have to work out somehow," he had said, feeling in his pocket for his cigarette case. "It has to."

They spent the first month with Fischer in his moderately large flat in Saltsjöbaden. In the camp, they had spoken Latvian with each other; now, when Fischer was around, they had to speak German. They felt as though they had started taking a step but had not yet found a place to land. After a month, Fischer found a flat for them close by, and they were finally able to finish taking the step.

Though Nina knew that Fischer was kind and that he was helping Maksis, she sometimes found herself resenting him, feeling that he was the reason the family had been separated. She concentrated on pushing away such thoughts, knowing that she was being illogical, but she missed Maksis and she missed Elza. Most of all, she missed Ernests. If she could not blame God, then she had to blame someone else.

More than anything, she wished that it was possible for them all to be living together. While she thought of Stockholm, the things that Elza had written about – the Palace, the Town Hall, the narrow cobblestoned streets of the Old Town, the islands, the boats, the water wrapping itself around the streets – all merged together into something that she thought she recognized as Stockholm. But she knew that the images could never be more than her own painting built on memories from the window of a train. She occasionally saw Elza and Maksis and the children, and even herself, in the painting, but there was always something separating her from them – a tongue of water, a park, a building.

By the time the autumn of 1945 was covered in white brittle frost, Maksis and his family had moved again. For Ilona, the move was simply confirming what life was all about. Jānis was still missing Grosīte. The new flat was on the top floor of a three-storey house in Lännersta, in the Stockholm archipelago. The house, a timber building, stood alone on the edge of a large finger of lake. Behind it, almost fifteen kilometres to the west, was the centre of Stockholm. Further along the road, and spread out along the edge of the water, were several more houses, and beyond them, there was a small village. On the second floor of the house, there were two more flats, and the bottom floor was used by summer guests.

Ilona and Jānis had begun school. Ilona saw how all the other children believed in permanence while she no longer was sure that she knew what the word meant. She stood next to them though removed from them; gradually, some of the strands of that permanence wrapped around her and drew her closer. Jānis continued to miss his grandmother, but eventually the strands even reached around him. Imperceptibly, *now* was becoming more important than *then,* and Jānis, like Ilona, began to believe that there might actually be something after the *now.*

While life slowly started to rebuild itself in the house by the water, Maksis continued to worry about his little sister. He read her letters, searching between the lines for anything that would tell him how she really felt. He suspected that she was not happy in Vara, but he wondered if she would be able to be happy anywhere. Without Ernests.

He wrote: 'How are you, Nika? Really. How can I help you?'

But he never received a direct answer, and he continued weighing her words, one against the other.

He considered taking things into his own hands. He had got to know the mayor of Skövde, a much larger town north-east of Vara, somewhat closer to Stockholm. The mayor spoke fluent Russian, and his son was a chemical engineer. Maksis had worked with the son on several occasions. He had also spoken with the father. Many times. Perhaps a mayor could do things that other people could not. Perhaps he had an answer. Maksis suggested to Nina that he could write to the mayor on her behalf. He might be able to have them moved from Vara to Skövde, and it was easier to get from Stockholm to Skövde. Eventually, they might even be able to move from Skövde to Stockholm.

Nina replied that he really should not worry and that they would stay where they were. Maksis shook his head and sighed. He could do no more.

VIII

The war had ended, and people were still trying to find themselves and each other. Some succeeded but many did not. Never before had so many people died or been made homeless. The Great War had been the war to end all wars, but there had been a chink in the rhetoric, and people had been pushed into war. Again.

As the 1940s moved towards, and then beyond, their middle point, people, still dazed and confused, tried to rebuild their lives. They no longer believed in any kind of rhetoric; many had lost their belief in everything. They had been promised peace, but they now knew that *peace*, like so many other words, was layered with different meanings for different people. America was worried about communism spreading and eating up the entire world, and Soviet Russia was worried about the American bomb. The two powers, tentatively sparring with each other, searching for weak spots, sought assurance and promises of support from other countries. Just in case. The world was once again dividing into them and us. The good and the bad. The war had ended, and the Cold War had begun.

In Stockholm, more than three hundred kilometres north-east from Vara, in the house by the water, Elza tried to convince herself that she was one of the more fortunate ones. She was free, and she was alive. Every time she looked out of her kitchen window at the dark water, only metres from the house, she was strangely moved by the beauty and the solitude, and yet she was being eaten away by loneliness. Maksis and the children were gone all day, and she was alone in the house by the water. She missed Nikolina; she missed her friends; she missed Rīga. Then she wondered: Was this freedom? Was she really free? She was no longer completely sure.

She wrote long letters to Nina, asking her to write more often, choosing to forget for a moment that Nina had already written only days beforehand. She wanted to visit Nina, but who would look after the children? She imagined Nina and Grosīte and Andris in Stockholm. She wanted them all to be together again. She wanted things to be the way they used to be. She thought about this a lot. The *used to be* was disappearing backwards into a misty haze; sometimes she was no longer sure if she remembered exactly how it really had been. Before. Before they all left home.

In October, months before the extradition of the Latvian soldiers from Sweden, Nina had written to her: 'I would love to visit you, but the train costs fifty crowns. If only I could find dependable work somewhere, I might be able to save the money, but I have not earned a single öre for over a month. It is not often that Svea needs my help, and the payments from Social Security are very small. But I will try to get to Stockholm somehow, because I so desperately want to see you all again.'

Elza thought how frustrating it all was. Only three hundred kilometres between them, and both of them longing for each other. Had it all been worth it? The thought was dangerous, and her mind moved around it cautiously, pretending that it was not there while being entranced by its presence. They could have been killed anywhere between Rīga and Sweden. No one would have known. No one knew that they were in Sweden. No one knew of her dreary emptiness or of the water and the silence and the solitude that were closing in on her, driving her into some dark, godforsaken corner.

She wrote to Nina that they would certainly all be back in Latvia by the following summer. She hoped that this would be the case, and the more she hoped, the more possible it became. Finally, she believed that it was true. They would be going home in the summer. The darkness lightened and she was able to smile at the water and almost enjoy the solitude. Soon she would be packing. Soon they would be going home.

Nina wrote back to her: 'You wrote that we will all be back in Latvia this summer. Is it possible? We are quite isolated here, we do not have much idea what is going on in the world. Have things changed so much in Latvia? Is it really safe to return? Your words – this summer, we will be back in Latvia – have been such wonderful music to our ears. If you know more, please write.'

As much as Elza wanted it to be the truth, she knew that it was not, and she knew that there was nothing more that she could write. She thanked Nina for the extra food coupons and said that she may have heard wrongly about Latvia and summer. Factions within the Swedish government wanted to send the refugees back home, but they knew that they did not have the right to force anyone to leave. Perhaps she had merely leapt beyond what people wanted and what they were permitted to do, to a place where her own hopes created the most positive outcome. If she just kept hoping, just a little longer, just a little harder.

IX

On Thursday, the fifteenth of November 1945, I step off the train at Stockholm's Central Station. I cannot believe that I am actually in Stockholm; Maksis sent me the train fare, and Mother said she would look after Andris.

Now I stand for a moment on the platform, looking around at the people and the train lines and, beyond the station, at the buildings that are Stockholm. I am carrying a small brown bag – I am only staying for a couple of nights – and I look for the exit. Maksis had written: 'I will meet you at the third exit.'

My heart feels both light and constricted; I cannot think of anything else than that I will soon be meeting my brother. Only a few more minutes, another flight of stairs, another door...

He is standing just where he had said he would be. He is watching the people coming through the door while he waits for me. Everyone else in the huge hall disappears as he comes towards me. I drop my bag and throw my arms around him. It is as though I have come home. I have missed him so much. We hang on to each other, and the people part and walk around us. I feel as though we are on a square of pale blue sky that is all our own, and that all the images and noises are somewhere below us.

He lets go of me and laughs, picking up my bag. "It's so good to see you, Nika!"

I think of when we last saw each other, all those months ago, and my hand tightens around his. I remember Petrograd. Why does life have to be so complicated? I look at him. "Do you know how much I have longed for this moment."

We are in front of the station; it is cold with the feeling of imminent snow. He nods. "We have all longed for it, Nika."

From the station, we take a bus; after a few kilometres, we get off that bus and get on to another bus. On the second bus, Maksis takes out his cigarette case and picks out a cigarette. It is all so familiar: the cigarette case, his fingers playing with the cigarette, the lighter and then the red glow on the tip of the cigarette. I watch the smoke curling up towards the roof of the bus. Home is beginning to wrap itself around me. All I need now is Ernests.

"You know that Ginters is here in Stockholm?" The hand with the cigarette resting on his knee while he looks at me.

No, I do not know.

"He got across a few weeks before us. He's working again. Here, in Stockholm." He draws on the cigarette. "He told me to say hello to you."

The question hangs in the air. "Does he...? Does he know anything at all about Ernests?" Thinking that if he did, he would have said.

Maksis shakes his head and puts his hand on my knee. "He has some contact with the Latvian Red Cross. He said that he will let me know if he hears anything." His voice runs off into a silence, and the silence continues until he says, "We'll be getting off soon, Nika."

And I remember all those years ago in Petrograd when he talked about *getting back*, and I think how wonderful it would be if we were able to step away from all the craziness caused by war, and if we actually could *get back* to how things were before.

The bus pulls to a stop, and we stand up, and I follow my brother off the bus.

X

The vicar comes in the evening and sits in the lounge room on the edge of a chair. He uses all the expected phrases – 'my sincere sympathy', 'she will be greatly missed', 'a wonderful woman,' – and sips black coffee quietly, without any slurping. He is too young to slurp.

Yes, he knew Fru Abolins. He used to see her occasionally in his congregation, and she always had something nice to say to him. He has his black hymn book, and a few suggestions jotted on a piece of paper. He makes some marks on the paper, and then he takes a small calendar from his pocket.

"The first Tuesday in September," he says. "Eleven."

Andris shrugs mentally.

Diane thinks: That's still two weeks away!

The vicar makes a note in his calendar and returns it to his pocket. "The hymns?" he wonders, taking another sip of coffee.

Andris suggests **Nearer, My God, to Thee**. So much about her life had resembled the slowly sinking Titanic; it was probably appropriate.

The vicar makes a note. "And anything else?"

Andris flicks through the hymn book lying on the table. Occasionally he stops and reads a few lines, and then he turns the page again. "Why not **Great is the Earth**?"

The minister takes the book from him and turns to hymn 21. He clears his throat and sings softly: "Great is the earth, wonderful is God's heaven..." Then his voice tapers off, almost as though he is thinking of something else, but it comes back again with the last line. "... we go to paradise with song".

Yes, she would like that, Andris thinks, taking the hymn book from the vicar, reading through the hymn. A hymn for pilgrims. Surely she was a pilgrim if anyone was. Pilgrims are always on the move towards something. He wonders: Did she find it? That which she was looking for.

He indicates to the vicar that he is happy to include hymn 21.

The vicar talks about music and makes a few suggestions. He has done this many times before; he knows what people like. The service will not be long, but it must have dignity. He pauses in his train of thought. No, more than dignity: it must have a soul.

XI

It is New Year 1946. Outside, it is snowing. From the kitchen window, I can look across the flat expanse of the Vara plain. Mother opens the door, and the cold air sweeps through the little cottage; she has been out to the woodshed. Andris is playing with a small wooden horse on the floor.

The door closes, and a rush of warmth returns to the room. I think of the cold that began already as summer was fading into autumn, and how, since then, it has continued to cut into my body, and how I can never really feel warm, in spite of all my clothes. I pull my shawl closer around me and read the letter I have been writing but have not yet finished.

'Dear Ezīti,' I read. 'You are probably wondering why you have not heard from me for so long. I have not been myself; at times, I feel as though I am slowly separating into thousands of small pieces. Everything that has been happening these past months has affected me very badly. Perhaps I should not read the newspapers, because then I would not know what is happening, and I would not have to worry.'

I think of the newspapers with the photos of all the starving young men behind barbed-wire fences. Underneath: *Hunger strike continues.*

I have finally learnt some Swedish. I am able to pick out words and sentences in the newspaper. Fru Swantesson gives me the women's magazines she has read and no longer wants. They have lots of pictures, and there are few difficult words. The three words under the picture are no longer a problem for me. I have seen the words *hunger strike* written many times these last few weeks. The thin, haunted men behind barbed wire are all in Sweden.

I remember the faces, somewhat blurred, young and full of despair. There are more than one hundred men, mainly Latvians. Like Ernests, they had all been conscripted by the Germans; when they finally managed to escape, as the war was disintegrating, they had fled to Sweden. They had hoped for refuge, but now they are considered to be prisoners of war. They had fought with the Wehrmacht, so they must be handed over to Soviet Russia. The Swedes cannot imagine the things that the men are trying to tell them: things about tunnels and chasms and about people disappearing into bottomless holes. There are rules and regulations regarding the treatment of prisoners of war. The Swedes are well aware of these regulations, and they assume that the Russians are also aware.

All the while, my thoughts keep going back to Ernests. He could have been in one of those grainy photos. He could have been one of the prisoners refusing to eat, unable to sleep because of the nightmares. He could have been one of these men who preferred starvation to the fate awaiting them. I cannot stop thinking about the men behind barbed wire; while I think of them, I think of Ernests, and I wonder where he is and whether I will ever see him again. My mind moves away from Ernests, still unable to understand how people, who have taken such good care of me and my family, will soon be complicit in ending the lives of so many men. The thoughts move around in my head, thoughts with questions to which I have no answers.

I sigh and return to my letter: 'This Christmas was so empty. Remember last year when we were all still together with our hopes and expectations. But everything will...'

Here the letter stops. I pick up my pen while I am still looking out the window. I think for a moment. What will everything do? Could I be sure that the sun might be shining just around the next corner? Now, when men are standing in long lines waiting for execution? I sigh and continue writing.

'But everything will work out eventually. It will take time, and we must be patient. Think of all that we survived together! We cannot let ourselves fall apart now, even if, at times, it would be so easy to simply let go. No, Ezīti. We have come this far, and we must not give up. We must continue to hope, because without hope there is nothing.'

I have spent so much of my life hoping; I am no longer sure if I have sufficient hope left within me. There must be a point beyond which there is no more hope, beyond which there is nothing. I wonder whether I have already reached this point. I look at my fingers turning the pen around and around between them, and I wonder if I am the same as the pen being turned around and around and around.

A wave of anger sweeps through me. I can feel it racing through my body and out to my very fingertips. I can feel it sinking down to my feet and pushing through the top of my head. I let go of the pen, stand up and walk to the window. I breathe deeply. Everything beyond the window looks calm and still, almost like a painting. Why was my life not like that? Like a painting. Calm without dark shadows. Why was I always running from one place to somewhere else? I turn around and brush the hair out of my eyes. Andris runs past with his little horse. He is making what he believes to be horse sounds. I try to smile. Perhaps I have no choice; perhaps this is what life is all about after all. Running. Running in all directions.

I think of the letter I had received from Elza just before Christmas. It had worried me; she had seemed so miserable.

'It is so dreadfully cold here,' she had written. 'And there is nothing I can do about it. We have no water in the tap; it has completely frozen, and the drain isn't working either. The pipe has cracked...' In between all the complaints, she was crying out: I need you! Why don't you do something?

I can hear her, but there is nothing I can do. We are in a tiny cottage next to a pigsty, on the other side of Sweden. Her house with the frozen taps, near the lake, is too far away for me to reach. I write to her and talk about hope while her voice fills my head, asking why we cannot all be together.

Then I find myself thinking of Christmas, and how out of place I had felt. We had been invited to the rectory in Kvänum, a small village near Vara. The vicar and his wife had been very kind to us since we arrived. They had visited us twice in their red-brown buggy pulled by a black horse; each time they had had presents of food and, once, a small toy for Andris.

There were many people at the rectory, and, for us, most of them were new faces. They smiled at us. Politely. Curiously. They knew that we came from somewhere else and that we spoke another language.

"Russian?" one man asked. "You're Russian, aren't you?"

And I shook my head as he moved further down the table, collecting food on a white plate with a gold border, quickly forgetful of nationalities and languages.

I held on to Andris' hand, telling him to behave while the vicar brought us white plates with gold borders and explained that we were to collect food from the table. My eyes swept over the table where a starched white cloth was almost hidden under turkey, ham, sausages, meatballs and fish, all elegantly arranged on large platters, nudging potato and cabbage dishes, different breads, cheeses, dried fish, pickled fish, grey-green gherkins, pâtés and many foods I had never seen before.

I wanted to be transported elsewhere, but I knew that that was not likely to happen. I was locked into that one moment, with the vicar handing me a white plate. I knew that I would have to take the plate and that I would have to walk around the table like everyone else, and that the moment would stretch and would engulf everyone and everything, and no matter where I looked, there would be no way out.

I took the plate from the vicar and hesitantly joined the queue around the table. The vicar's wife came over to me, entering the moment, pointing out the different foods, describing them for me in German.

Someone touched me softly on the shoulder. "So, you're German?" In German. Coldly? Judgementally?

My hand, reaching for bread, stopped halfway in mid-air. I

shook my head. "No, I'm not German, nor am I Russian. I'm Latvian." I thought for a moment what it meant; I did not expect the man in front of me to understand. He had always been Swedish. No one had ever tried to make him something that he was not.

"I'm sorry," he said.

Was he confused? Apologetic?

"I've never met any Latvians before."

I write: 'It had been wonderful if we had been able to celebrate Christmas together; perhaps then we could have stepped out of the present into something that may have resembled the past. Our past. But, Ezīti, can you imagine? There were gifts for each of us under the tree, and on the tree there was a Latvian flag. Grosīte was so overcome that she actually wept.. We had not been expecting such thoughtfulness.'

I put my pen on the table and reread the letter. Of course, I must thank them for the gifts they sent us. I should have started the letter with my thanks, especially when we were unable to send them anything. I wonder if I should tear up the letter and begin again, but I decide against it. Andris is still playing with his horse, one of the gifts not yet acknowledged. Mother is busy stirring something on the stove. Outside it is still snowing.

Beyond the cottage is the road, and beyond the road are the fields. But everything is completely white, and the road and the fields seem like one large expanse. I sit, wishing that we could be with Elza and Maksis, and my thoughts weave in and out of the idea of us moving to Stockholm. For a moment, I wonder if it would be possible. I know that Elza wants us to move there, and I know that we want to be there. With them.

Mother stops her stirring and looks at me. "She is really not coping, Nika." She wipes her hands on her apron and sits down on one of the high-backed, wooden kitchen chairs. "It had been better if..."

I know what she is going to say; she has said it so many times before.

I finish the sentence for her. "...we were there. In Stockholm."

I shake my head slowly. "I know that's what we all want, but..." I sigh.

Mother looks at me quickly and then looks down at the table. "Perhaps I should go up there for a while. I could take care of the children for her."

I know that Mother is missing Ilona and Jānis as much as Elza is missing us. But I also know that, with Mother gone, it would be just Andris and myself. Would I manage? Mother assumes that I would manage; I have always done so in the past. Why not now? I continue to look at the snow and the expanse where I know that there are fields and even a road, but where everything is white.

XII

When she returned to Vara in the late autumn, after visiting her brother in Stockholm, Nina felt for a while that the distance between herself and her brother may have shrunk a little as the memory of familiar faces and voices cancelled some of the spaces and pulled Vara just a little closer to Stockholm. While she continued to think of Maksis and Elza, her mind sorted through the many sights and sensations of Stockholm – images that had now replaced those in her imagination – still not quite believing that she had actually seen the colours and the shapes and the water winding itself around buildings, and thinking how she had stood on the edge of that same water, knowing that somewhere to the south-east was her home.

But, as the months passed, there were also other memories. Next to her bed, she had placed a small cardboard box, purple with shiny gold writing. Once, it had held chocolates: round and square, many wrapped in brightly coloured foil. She remembered receiving it shortly after they had arrived in Vara. The secretary of the Church Committee had given it to her with a bunch of summer flowers.

She had said: "We hope that Fru Kindal and Fru Abolins and Anders will be very happy here."

Thinking back, Nikolina remembered how the secretary had even curtsied as she had handed over the chocolates, beautifully wrapped in blue paper, together with the large bunch of daisies and red roses.

Now the box held only disappointments. Pale brown cards

beginning: It is with regret... Austere official stationery with letterheads and illegible signatures: Dear Mrs Abolins, I regret to inform you...; Madame, En résponse à votre demande de recherche...

German, Swedish, French, English. Everyone regretted her disappointment; no one was able to give her any hope. And in between the cards and the envelopes were all the drafts for the letters she had written in hope; yet the letters had only been able to find brick walls with no openings.

She opened the box, letting her fingers slowly move over the papers, lifting them out one by one. There had to be hope, otherwise life would fall into some kind of a meaningless vacuum. Somewhere, Ernests was still alive; she knew that, but no one could tell her where he was. Was he calling to her, and she was unable to hear? Had he returned to Rīga? She hoped not, but the thought floated in and out of her other thoughts, worrying her, nagging at her.

There were so many people missing and many of them were dead. Rozalija was sure that Ernests was among the latter, and even if he was not dead, the chance of his being found in the confusion and shambles of post-war Europe was less than any needle in the proverbial haystack. She would have comforted her daughter had she known how; instead she knitted, read her Bible and attended to the house.

Nikolina made up a box of things: socks and mittens with intricate patterns that her mother had knitted in grey and off-white wools; oatmeal soap wrapped in coarse brown paper; a small brown tin of ground coffee; a couple of tins of preserved meat; some biscuits in a cardboard box with the word *Kex* printed across the top; two packets of cigarettes; some powdered milk; some sugar cubes and a Latvian newspaper. She was going to include a note, but after sitting for a long time and not being able to write anything, she finally wrapped the box carefully in brown paper, without any note, and sent it to the Red Cross in Stockholm.

She asked them to forward the box to a displaced Latvian

soldier in a camp in Germany or Belgium, to someone without a family. Someone without anyone. If she could not find Ernests, she might be able to help someone else. As she packed the things into the small box, her hands had moved over the various items, filling each of them with her love and her sorrow and her longing. She had thought all the time of Ernests while she imagined a stranger opening the box. Perhaps her mother was right; perhaps Ernests would never be found. She was still searching for the needle in the haystack. She did not want to give up, but the light was waning fast, and she was no longer sure that she would find it in time.

XIII

As 1946 began to gain in confidence, Nina reread all her brother's letters offering help. She wanted to be in Stockholm with Maksis and Elza, but she knew that it was not practical. Maksis already had three people to take care of; he did not need another three. Nina wondered for a while about Skövde, but it would just be another new place, with more new people. She did not feel that she could start again somewhere else. Without Maksis. Without Ernests. She and her mother would manage on their own. She would try to find work. They would become independent. She turned the word *independence* over and over in her mind. It had meant different things, at different times of her life. She had always thought of herself as being independent, but there had always been others watching out for her: Ermonis, Jānis and then Maksis. And Ernests. Her thoughts began to move in many directions, and she lost the thread of what she was thinking. Where was Ernests? Was he still alive? She put her hands to her head. Should she be thinking of him as alive, or was he already dead?

Her thoughts cleared like small clouds rushing across an expanse of sky, leaving only a flat grey-whiteness behind. She remembered how Latvia had been independent once, and she thought of all the euphoria that had swept around them in 1920. With her thoughts back in Rīga, weaving in and out of ecstatic, celebrating crowds, she thought yet again of Auguste. She had not been able to write to Auguste, not to anyone at home. It would have been too dangerous for family still in Latvia; the thin

Latvian newspaper published in Sweden had made that very clear. Nina knew nothing about family and friends, and her family knew nothing about her. No one knew that they had survived the crossing to Sweden and that they were safe. Even Auguste knew nothing about them. Nina tried to concentrate on her thought: a blurred image of Auguste standing at the kitchen window, looking out on the garden. What was she thinking? Had she regretted her decision? She moved away from the window, but Nina could not see her face properly. Then she wondered if she was already beginning to forget and if the past was being pushed aside by the present. She shook her head, wondering at the same time if things may have turned out as her aunt had thought they might: that Ernests had actually returned home to Latvia. Nina knew that he could very well have returned home. But why would he return home if he knew that they probably would not be there? And when home was no longer home?

Nina's thoughts returned to the word *safe*. Most of her childhood had been spent being flung in and out of the word like a yo-yo on a very long string. She looked around her. She knew that she was safe now. She was not with her beloved brother, but she was safe. Occasionally, Svea Swantesson paid her to clean the big house. When she was there, she was able to have Andris with her. If Janne was at home, he would take Andris with him on the tractor or in the truck. No one seemed to mind. This was yet another reason why she knew that she should stay where she was. She remonstrated with herself, thinking of Petrograd, of Orsha and of the Year of Terror. She had to be thankful for what she had; eventually, she would be able to visit Maksis and Ezītis again.

For a while Rozalija had talked about visiting her son, but she had been having occasional dizzy spells. As they became more frequent, she admitted to herself, and then to Nina, that she would not be able to travel so far on her own. She would have to be content knowing that her only surviving son was safe in

Stockholm; perhaps that was all that was necessary.

With the reality of her mother's mortality no longer safely contained in a place where her thoughts did not normally go, Nina took her mother to the doctor, who listened while Rozalija explained how she often felt light-headed and even faint, and how she sometimes felt like a spinning top, even though she was standing quite still.

The doctor examined Rozalija while Nina sat on the chair in the corner of the room, her handbag on her knee, thinking about endings, unwilling to accept their inevitability. She was still trying to tell herself that everything would continue, without any endings, when the doctor returned to his desk, leaving Rozalija near the examination couch, buttoning her blouse, tucking it carefully into her skirt.

"Old age," he said, making a note on a paper lying there. "Definitely nothing for Fru Kindal to worry about; just a matter of taking things easy."

Nina thanked both the doctor and God, and her thoughts, released from analysing the inevitable, returned to flirt with other anxieties. Yet another letter had arrived, this time from Stockholm. Like all the others, it had thanked her for her enquiry but regretted that there was no information about either person noted in her letter. They would contact her, should anything come to hand. A similar letter had arrived from the English authorities. In a moment of desperation, she almost considered writing to the Russians but changed her mind before the thought had fully taken shape. Instead, she wrote to Elza and told her that they should not be worrying about things that were beyond their control. She wrote that everything would work out. While she wrote, she wondered if both Ernests and Lucija were already dead, and if she might never ever know.

In her diary, she wrote: Why doesn't anyone know where he is? Surely there is someone who has heard his name or seen him? I have to keep believing that he will be found, otherwise he may as well be dead. I must hold on to this one hope. If I let go then I know that he will disappear for ever. Mother does not believe that he is still alive, and she says that I should not believe anything else. She fears that I will just be more hurt later on when he does not come back. Come back? There won't be any coming back, because there is no place to come back to! Perhaps that is what has happened? Perhaps he has gone back to Rīga? If he thought that we were still there, why wouldn't he go back? But he knew that we were going to try to get away. And why would he go back, knowing what has happened there? There are so many questions and so very few answers. At times, all I want to do is to scream out: Ernests, we're here! I scream a lot in my head, and I hope that he can hear me, wherever he might be. I know that Mother is wrong. I know that he is still alive. Somewhere.

XIV

As January, 1946, moved towards its end, I became anxious and depressed. At night, I was unable to sleep, and, during the short hours of winter daylight, I was like a robot, doing all those things that had to be done while my mind was elsewhere.

Everyone knew that the Baltic soldiers were to be deported to Russia; their faces, newspaper-distorted, were constantly before me. I could not understand why the Swedish government was only listening to Stalin. Even the Swedish king had asked Stalin for more time, hoping to give the government a chance to reverse its decision. But Stalin was adamant, and the government was adamant. It was as though the government was on an island far beyond Sweden, and it could not hear the people or the media. It could not even hear King Gustaf. We knew that there was deportation and there was execution; in the wastes of Siberia the two fused together and became one.

I pushed my hair back from my face. In spite of the freezing cold, I was perspiring. Heat was radiating in waves from the stove in the kitchen as Mother and I slid the trays into the oven – trays covered with pale rounds of unbaked dough – and, later, pulled them out, hot beneath the crisp, light-brown bread. The whole house was already full of the smells of newly baked bread and burning pine wood. I enjoyed the smells; they were warm and comforting while, beyond them, there was an icy chill persistently trying to push itself through all the warmth.

I knew that many of those behind the barbed wire were still boys, some of them born as late as 1926, but I was reluctant to take the thought any further, not wanting to enter that space where the soldiers were waiting for the Swedish government to change its mind. They wanted to hear that the government finally understood about the tunnels and even the chasms and how extradition was simply another word for execution.

I thought, yet again, that this is where Ernests could have been, had he managed to reach Sweden still in uniform, and my stomach tightened with anxiety. I knew that Russia would treat them all as traitors; anyone who had lived through 1940 and 1941 knew that. I remembered all the thousands of people taken away in black trucks. I remembered the false accusations, the executions and all the people who just disappeared.

So many people had tried to explain this to the Swedish government. Both refugees and Swedes. There had been all kinds of demonstrations and letters, but the government was committed to Stalin. The agreement had been made in secret months ago. I heard that the prime minister had even silenced the media while he had reinforced security at the camp. Somewhere within all those layers of thought and power that comprised the government, there must have existed a very small doubt. Perhaps there was a very small nucleus of a suspicion floating there, uncomfortable and persistent. Perhaps it suggested that the demonstrators and the letter-writers and the Baltic refugees might actually be right. Perhaps it whispered that deportation for these men was actually a death sentence. Why otherwise were young boys trying to kill themselves?

But if the people in the government were aware of such thoughts, they did not say anything; as far as they were concerned, there was only one choice.

I closed my eyes. My face was burning, and I knew that my hands were trembling. These people in the government had not experienced Latvia's months of terror. They had not hidden behind locked doors, listening to heavy footsteps outside in the street while they crouched, not breathing, waiting for the knock, feeling the cold sweat beneath their clothes, yet somehow still aware of the clock ticking and the fly fighting against the stickiness of the spider's web. They had not seen the trains heading west, the windowless carriages packed with prisoners, nor had they seen the tortured, mutilated bodies lain out, side by side, each with a bullet wound to the head. I wondered if these people knew what real fear was; they had never seen the opening to the tunnel, much less been forced into the darkness and the crooked passages. I wanted them to understand, and perhaps as individuals they did, but clustered together, their shared mind was unable to equate what was real with the imagined complexities of power. I was clinging to my belief that people were basically good; I knew that it was only when political ideas took over the crowd that insanity was created and there was nothing left but tunnels and chasms.

I thought of this then, standing in the warm friendly kitchen, and again, on the twenty-fifth of January, when one hundred and forty-six Balts were forced to board the Soviet ship, *Beloostrov*, in Trelleborg harbour.

As the prison buses pulled up at the harbour, within the area enclosed by high fences of barbed wire, a Latvian lieutenant stabbed himself in the neck with a concealed dagger. Another boy, his right hand firmly held by a Swedish police, thrust his left hand through the window of the bus. Things were beginning to disintegrate, and the police, many of whom secretly felt that the extradition was wrong, hurried the men from the buses towards the barbed-wire-covered gangway. As the line of terrified men was sucked into the narrow tunnel, the boy's arm was quickly bandaged. A doctor decided that he was well enough to travel, and he was carried on to the ship on a stretcher. The lieutenant no longer had to worry about the ship or the ship's destination; he died before reaching hospital.

Later, in an attempt to justify what had been done, a politician explained apologetically that the government could not discriminate against Soviet Russia.

"We cannot regard the Soviet Union as being a country of barbarians," he had said with a weak smile while a journalist made notes in a small notebook.

The Swedes had simply done what they had been told to do,

and now the Balts were no longer their responsibility.

XV

He phones his aunt and speaks with both her and his cousins. His aunt does not think she can manage the trip from Stockholm, but his cousins will be there for the funeral.

He phones his mother's Latvian friends: people who fled around the same time and who had later become united in a foreign place. None of them knew each other in Latvia, but, in Sweden, they had developed close and protective relationships with each other, relationships that were the threads linking them back to their home. When they were together, they could speak their own language, sing their own songs and talk about their own memories.

The conversations become lengthy and drawn out, each person needing to know. Why and when. No, she did not have a heart problem; no, it was not expected; yes, he would miss her very much. He crosses another name off his list and dials the next number. He is very tired, but he knows that he will not be able to sleep – there are too many memories, too many images.

He had not realized that she had so many friends; all these names and faces that were part of her new home. No, it was not a new home; she had lived here for more than forty years, but it was not really home. She never spoke of herself as Swedish; she never really belonged. She was like the pilgrim. Her mantra, like the Jew's *Next year, Jerusalem*, had certainly always been *Next year, Latvia*.

But it never happened.

XVI

It was already February, 1946, and she sat at the small kitchen table with the letter still in her hand. She had read it several times, but she kept reading it, trying to convince herself that it was actually real and that she was not dreaming. There was no longer a line between what she dreamt and what was real. It was her brother's writing, and she could feel the paper between her hands.

'My Dearest Little Sister. All of us here in Stockholm are celebrating! Ernests is actually alive and well; he is in Belgium with Roberts Dzirnis, the assistant from the museum. It was Dzirnis' wife who wrote and told me that Roberts and Ernests are at the same camp...'

There were tears streaming down her face. She had always been so sure that he was alive; she had known it all the time. While she was scrambling through the haystack, she had always believed that the needle was there, somewhere within reach. She thought of Roberts' wife receiving the letter, opening the envelope, reading those few precious lines from her husband. As Nina held Maksis' letter in her hand, she was overwhelmed by a feeling of closeness with this woman with whom she had shared the same fears and the same hopes.

'When she wrote, she had only just found out about Roberts, and she wanted everyone to know. You can write to Ernests via Latvian Red Cross, Corporal Roberts Dzirnis, 377 Avenue Louise, Brussels, Belgium. No one yet knows how long they will remain in Belgium; there is talk of them being moved to some place in Germany. Write as soon as you can, Nika, and make sure that you send the letter airmail. It should not take more than two days before Ernests has your letter in his hand. Think of that! Only two days!'

She finished reading the letter and then read it once again. Perhaps she had misread something? But, no – Ernests was safe. He was in Belgium. She handed the letter to Rozalija, who sat down at the table.

Rozalija had never expected Ernests to be found; she was always quite sure that he had been killed somewhere between Latvia and Germany. She wiped her apron across her face, unable to speak. Then she leant across the table and put her hand on her daughter's shoulder. "Thanks be to God!" she said.

Nina walked across the room to the sink under the window and turned on the dull brass tap. The water was sharply cold, and she splashed it over her tear-stained face. Then she wiped her face and her hands on a towel hanging near the sink. With a tiny smile flickering around the edges of her mouth, she pulled out one of the drawers in the dresser and took out her writing pad and ink.

'Dear Mr Dzirnis,' she wrote, thinking that it was now the eighteenth of February, 1946, and that she had not seen Ernests since the end of August, 1944. The words looked crisp and clean on the empty page. She hesitated for a moment, and then she continued, the pen nib scratching softly on the thin paper.

'I have received news that you are in the same camp as Ernests Āboliņš. If it is true that you really are with Ernests, then please give him our inexpressible affection and love. Both his wife and his little son, Andris, are safe and well and are eagerly looking forward to hearing from him. Recently, I sent a parcel to the Latvian Red Cross. At the time, I did not know anything about you or Ernests, and the parcel was intended for an unknown Latvian soldier. However, if you have received the parcel, and if you have not yet given it to anyone else, and if my husband is there at the camp, I would be grateful if you could give it to him... '

XVII

It was the fifth of February, 1947, and almost a year had passed since I first heard that Ernests was still alive. When I received that letter from Maksis a year ago, I had expected Ernests to turn up immediately. I even told Andris that his father was coming home, and then I waited impatiently for the letters telling me that he was leaving Belgium, leaving Germany, entering Sweden, arriving in Vara. But bureaucracy is not impatient. It takes its time. There were many steps to be taken before Ernests would be able to walk through our door.

From Belgium he was sent to a camp for displaced civilians in Osnabrück, where he remained for many months. An entry visa for Sweden had to be first applied for and then approved; other papers had to be completed and stamped. From there he was sent to Lübeck, and from Lübeck, he was eventually taken by ship to Landskrona in southern Sweden. He arrived in Landskrona in January 1947; even then, there was paperwork and medical examinations. Time was not important to the people with stamps.

In February, it was still winter-cold, and outside the window, the fields were icy white, merging without lines into a sky of the same colour. I was surrounded by a cold that pushed in on me from all angles as I put another piece of wood into the stove and closed the metal door with a bang.

The hands on the square brown clock on the bureau moved slowly. It was already midday, and soon the afternoon light would be upon us, and then it would be dark. The fields and the sky and our little house would still be the same; it would be the colour that would be different. Or the absence of colour. Earlier, my mother had been baking, and smells of pirogi and cottage cheese cakes still hung around the house while, beyond the house, the cold stretched in all directions.

I watched the hands on the clock. I knew exactly when he was leaving Landskrona and when he would be arriving in Gothenburg. I could see him getting off the train, looking rather lost, not understanding all the words racing around him. He would not have much luggage, just a bag with his few clothes and papers. I wondered if he had he changed much. Pulling a hand through my hair, I knew that I had changed; It is difficult not to change when confronted by dark tunnels and uncertain stretches of water. I knew that he would have also changed – all that he would have seen and survived.

I thought of him in Gothenburg sitting in the warm waiting room or on the cold, open platform. We did not expect him until the late afternoon. Janne was collecting him from Vara station with the horse and carriage, and I knew that I could have gone with him. He asked me several times, but I was hesitant. I was not sure if I wanted to meet Ernests outside a station with lots of strangers. I had waited for this day for so long. When others had said it would never happen, I had clung to hazy images of Ernests walking towards me, his arms ready to embrace me, his eyes telling me how much he loved me. The images were all born in another time; they were images I could not share.

When he arrived as the darkness was turning the snow into grey and black shadows, I heard the carriage stop outside the cottage. The horse whinnied. Janne called out to me, but he need not have done so. I had been waiting for this moment all day, every day for almost three years. I opened the front door, moving from my own past into our future. The last time I had seen Ernests, we had been in Latvia, and now I was about to meet him again in a strange country with a strange language. It had been summer when he disappeared, and now it was winter.

I walked out on to the steps as he stepped down from the

carriage. I saw that he looked thin, gaunt, tired. He walked towards me, the snow crunching under his boots, as our two different pasts fused into the present and an uncertain future.

He had sent the letter from Belgium to Ginters on the twenty-sixth of February 1946, and then he had waited. They had been told that they would soon be released. Those who had family in Germany would be released first. Somewhere between the end of 1945 and the spring of 1946, the people in charge of the camp had finally understood that the Latvian soldiers in the German uniforms were actually not Germans. They were not Nazis. They were just victims like so many others. And the beatings and the target practice had stopped. No one could say exactly when. Life was not easier, but the terror was gone.

'Dear Mr. Ginters,' he wrote. 'I was unbelievably happy to see your name in the *Latviju Zinas*, among the names of the new Latvian Red Cross committee. I have already written to you once before; however, I'm not sure if you received my letter. I am in a POW camp. They are telling us that we will soon be released, first those who happen to have relatives in Germany, but nobody really knows. Since I have been away from our homeland, I have not heard anything of my family. Roberts Dzirnis, who is here with me, has also written to Sweden; so far he has not received any answer. Please write to me. I wait impatiently for news from you. With cordial greetings, Ernests Āboliņš POW Camp 2227 A667208 cage II 800 Control Unit BAOR (via Great Britain).'

While Ernests was waiting to hear from Valdemārs Ginters, Dzirnis finally made contact with his wife in Sweden. After months of brick walls and closed exits, everything began to open up, and a visible path appeared, connecting Ernests and Nina.

For a while they were like two strangers, each with a different story. Their hands sought comfort in the touch of skin against skin, body warmth against body warmth. Their eyes followed each other moving around the room, or while they sat opposite each other at the table. They needed to relearn all the shapes and gestures that had once been so familiar.

"I love you," he said one evening when they were sitting within the warmth, looking out at the cold.

"And I love you too," she had answered, her hand touching his.

"You were with me all the time," he continued, his hand closing around hers. "Did you know that?"

She nodded, smiling at him. There had already been so many tears, but somewhere, behind the smile, there were still more tears wanting to be released. She leant over and kissed him on the forehead, needing to re-absorb his presence. Yes, she knew that they had never left each other. Not really. It had been the one thing that had kept her going, knowing that he was still alive, somewhere.

Ernests knew that he needed to rediscover his son; a son who had no idea what a father was. He had smiled when he heard how Andris had wondered whether his father was a man or a woman. It had been a long time, and their lives had gone in different directions. He picked up his son and placed him on his knee. The child resented the smell of cigarettes, and he looked uncomfortable, wanting to get back down on to the floor. Nikolina could see that fusing two pasts would not be easy.

A month later, Ernests left Löjtnantsholm and took the train to Stockholm to see his cousin, Maksis. It was somewhat of a relief; the little cottage was too small. The walls had been straining to reach around yet another person. Ernests was hoping that Maksis might be able to help him find work.

He remained with his cousin and his family for almost two weeks, and, when he finally left Stockholm, he took the train to Jönköping on the east coast; Maksis had arranged for him to meet someone there who needed an architect. Sitting in the small, sunlit office, Ernests listened to a man in a dark-grey suit tell him that the job was his if he wanted it. While he listened, he concentrated on the square patch of buildings framed by the window, knowing that he would not be able to take the job, realizing all of a sudden that his self-confidence had completely disappeared somewhere between Rīga and Sweden. He wondered if it had remained on the battlefields or in some cold corner of the camp, behind barbed-wire fences. He looked at the man in front of him and apologized for all the inconvenience. He said that he would not be able to take the job while he thought how much he really wanted it. On the long train journey back to Vara, he could only think of all his hopes running out into the cold, grey wetness of early spring.

He was restless and no longer in control. He had not been in control for a long time, but he knew that he had to do something about getting his life in balance again. Also, the cottage was too small for all four of them. The Welfare Agency made an assessment: he was too weak for heavy, physical work. But there was work at the porcelain factory, so they contacted all the right people and made an appointment for him.

At the end of April, he took the train and travelled the thirty kilometres to Lidköping, north-west of Vara. He was prepared to take whatever work he was offered. If he was ever to return to his profession, he would first have to regain his confidence, if that was possible.

Only days after arriving in Lidköping, he was employed as a kiln-operator at Rörstrand's Porcelain Factory. As he could not travel between Löjtnantsholm and Lidköping every day, he rented a furnished room from a man called Hallberg, in a house on Kopparslagsgatan on the west side of the river, Lidan, close to the factory.

Lidköping was a medium-sized town sprawled around the mouth of the river, at the point where it emptied into Lake Vänern. Ernests could not see across to the other side of the lake, and Hallberg told him it was the largest in Sweden. Where Lidan and Lake Vänern mixed their waters, boats from Gothenburg and even further afield sat patiently, waiting to be loaded or unloaded. Of an evening, Ernests would walk along the edge of the river, looking at the boats and the cranes, listening to the lazy creaking of the timbers and the cries of the seagulls overhead.

If he continued along the west bank of the river, moving away from the lake, he passed a cluster of small brick factories on his right, before reaching the wide expanse of the town square with a beige-yellow building at its centre. On market day, the whole area was patterned with carts laden with pale-green cabbages and brown potatoes; barrels of pickled fish; improvised tables covered with rounds of cheese, bread, eggs, jars of vegetables in brine and vinegar, sausages of all different sizes, bags filled with wheat and rye, and, on the ground, tubs of silver-grey fish with glazed, unseeing eyes. In the summer, flowers in tin buckets added swathes of pink and red and white and yellow while, everywhere, the conglomeration of smells wrapped around everything and everyone.

Ernests enjoyed the noise and the bustle of market day. Sometimes he would wander around, breathing in the smells and the curious sense of both belonging and being anonymous. Other times, he would buy a small wedge of cheese or a piece of sausage or, in the summer, small new potatoes and sweet-smelling dill weed. Then he would sit on the steps of the beige-yellow building, with his parcels next to him, a cigarette between his fingers, watching the movement while listening to all the sounds.

He had heard that the timber building had once been a hunting lodge on the peninsula jutting out into the lake. It had belonged to a nobleman, a close friend of one of the kings, and eventually it had been been brought into the town to decorate the town square. It was squat with three levels, each level smaller than the one below, and at the top Justice held her sword and her scales, looking out over Lidköping. The building had once housed the courthouse, and the police used to be there as well. There had even been a proper holding cell with bars and a lock. On ground level, there was a museum, and Ernests reminded himself that he would have to visit it some day. The other levels contained offices or meeting rooms; Hallberg was not quite sure, although he could still remember when it had been a proper town hall with councillors and people putting stamps on sheets of paper. Sitting on the steps, thinking about what Hallberg had said, Ernests felt as though he was straddling both the past and the present, but the more he thought about it, he decided that the present was merely an illusion and that life moved in ultra speed from what had not yet happened to the past.

He knew practically no Swedish, but he spoke German, and he hoped that he would soon be able to get a better job. On the weekends, he took the train to Vara where Janne or one of the farmhands met him. Life was slowly pushing itself through unfamiliar undergrowth, finding new paths. Soon they would all be able to live together again, but first, he needed to earn some money.

XVIII

There are things one does not talk about. Looking inwards into what some may have called his soul, he knew that there was no longer any connection between what was on his inside and what was on the other side. It was more than not knowing the language; it was a matter of no longer connecting. Anywhere.

He lit another cigarette. There are many things one does not talk about.

When they were moved on to the ship in September 1944, the disbelief and the anger and the frustration finally gave way to passive acceptance. As they sailed up the Daugava and into the Gulf of Rīga, he knew he had to accept that he was no longer Ernests Āboliņš, the husband of Nikolina and the father of Andris; he had become soldier Ernests Āboliņš, part of the 15th Waffen Grenadier Division and known only by number 19058-C. Numbers do not have families, nor do they have feelings or needs or hopes. They are just numbers, and they simply do as they are told. They cluster together with other numbers, forming different and new patterns, or else they run along in long lines, creating results that are often based more on subtraction than on addition.

As the ship moved north-west towards the Baltic Sea, he had stood at the railing, following the hazy coastline of his country. While his eyes tried to focus on the blurred grey line that occasionally became even more indistinct, his thoughts were only centred on his family. He knew that they were going to try to escape, and he was supposed to have been with them. He and

Maksis had discussed the plans in detail; Maksis knew someone with a farm on the coast, somewhere near Kolka. It was all arranged. He wondered whether they had already escaped or whether they were still in Rīga. Perhaps they had remained in Rīga, hoping that he would return. He covered his face with his hands, thinking how impossible everything had become. But, like an insect in a bottle, it was pointless flinging his head against the glass. If there was no way out, then there was no way out. For a pacifist, the uniform was uncomfortable. He no longer recognized himself; he was no longer himself. He was someone else, and the real *he* was standing to one side, looking on. The 15th Waffen Grenadier Division was one of Himmler's creations. With the war closing in on Germany, Himmler intended to use the Latvians to defend the Pomeranian Wall against the Russians.

After leaving the ship, they spent several days in a town somewhere in northern Germany; then they were sent south-east into Poland, walking many kilometres every day. Autumn was closing in, and often they walked through cold, blinding rain or against winds that stung their faces while pushing them almost horizontal to the ground. He wondered how Nietzsche could have believed that walking gave rise to great thoughts, when his own mind was numb and empty, and all he could think about was the road in front of him and what he was likely to find at the end. He knew that everyone was moving in on the Germans and that the Russians had moved in on Latvia. All he wanted was for the war to come to an end.

But it had not yet ended. He stumbled through long days and nights of grey boredom tinged with sharp-edged anxiety, knowing that the tediousness of waiting and watching was better than what was to come. When it came, with so much discordant noise and shouting and thick, heavy smoke hanging pall-like over everything, he wondered, yet again, at the insanity of it all. The dead men looked at him with empty eyes, and he thought that it did not much matter where they were from, not once they were dead.

Even the landscape had died. He would understand if it rose

up against everyone in its dying agony, but that did not happen. The landscape was also safely within the bottle.

Then it was winter, and all the devastation was soon covered with white. They trudged through metres of snow, and blew on already-frozen hands. Hands with statue-like fingers that refused to grip around rifles. Sometimes, they felt that it did not matter as they were already too blind to see anything. But the Germans were becoming desperate; the Russians, with their tanks, were bearing down on them from the east, driving them west, back across Germany. The Russians were relentless, and many men remained in the whiteness while some of those who moved on envied them. Ernests did not envy them; he did not envy anyone; all he wanted was for the war to finish. He now understood a lot more about the abyss and why it was looking back at him. He tried to move his gaze, but there was nowhere else to look. Many of the men being pushed west no longer had rifles, and those who did often had no ammunition. When they could, they took rifles from men who no longer needed them, but rifles were not much help against the persistent Russian tanks.

When there were short, unexpected moments of respite, they fell exhausted on to the frozen ground where they slept like dead men for an hour or so, until the moment had passed, and it was time to move on. The pieces of canvas, pushed down into each man's pack, were now rarely joined together into a tent. There was never enough time. Some men wrapped themselves in their own pieces, but, even then, they would usually wake with their heads frozen fast to the ground beneath them.

There were still Latvians hoping that Germany would win the war and banish Russia from the Baltic countries. Ernests knew that it was not going to happen. But something would happen when Russia and the Allies defeated Germany. He tried not to think about it. He had no idea where Nina and Andris were. He did not know if they were still in Latvia or if they had escaped. He remembered Nina's dream, and how they were planning to leave Latvia before everything had collapsed, like some flimsy structure built of glossy playing cards with printed images, and he had been taken away. He thought of Schopenhauer's idea that every parting is but a foretaste of death. Yes, he would agree with that, but he was not sure whether or not he would experience the resurrection.

As the war broke into its final, awful days, the battalion Ernests was with surrendered to the Americans somewhere near the Elbe River. So many men had died. For what? Ernests had no idea. He was sent to Zedelghem 2227 in Belgium. He and fourteen thousand other Latvians. It did not matter that they had been forced into the German army. That was completely irrelevant when everyone wanted blood. Someone had to pay for the confusion and the turmoil into which the whole world had descended. A German uniform was sufficient condemnation.

All around him the earth was spewing broken buildings and haunted, broken people on both sides of barbed-wire fences, and he was one of those people, now caught behind two tall fences of barbed wire. There were thousands of Germans in the camp, but 2227 was just for Latvians. Not that it made a lot of difference; they were treated the same as the Germans. They tried to explain why they were in German uniform, but no one wanted to listen, because everyone was hating. Many of them were beaten; some were used for target practice. He could still remember the terror when the red-faced sergeant appeared in the yard.

"Hey, you and you and you, come here!" Was there a smile on his face? Ernests could no longer be sure.

'You and you and you' were never seen again. Each man wondered quietly when it would be his turn. No one talked about it; words might only give their fear physical substance. If they pretended it was not happening, then perhaps it would not happen. Not to them.

There was never sufficient food, and the tents provided for shelter gave little warmth. Ernests wondered if he would ever get back to Latvia. He wondered if he would ever see his family again. He began to despair of there ever being a resurrection.

Then, towards the end of 1945, while looking through a well-thumbed copy of *Latviju Ziņas*, he saw the name Valdemārs

Ginters. It was as if all the clouds had skidded off the sky, letting the sun stream through in one long shaft of bright light. Someone he knew was still alive.

Ginters' name was mentioned together with a Latvian Aid Committee in Sweden. From what he could understand, the Committee was working together with the Red Cross, trying to reunite people. Ernests sat with the newspaper in his hand, looking over the hundreds of small tents to the high fences of barbed wire and the guards with rifles at the ready. What if he had never seen the newspaper? What if he had seen the newspaper, but not Ginters' name? He breathed in deeply. He had a reason to continue living. If Ginters was alive, then, perhaps, Nika and Andris were also alive.

His thoughts swept back to that day in August 1944, when they had gathered at the church for Andris' christening. It had been a sunny, almost warm, day with an orange-yellow feeling of encroaching autumn, but beyond the blue and the yellow, there had been an uneasy feeling of grey. It was the same grey that had settled over the whole city and was already spreading east and west, like oil spilling from some invisible can. After the short ceremony, Ginters and Lucija had both signed their names as godparents. He remembered shaking hands with Ginters on the steps of the church, both of them trying to remain positive about the future in spite of the advancing greyness. Then, two days later, he was captured.

He pushed his hands through his hair as the images folded in on each other, and he was left with only the reality of the newspaper in his hand. Surely seeing Ginters' name was a sign? A sign that he had reached the bottom and that he was now on his way up. Perhaps there was a God up there after all.

There was a restriction on how many letters could be written and how long each letter could be. All letters had to be written in one of the Allied languages or else in German. Ernests wrote a letter to Ginters in German. He wrote on a specially provided letter-form, because all letters had to be approved before leaving the camp. He wrote how happy he was to have seen Ginters' name in the newspaper, and then he reread what he had written and thought that *happy* was not sufficient to describe what he felt. There was no word that could describe what he felt when he saw Ginters' name in the newspaper. He hoped that Ginters understood.

When he received no answer, he wrote another letter to Ginters in February 1946. While his letters were trying to find Ginters, Ernests received Nina's letter. When he received it, he was about to be moved from the prisoner of war camp in Belgium to a displaced persons' camp in Osnabrück, run by the United Allied Nations Relief and Rehabilitation Administration.

'My Dearest Nika,
You cannot begin to imagine the great happiness and surprise that filled me, when Roberts Dzirnis handed me the card you had written. It was the first of March, and my first thought was that my dear family had actually managed to escape! It is an unbelievable miracle that, after eighteen long months of not knowing anything, I have at last discovered where you are. Last autumn, I heard that Ginters was in Sweden, and I have written to him twice, but, as yet, have not received any answer. Dzirnis also wrote to the staff of the museum, and I know that he mentioned my name as well. I have no way of knowing if the museum has any contact with Ginters, but we must probably assume that he has not received the cards I sent to him in Stockholm. We are very limited as to how many letters we may write; however, last week things definitely took a turn for the better when we were moved to Germany. This is the first step in the release process. We are now at a camp in Osnabrück, and, after further approvals and paper-work, we will be set free. We will then be given recognition as civilian refugees. Those who have relatives in Germany will be allowed to stay with them.

My dearest Nika, you must try to find out if I will be able to join you. I have heard that those with family in Sweden can be given an entry visa. Write to me, my dear, and let me know how you are and how you are managing. Is my mother with you? Who else is in Sweden? Where are you living? I could not find the place on the map. Which is the closest large town? Don't worry about me, my dearest. I am well. I am coping, and the most difficult time, winter, is thankfully now behind us. The weather is warm, and even the room where we are living is pleasant. The area here is hilly, and it is very beautiful. Oh, my dear, dear girl! Things never work out the way we expect them to, do they? And our little Andris is now two! Give him my love with many, many hugs and kisses. Already, I am looking forward to your letter. I wanted to write to you much earlier, but I was not sure if you would receive my letter as we were already preparing to move from Belgium. However, I suspect that we will be spending quite some time in this camp. Give my regards to our friends and to all those you know. To our soon-to-be reunion, my dear.'

XIX

It is almost the end of April 1948. Ernests has been in Sweden for more than a year, and is now working as a photographer for Rörstrand. He is pleased to have been able to leave the kilns behind him, but he made some friends while working there, including some other Latvians – among them, Edvards Tipsis and Augusts Ābeles. The Latvians have their own stories; the Swedes have the stories of those they know or of those someone else knows.

He has bought a bicycle, and he often visits Tipsis or Ābeles after work. They are both married, and Edvards and Marianne have small children. Augusts and Anna share their very small flat with Anna's mother. Ernests thinks of his own mother and asks himself, yet again, why she did not leave when she had the chance. They have had no contact with her. He does not know if she is still in Rīga. He does not even know if she is still alive. He thinks about the idea that existence can never be in the present because, by its very nature, it must always be relegated to the past. All he has is his mother's past; he does not even know if she has a present.

He wrote to her in October 1944, just after he had arrived in Germany: '... how are you managing? How are Nika and Andris? Are you already at Kurzeme, or are you still in Rīga?'

He sent the letter both to Rīga and to the house in Saunaga. He also wrote to Nina and Maksis. By the time his letters finally arrived, everyone would have already left Latvia. Everyone except his mother. He never received an answer, not even from his mother. Later, he wondered about this a lot. Perhaps his letter to her never arrived or perhaps it did, and she answered it, and her letter to him never arrived. Or perhaps it arrived after they left the camp in northern Germany and had moved south into the nightmare that people call war. He knows nothing about her present.

He lights another cigarette and nods his thanks to Anna, who has poured the coffee. Here, he does not have to say anything; what is inside him is also inside them. They may not have been where he has been, but they have lived the fear and they have seen the devastation; they do not need to talk about it. He stubs out his cigarette in the ceramic ashtray and stirs three lumps of sugar into his black coffee. Anna is talking about seedlings and seed boxes. He leans back in the well-worn sofa bought from the Salvation Army, and savours the feeling of heat moving down through his body. His life has taken a one hundred and eighty degree turn; it will never be the same again, but he knows that it could have been worse.

At night, after work, he sits in his room on Kopparslagsgatan and reads Nietzsche and Schopenhauer. He also reads Kierkegaard and Jung. He reads the books in German. One of the books has been with him since Rīga. It was in his pocket with his camera, the night he was captured.

A flat in a house on the east side of the river becomes vacant, and Ernests signs the tenancy agreement that includes an extra room for Rozalija. The house is in the middle of a group of similar houses, all from the early part of the nineteenth century. The area is known as Limtorget, and the houses are those that survived a fire that swept through the east side more than a century ago. It is within walking distance of the river and the town square. It is further from Rörstrand than the flat where he has been staying this past year, but the distance is of little consequence when he thinks that now they will be able to be together.

He pushes the signed paper back across the desk. The thin, sallow-coloured man on the other side eyes it quickly, smiles and offers his hand to Ernests. As Ernests takes the man's hand, he is hoping that the handshake will be the beginning of a better life.

They move in at the end of April 1948. Janne now has a Volvo, and he drives them from Löjtnantsholm with the trailer bumping noisily behind them. Ernests sits with Janne in the front, while Rozalija, Nikolina and Andris sit in the back. Nikolina thinks of the trailer obediently following along behind with everything they own: a couple of beds, a table, three chairs, three bags, a couple of boxes of books. She reflects how easy it is to accumulate things; when they arrived in Sweden, almost four years ago, they owned practically nothing.

The flat is downstairs in the little red timber house. In front of the house, there is an open area and a water pump; at the back, to the right, is the privy; to the left, there is a long stretch of garden with fruit trees and vegetables. On the other side of the open area, there are other similar houses. There is a dirt road running through the little community, past the pump.

There are two flats downstairs, one on each side of the front door. Upstairs, there are three rooms for three tenants. In one of these rooms, Rozalija unpacks her few belongings and then comes down the stairs to help her daughter. Andris is already running around in the garden outside while Nikolina is busy scrubbing the kitchen floor. Ernests and Janne have unloaded the trailer – the small pile of disparate things looking vulnerable and exposed in the bright spring sunshine – and are now sitting on a couple of the chairs, smoking. Ernests calls out something to Andris, who looks up for a moment, smiles and then disappears between two apple trees. Inside, Nikolina is also hoping for a new beginning.

XX

It was 1951, and the four of us had been living at Limtorget for three years. Andris had already started school, and the days seemed suddenly longer and less regulated – like a piece of string no longer pulled taut but lying loose and twisted on the ground.

In the afternoon, Marianne Tipsis would sometimes call in on her way home from work, leaning her bike against the side of the house, her shoes crunching on the loose gravel as she walked to the front door. She had been working at Rörstrand for several years; she wanted me to start there as well.

"Think about it, Nika! You have more free time now, and the money..." She looked around the room. We were sitting in the kitchen.

"You could use the money, couldn't you?" She finished her coffee, setting the cup back on the white saucer, moving the teaspoon until it was parallel with the edge of the table. "Let me know if you're interested; I can always put in a word for you."

She put in a word, and I began work at the factory, where I was given work inspecting fired porcelain for flaws, polishing off small jagged irregularities and smoothing edges. It was hard on my hands, but Marianne was right, we needed the extra money.

Shortly after he started working there, Ernests had told me that Rörstrand was one of Sweden's most important industries. I was impressed, but, when I asked him about the name, he had looked uncertain and had shaken his head. Then, weeks later, reminding me of my question, he told me that the factory had begun in Stockholm, in a castle of the same name.

"The castle was on the edge of a lake, and the shores were overgrown with reeds." He had laughed, possibly thinking of all the information that can be contained in a name (*rör*:reeds; *strand*:shore), and then I remember him leaning back in his chair before continuing. "But that was a long while ago. When Stockholm needed more room, the factory was moved to Lidköping." He reached over and poured himself some more coffee from the coffee-pot on the table. "That must have been fifteen, twenty years ago."

I liked the connection with the castle as it reminded me of Rundāle; I also liked working at Rörstrand, and, although the work was hard, I enjoyed the suggestion of independence and the company of the other women. Occasionally, Ernests and I would walk to work together while he pushed his bicycle. We would walk along the edge of the river and then across the bridge, and it felt as though we were young again, and all the difficult years in between had never existed.

XXI

They knew that most of the news that trickled over the Baltic Sea from the East was propaganda, but it did not always look like propaganda, not until it was pulled apart and dissected. Often it would paint life as they wanted it to be, and, for a moment, they would sometimes pretend that it was the truth while they blocked their minds to everything that was telling them otherwise. Soviet Russia was inviting the refugees to return; there would be no retribution; the past was forgotten. Life in all the Baltic countries was now perfect. They looked at the pictures and read the words that wove around things like happiness and gratitude and high living standards. Many Swedes believed the news to be authentic, and they wondered why the Baltic people would want to stay in Sweden when things were obviously so good in their own countries.

Nikolina could not help thinking of all the Latvians who had been removed to Siberia and of those who had now fled to places beyond Latvia. Thousands of Russians had moved into the Baltic area of their own accord, or had been moved there as part of a Soviet Russification policy. But there had always been Russians in Latvia. She thought of the Russians who had lived there when she was a little girl. Most of them went to the domed Russian Church where men with long, white beards could be seen against colourful paintings and where everything was wrapped in the wonderful smells of melting wax and incense. She remembered Shurik, Katarina and Polina, who all lived on Kalnciema iela and with whom she often played before the war swept everyone away in so many different directions. She remembered Nonna Doletskaya, whose husband was a blacksmith and who sometimes gave her hard pieces of shiny red-brown sugar, wrapped in brown paper.

Later, more Russians came to Latvia, fleeing ahead of the Revolution. But that was long before 1940. After 1940, nothing could be the same again. The Russians who came were different. Those in charge started moving Latvians as far away from Latvia as possible, but then the Germans came, and the Russians had to wait several years before they could continue exchanging Latvians for Russians.

She had heard that many officers from the Red Army had remained in Latvia and that their families had later joined them there. Also, Communist Party officials had been sent from Moscow to enforce control, and they also remained. She thought of all these people, and she thought that now there would be many more Russians in Latvia, living in houses that had once belonged to Latvians, simply because the houses were empty and vacant: simply because Stalin wanted Latvia to be completely absorbed by the Soviet Union. He wanted to pretend that Latvia had never existed.

In the early 1950s, they all travelled to Stockholm by train and spent a week with Maksis and his family in Lännersta, in the house by the water. By then, the children were no longer children and everyone was older.

It was summer. While they sat on the sun-drenched grass near the side of the house, watching other people's children playing on the edge of the water, listening to their quick, sharp cries and their bubbling laughter, they tried to make believe that things were just the same as they had been all those years ago, before their lives had been pushed into another orbit. But they knew that such pretence was impossible, and, instead, they tried to talk about the *now*. Later, they took the bus into Stockholm and looked at the City Hall and the Royal Palace and the narrow cobbled streets running down to the water. They even went to the Opera, where they sat in the darkness, absorbing the presence of the people all around them, and watched *Die Fledermaus* while the music and the costumes and even the building itself pulled a layer of something else over the *now*, removing all the sharp, uncomfortable edges.

Then, the day before they left to return to Lidköping, Maksis told them that he was going into business with a friend he had met, Lars Hultman.

Maksis had enjoyed working with Fischer, but he really wanted to start his own business. Hultman, a somewhat failed, but still reasonably well off, dental technician suggested a partnership. Hultman, no philanthropist, saw an opportunity to make more money, while Maksis saw the chance of finally being able to realize his ideas.

Hultman found some rooms in a building on Lidingö, closer to central Stockholm and north-west of Lännersta. Then he registered the business name, S&V Engineering. While Maksis concentrated on making his ideas tangible, Hultman began to count the money that had not yet begun to appear. Travelling between Lännersta and Lidingö took time that could be used more profitably, so Hultman found Maksis a flat on Bodalsvägen close to the business, and Maksis and Elza and the children left the archipelago behind them and moved to Lidingö.

Although Hultman was really only interested in profits, he did realize that Maksis would need to be able to support himself and his family. He decided to lend Maksis a certain amount of money each month; later, when the business started to bring in money, he would begin to withdraw the loan from Maksis' share of the profits. Hultman had a friend with a background in law and who claimed to know everything about taxation, and he helped draw up the contract. As the money was a loan, there would be no tax to pay.

The business slowly expanded. Hultman found a large workshop in Norrtälje, north of Stockholm, where they could begin manufacturing, and Maksis split his time between Lidingö and Norrtälje. In the summers, he and his family spent all their time in Norrtälje. Surrounded by sparkling water, the smell of salt and seaweed and boats, sandy swimming spots and sun-kissed open spaces, Norrtälje *was* the Swedish summer. Life was beginning to look very positive.

Then the Taxation Department became involved and the direction changed, suddenly and without warning. The Taxation Department was not particularly interested in talk about loans and repayments; it insisted that the money Maksis was receiving was actually a wage. And wages needed to be taxed. Hultman's friend had vanished, and no one – not even Hultman – knew where he was. Maksis was told that he would have to repay all the money owing to the Department. Maksis did not own so much money, but the Department was both understanding and patient and drew up a repayment plan. Maksis knew that it would take years; he also knew that until the money was repaid, the family would not be able to take out citizenship. Life had unexpectedly taken on some very grey tones, despite summer and blue skies.

Then the Taxation Department remembered Lars Hultman and reminded him of all the outstanding payroll tax, which also had to be paid. By this stage, Hultman was regretting he had ever listened to his friend, but there was not much that he could do. He paid the tax, and he and Maksis weathered the storm, but Hultman's dreams of making amazing profits had moved well and truly beyond his grasp.

XXII

When I was still little, I do not believe that there were any hard shadows or worried looks. Or fear. It was a time when people greeted each other with a smile, when children played happily in the streets and when the grocer gave away sticky sweets. It was also the time when I discovered Minna in the barn with her four small kittens.

The father of Minna's kittens was Pincis. He was a large black cat that had always lived in the barn. After the kittens arrived, Mother decided that she no longer wanted lots of cats in the barn; she would only keep Pincis and the male kitten. I did not know what Mother had decided, but I soon noticed that three of the kittens were no longer there. Had they wandered off? Had the fox taken them? No one seemed to know. Then Minna also disappeared.

It was a windy autumn day when Minna disappeared. I looked everywhere for her, but she was nowhere to be found. Years later, Maksis told me that Mother had asked Father to do away with her, but this was too much for Father, and he gave her to a friend of his, hoping that his friend might be able to do what he could not do and not tell him about it. But the friend was just as hesitant as Zacharias; instead of drowning Minna in the pond, he took her into central Rīga and left her there. On her own.

I wept when Mother told me that Minna had run away. Mother was quite certain that Father had taken care of her. Father thought that his friend had taken care of her, while the friend was hoping that she might be able to take care of herself. I spent hours in the barn, looking after the remaining kitten and commiserating with Pincis. The weeks passed, and there was no Minna.

Then, in early January, when everything was white and it was bitterly cold, a sound at the door caused Father to get up from his chair near the stove and open the door. Outside, on the top, snow-covered, stone step was Minna. She was very cold and very thin; as soon as the door opened, she ran into the house, leaving wet patches behind her on the floor. Somewhat startled, Father closed the door, and, like the father whose children followed the path of pebbles, he was unable to hide his relief and his delight that Minna was actually alive. I remember Mother giving Father a strange look while I shouted for joy. Picking up a very wet and cold Minna, I hugged her poor emaciated body against my own. Pincis purred around my feet, and, when I finally put Minna back down on the floor, he stayed close to her, protecting her, never wanting to lose sight of her again.

XXIII

They go to concerts: Beethoven, Mozart, Rachmaninov, and then they walk home via the town park, talking about what they have seen and heard while Ernests holds a cigarette between his fingers, moving his hand up and down, making a point about the music, the people and even the park. He argues that music is bigger than everything, and that it incorporates everything.

"Everything around us," he says, throwing out his arms; the small glow of the cigarette making a sudden sweep against the dark. "There is nothing that is not music."

She does not disagree, because she feels the same. There are no words to describe music; it just is, and everything else is beholden to it and moves in time to its rhythm.

When there are no concerts in the town, they listen to the radio. They both yearn to be part of that which cannot be described by words. They often listen, their eyes closed, somewhere between that which can be described and that which cannot be described.

The radio also speaks of other things. In 1953, it tells them that Stalin has died of a stroke. The music around them takes on a different feel as it moves from a minor to a major key. Nikita Khrushchev comes to power; by 1957, there is the slightest sense of a fresh breeze blowing from the east. Thousands of political prisoners have returned home from Siberian camps, and artists and writers are wondering if they may now be able to express the truth as they see it. Borders are squeezed open, just a little; some Soviet citizens are permitted to travel abroad, and Westerners are allowed to enter Soviet countries.

But Nina knows that she would not be able to return to Latvia – not yet. Not while Latvia is still part of the Soviet Union. She welcomes the changes, but they are still not sufficient. She is sceptical and still afraid. After almost ten years, she can finally write to friends and relatives. Short letters not saying much more than that they are well. That they are in Sweden. That Ernests is with them. Earlier, she had not dared to write – not to anyone.

She writes to Auguste, carefully choosing her words, but the letter is returned. She writes to Paulina and Hermine. Finally, a letter arrives from Paulina, telling her that Auguste passed away a few years earlier. The letter is unemotional as Paulina would have expected it to be opened and read by others with black pens. She has only written what is necessary: that Auguste has died and that she is buried, and that she and her husband, Peteris, visit the cemetery occasionally and put flowers on the grave.

But the emotion that could not be put into the words has woven itself into the paper, and now it bursts out, rushing at Nina. She puts her head in her hands, pushing her fingers hard against her forehead, trying to focus her thoughts on all those things over which they no longer have any control. She knows that Auguste would have spent her last years wondering where they all were, wondering if they had reached safety, wondering if her son had survived the war. The tears are burning behind her eyes. There are so many tears. They have been there for years. Perhaps they will eventually wash out of her eyes, and they will create a flood that will sweep everyone and everything away.

Had it all been worth it? She thinks back to the last time she saw Auguste. She remembers that it was autumn, and the flowers had begun to fade. What would have happened if they had stayed? Would Ernests have found them? Would they have found Ernests? What would Russia have done with him, after he had fought with the Germans? Against the Russians.

She sits, holding the letter in her hand, thinking about her aunt's decision all those years ago, wondering, as she had on so many other occasions, what it is that actually governs our lives: free will or predestination.

XXIV

In 1952, Ernests introduces photo-etching to Rörstrand. The method has been used by the German porcelain industry for some time, but it has never before been used in Sweden. The laborious work with transfers that previously took several weeks can now be completed in one day. Someone else takes over the photographic work Ernests had been doing, and he moves into the laboratory.

But, as 1952 rushes towards 1956, signs of friction begin to appear between Ernests and Rozalija. Feelings of pain and frustration rise like small bubbles, many of them finally breaking and frothing on the surface. Nina thinks that she recognizes the darkness from where these bubbles come, but she is unable to do anything to stop them, and, before long, they fill the house, blocking all the exits. Then Rozalija packs her things and moves to the other side of town, to the long single-storey housing complex where Marianne and Anna still live. After she leaves, the remaining the bubbles burst, making small rivulets of water that soon disappear into the dry summer soil.

Nina misses her mother, but she is thankful for the peace. She wonders if there would have been any bubbles had life been different. She knows what Ernests and her mother have always meant to each other, but too much has happened, and now there are too many things in the way. She understands that Ernests misses Auguste and that Rozalija's presence reminds him of all the questions with no answers. Why did his mother remain? Why did she not leave when she had the chance? Perhaps it is all the things that happened – and did not happen – that have caused the bubbles to form.

A new tenant moves into Rozalija's room upstairs. Summer turns into autumn and then into winter. Nina is no longer working, and, twice a week, she crosses the river to visit her mother. It is a long walk: the housing complex is on the southern outskirts of the town.

Then, in 1956, Ernests and Nina and Andris leave Limtorget behind them. Their new home is on the opposite side of the river, in a grey-white building, one of many standing in a long line on Rådagatan. The buildings are all owned by Rörstrand, and the flats are rented out to employees. Ernests' name had finally wended its way to the top of the waiting list. Limtorget may have been idyllic, but it was confined and primitive; Rådagatan is centrally heated, and the rent is subsidized.

Now they have a two-room flat on the top floor of a three-storey grey-white building, and, because all the buildings look alike, Nina is thankful for the numbers clearly marked at the front. They are on the west side of the river, but they cannot see the river from where they live, and, although it is further to walk to the factory, it is closer to where Rozalija is now living.

Nina finally makes contact with Lucija. She receives a letter from the Red Cross in Germany, telling her that Lucija had been in Germany but that she later moved to America. They send her an address in America. To someone who might be able to help her. Nina writes, and then she waits for an answer. It takes a long time for the answer to arrive, but at last it does. It is a letter from Lucija. She is in America, and she is married to a Latvian she met at the camp in Germany. America is all that she had dreamed of. And even more.

Nina writes to her: 'Tell me everything.' Eager to hear about dreams made real.

Lucija writes again and again. Nina and Ernests talk about what Lucija has written. Perhaps there are more opportunities in America? Perhaps Ernests would be able to find work that suits him? Nina cannot help thinking of the language that she does not speak. And she also thinks of her brother. They contact the

American Embassy in Stockholm, and the Embassy sends them the application forms. They are standing, their feet on each side of a chasm. Are they really serious about making such a move? They fill in the application forms and post them. The man at the post office notes the address.

"The American Embassy," he says, hoping for more information that does not come.

It is not a large post office, just a room on the ground floor of a block of flats. The postmaster, a tall, thin man, with metal-framed glasses and dressed all in black, sells stamps and weighs parcels and handles giro-payments and changes pension slips into cash. He manages everything on his own, and he knows everyone in the street.

"Fru A-Bolin," he says as Nina opens the door, black handbag over her arm, her letter clenched in one hand. "What can I do for Fru A-Bolin today?" Then he looks at her, waiting for something more. "The American Embassy," he says.

Nina smiles at him and watches while he carefully places the stamp on the large brown envelope. Then the bell on the door tinkles, and another customer enters the space.

They wait to hear from the Embassy, three people squashed between only a few walls, and each day they think: 'Today? Perhaps we will hear something today?'

But no official-looking envelopes fall through the narrow letter opening, and there are no cards telling them to collect registered mail from the post office. The flat – a small hall, living room, bedroom, tiny kitchen and an even tinier bathroom – seems to become even smaller while they wait.

Living so closely to one another can only work if everyone accepts being part of a well-oiled machine. Personal space is reduced to that one part. When the well-oiled machine itself begins to spatter and hiccup, then nothing works properly any longer; problems that were never perceived as problems become the focus. Eventually, the machine stops working.

They have still not heard from the Embassy, and the world is swirling itself into a tight funnel around them. Nina asks herself why, but she has no answer. The swirling continues until she cannot even see the smallest pinpoint of light. Ernests has changed. He has become short-tempered and is often angry. Nina begins to understand why the bubbles, floating between her husband and her mother, had risen to the surface and why they had finally burst. He is now smoking continuously, one cigarette after another. He complains about the cost while he thinks of his tobacco at Rundāle. Nikolina dislikes the smoke and the smell. She disliked it when they were at Limtorget, but, even then, she knew that there was nothing she could do about it. Stale cigarette smoke fills every crevice of the flat, refusing to be blown out of windows opened just for that purpose, green pot plants lifted down from window ledges and placed carefully on the timbered floors.

But something is nagging at Nikolina, like the sound of a far-off train, disturbing her consciousness with its increasingly sharp sound. She no longer recognizes her husband. He is not the man she married all those years ago. She makes excuses for him – there are so many excuses she can make for him – but eventually the excuses become thin and worn-out, and she begins to ask herself if this is the way she wants to spend the rest of her life. She still loves him, but she cannot live with him any longer. He is destroying all those memories that she needs if she is to continue surviving. She can see the family descending through bands of greyness into total blackness. She refuses to let that happen, and she considers divorce. The word is knife-sharp and cruel, and it fits uneasily in her mind, but she can see no other way. She lies awake at night and worries about what she is going to do. She no longer sees America as an option.

He is still working, but he is tired and always irritable. In late 1956, he suddenly faints at work. He is standing at a bench in the laboratory when, without warning, he falls to the floor. A man at the other end of the room hears the heavy thud and the scattered sounds of things being swept from the bench. He immediately drops what he is doing and calls out to his friend who is washing glass beakers in a deep sink. The first man notices that the gas on the bench is still switched on. He leans over immediately and turns off the small tap, and then the two men carry Ernests out of the laboratory into the recreation room. Another man hurries in after them.

Ernests has now regained consciousness, and the men give him some water to drink. He is very pale, and there are beads of perspiration on his forehead. One of the men takes down the first-aid box. He flicks through the instruction book, not quite sure what he is looking for.

The man who had switched off the gas says, "The gas was on. It's probably the gas."

Someone goes over to the window and opens it wide, letting in the cold outside air.

At the hospital, the doctor in his white coat, not having any other answer, nods his head thoughtfully and agrees that it may have been gas poisoning. He suggests a few days' rest and writes out a certificate.

Rozalija has now left the housing complex. The lease expires on her room, and she is forced to look for other accommodation. In desperation, she moves back in with her daughter and her son-in-law. No one really expects it to work. Not now. Not with Ernests the way he is. But, somewhere, deep within them, beneath all the froth and broken bubbles, they all want it to work.

Rozalija's health has deteriorated, and she is very weak; she is already over eighty. Nikolina stands between her mother and her husband, trying to help both of them, tied by responsibility to each of them. The flat is too small for four people, but they are all prepared to do their best. Four people holding hands, jumping off a cliff together. While they are still in mid-air, Nikolina writes to Lucija and says that she does not think that they will be able to move to America.

Ernests is tired all the time; he has forgotten what it is like not to feel tired. Often he feels disorientated and even dizzy, and he worries a lot about the fainting episode, knowing that it was not the gas. When he returns to the doctor, there are no answers, only the sterile, white surgery and a doctor already anticipating the next patient.

Even if there are no answers, Ernests knows that he is not well. Paths have become tightrope-thin as he desperately tries to find and retain his balance. The pain pressing behind his eyes spreads into every part of his body, tying his stomach into knots, forcing it into uncontrollable spasms. His body wants only to find some anaesthetized state of nothingness, where there are no questions wanting answers that do not exist. Each day, he longs for the nothingness while he pushes himself beyond what is possible and cycles the couple of kilometres to the red brick factory by the river. The two kilometres exhaust him, and he sits in the laboratory, his head in his hands, willing himself to do all the things that he knows must be done, thinking all the time of that grey place of non-existence that is just beyond his grasp. The men around him shake their heads, their faces full of concern. They tell him that he should be at home, and he thinks how the doctor has told him that there is nothing wrong with him.

Some days, he accepts the impossible and remains at home. The days sometimes stretch into weeks and months before he pulls himself out of all the greyness and, once again, tries to return to work.

Finally, Nikolina contacts Rörstrand and begins working again, leaving her husband at home in the flat with her mother, while she tries not to think of bubbles bursting, knowing that she has no other option.

She is given work in the sorting department, where she deftly separates porcelain with small deficiencies from that which is top grade. Later, in the shop connected to the factory, people hunt for bargains among all the seconds, being content with what they can find there – an uneasy balance between quality and price – while Nina's fingers cannot forget all the very small differences.

1956 disappears into 1957, and then 1957 rushes towards 1958. In the flat on Rådagatan, Ernests' body continues to be pulled between clouds of grey vertigo and the violent reality of nausea when his stomach is turned inside out, leaving him ashen and exhausted. Occasionally, there is a reprieve, and he pulls on his coat and laces his shoes, and cycles to the factory; most of the time, the coat remains hanging on its hanger in the hall and his shoes remain unlaced on the floor. When his body can take no more, he takes a taxi to the hospital where the doctor insists that everything is all right and that there is absolutely nothing to worry about.

It is spring 1958. The afternoon is sliding towards its middle, when Andris arrives home from school. The flat is quiet; all he can hear is the sound of the hanger's metal hook connecting with the rod as he hangs up his coat. He listens to the quietness, feeling that there is something suspended in the middle of it all, something he does not understand. It is almost as though the silence has been strangled in the middle of shouting something, but he missed hearing what it was shouting.

He sees that his grandmother is asleep on her bed in the living room as he carefully pushes open the bedroom door and calls softly to his father. But there is no answer. As he opens the door wider, he sees that his father is slumped in the chair by the window. He feels that everything in the room is moving closer and closer, pushing him into an infinitesimally small space. Time has stopped for him. He touches his father's shoulder, his arm, his face. He is alive but unconscious.

They have no telephone, but there is a phone in the cellar, on the other side of the heavy door at the bottom of the stairs, and he runs back down the stairs, taking the stairs two at a time, leaving the door to the flat wide open. He knows the number to phone; he has done it many times before, and his fingers slot into the right holes, pulling the dial around, listening to the soft whirring sound as it clicks back into position.

At Emergency, the doctor wonders irritably why they are

there. He says that there does not seem to be a problem. He looks at Ernests with a very slight frown while he fingers the stethoscope hanging around his neck.

He says: "Perhaps Herr Abolins has been working too hard? Perhaps he needs to rest?"

Andris is thankful that his father had regained consciousness before the taxi arrived, but he knows how difficult it is to make any doctor understand that his father is ill. They have stood here so many times before, in front of a doctor who does not want to understand.

When people are jumping off cliffs, priorities have to change, and things take on new perspectives. Andris can feel the wind rushing at him as he tells the doctor that he will not take his father home. Not this time. He hesitates and says that his father is very ill. He has not been working too hard; he has not been working at all.

"He needs to know what's the matter with him," he says, looking from the doctor to his father. "He can't work any more. He's at home all the time."

He tells the doctor that his father has not been well for more than a year, almost two, even though he knows that all that information must be in the papers on the doctor's desk. His eyes move from the papers to the stethoscope. Then he is gripped by the absurdity of the situation: he is only fourteen. Though he is aware of the very wide gulf between himself and the doctor standing in front of him, he is also aware of the cliff, and he knows that he and his family are very close to the edge. Because they do not have any answers. He realizes that he is shaking, one hand on his father's arm.

The doctor is taken aback. For a moment, he forgets about the stethoscope around his neck. Between Andris' words, he has caught a glimpse of the cliff. He looks down at the white papers in front of him lying on the beige journal folder, and then he looks up again – at Andris and then at Ernests.

"Perhaps we should do a few tests; not that I feel anything is seriously wrong. Yes, he will need to stay, probably for a day or so."

Then their world, which is already teetering on the edge of a vertical downwards fall, loses its balance and slips into the darkness. He has a brain tumour. If it is not removed then he will certainly die. And if it is removed? No one has any answers. Everyone is hoping. That the operation will be a success. That he will still be Ernests after the operation. Everyone is trying to be optimistic, searching around in the darkness with torches, lighting up things that, in effect, are completely unimportant. Everyone has forgotten America.

The four people, still holding hands, separate. After much thought, Nina moves her mother to an Old People's Home. She knows that it will take all her energy to get her husband back on to the cliff.

XXV

Had the train stopped? Or was it simply moving at a faster pace? I was not completely sure, but the sound in my head had changed. When I closed my eyes, I was only aware of a huge, grey, jelly-like mass sprawling across my mind's space. I sensed that it was becoming larger, seeking spaces within spaces. I could feel its confidence. Yet, while it was consuming me, it was giving me a reason to hope. Ernests was still Ernests. It was this thing that was now reaching out from him, into my own consciousness, twisting possessively around both of us, giving new interpretations to everything. I could not believe that I had actually considered leaving him.

Since the tests and the diagnosis, we had asked each other why it may have happened. But there were no answers. While we had heard of scientists and doctors attempting to draw vague, hesitant lines between smoking and all kinds of illnesses, Ernests decided that the answer was somewhere on the icy winter battlefields of Germany. Sharply stabbing both his anger and his frustration, there was a long, thin needle of something else. He knew that the something else was fear, and it was trying to remind him of his helplessness. It was also whispering about predestination.

We became compatriots against the unwanted parasite in his head. Was it grey, yellow, red, transparent? We had no idea. The colour changed every time I closed my eyes, but we recognized each other. The thing and I had become enemies; all I could think of was saving my husband.

The operation was too complicated for the small red brick

hospital in Lidköping, its buildings sitting comfortably on the edge of the river, side by side with the town park. The folder with all Ernests' papers was stamped *urgent,* and was sent to the Serafimer Hospital in Stockholm, and because of the large block letters stamped black across the front of the folder, Ernests' name rose immediately to the top of the waiting list. Standing in that lift moving quickly upwards without stopping anywhere, Ernests could not do much more than contemplate four grey walls, covered only with fear and resentment, while he thought about what would eventually have to happen and about what might possibly happen. I imagined that this was how people sitting on death row felt, waiting for execution or for a reprieve, wondering which will come first. There was nothing I could do to remove the worry or the pain. It was just a matter of waiting.

Knowing the verdict did not change anything; it merely added an extra anxiety. Now there was both the thing, and the operation to remove the thing, rushing towards us like some frightening night creature, its enormous wings outstretched, ready to obliterate us. My nights were filled with nightmares set in cold, sterile hospitals, with men and women in surgical green, and jelly-like masses that expanded exponentially and filled rooms and buildings and threatened to push everyone off the very curve of the earth itself. I would often wake, bathed in perspiration, trembling, not knowing if perhaps the operation had already been and Ernests had actually been freed from the parasite that was sucking the life out of him. Sometimes I woke, thinking that Ernests had died and that all that was left was the awful, grey mass.

Later, everything from that dreadful summer of 1958 became like a watercolour painting where all the colours ran together, and the blues were no longer blue, and the reds no longer red, but each was a bit of both, and nothing was any longer as one had expected it to be. But, before the colours had completely merged, and while they were still hesitating next to each other, news from across the Baltic Sea about the success of collective farming and the general state of happiness filled personal letters from the

Soviet Republic of Latvia, inviting us all to return home. I did not have the energy to wonder how they knew where we were living, but it was frightening to know that it was impossible to completely disappear.

In the late spring of 1958, we finally received a letter from the hospital in Stockholm, giving us a time for Ernests' operation. The night creature had flown in through a window and was forcing its way through all the rooms. Nothing was real any longer, though we could feel the paper in our hands, and we could read the words. The operation was scheduled for the beginning of July, but Ernests had to be at the hospital earlier.

In mid-June, we travelled by ambulance from Lidköping to the Serafimer Hospital in Stockholm. A nurse and I sat in the back with Ernests, and I held his hand, trying to concentrate on the present, unable to stop my mind wandering along a tangle of paths, many of which were distorted, rounding back on themselves or disappearing into hazes where I was unable to follow. Others were surprisingly clear.

Ernests and I were in the park in Rīga, and it was summer. We were sitting on the soft grass near the canal, breathing in all the smells of summer. It seemed like a long time ago. We were young then, and we thought that the years of heartache were behind us. We lay back on the grass and looked up at the trees and the sky and, in the distance, the tower of St Peter's Church black against the blue sky. As we lay there, we talked about how our own small world was completely defined by that line of buildings and landscape-formations encompassing us, and how the line was always changing in relation to where we were. And when the line changed, our world also changed.

We were right about the horizon, but we were wrong about the heartache. I looked down at Ernests and wondered why our world could not have remained the same as it had been that day in the park. But then, things never really remain the same, not even the horizon. In 1941, when the Germans were attacking the

Russians, they destroyed the steeple of St Peter's Church. Nothing is for ever, and worlds can change so quickly.

During those few weeks, as summer became more and more confident, Nikolina remained in Stockholm, visiting Ernests each day at the hospital. Every few days, she wrote to Andris, who was staying with the family of his friend Berndt. Berndt's father, Folke Wictorsson, usually wrote back, filling sheets of white stationery with his looped, decorative handwriting, telling her that he and Willis had taken the boys to visit his relatives in the country, that every Sunday the four of them visited Rozalija at the Old People's Home or that Lidköping was the just the same as always. All Nikolina had to do was to look after Ernests; he, Folke, would take care of everything else.

At night, she stayed with Maksis and Elza in the little flat on Lidingö; in the day, she took a tram and a train to Rådhuset in Central Stockholm. After she had climbed the stone stairs from the underground station, it was not so far to walk to the hospital on Hantverkargatan. Sometimes, Maksis came with her, and they sat on the tram and the train, two ordinary, middle-aged people. Those who looked at them may have noticed the faded hair and Nina's off-white poplin summer coat and possibly the flat laced practical shoes, but would have quickly forgotten the hair and the coat and the shoes as new images cavorted seductively in front of them, demanding recognition. Later, perhaps when they were caught up with other things, all the images would fuse together into a memory about a tram or a train or people they had seen somewhere in Stockholm.

When they reached the hospital, Nina and Maksis walked through the double doors of the reception on their way to the stairs, their shoes making sharp, decisive sounds on the polished stone floor. As they moved further and further from the doors, the street noises became muted and the light from outside became less bright. They had passed from one reality to another, and though the two realities were somehow intertwined, they were, at the same time, completely separate.

She received a letter from Andris. He wrote that he had found summer work at a bakery, and she wrote back, saying how pleased she was for him. She was doing her best to keep Lidköping in one box and Stockholm in another, and she was counting the days until July. She wondered if there would be something after July or if that was when everything would end. She sat by Ernests' bedside, and they talked about what was and what had been. They very rarely talked about what might be. Yet, as they sat, her hand resting on his, they both knew that what was about to happen had already touched their present. It was not just the past and the present that was pushing its way into their thoughts, it was also that which had not yet happened.

Some days they walked in the grounds of the hospital, feeling the summer sun on their faces, breathing in the smells of the garden and the warm brick buildings. They would sit on brown benches and remember other benches in other places. They were hurtling towards a solid wall, and neither of them knew if there would be a way through it.

"I love you!" they said to each other, feeling a need to say all those things that might be crushed by the wall. She talked about Rīga and Rundāle; she talked about music, about happiness and longing. She said that he had always been her best friend. He held her hand and said that there would be a way through the wall, and that there would still be a future, after the present.

On those days when nurses in starched white stood quietly at the end of the bed, and doctors and their students discussed Ernests in long broken lines of Latin, Nina would sometimes leave the hospital grounds and walk across to the City Hall. She would look up at the impressive red brick building with its tall tower and the three golden crowns resting at the top, and then she would make her way to the back of the building. Here she would often sit on the grass, watching the pigeons looking for food, and, beyond them, the dancing light-patterns rippling between the boats on Lake Mälaren. Her thoughts, though, were always with Ernests.

When they slammed into the wall in July, one of the surgeons from the operating team took Nina aside and told her that the operation had been a success. He was not the head surgeon; he was not even the assistant surgeon. He was just one of the members of the team, but he told her that they been able to break through the wall. He said that everything had gone according to plan, though it had been the assistant surgeon who had done the operation, not the head surgeon as Nina had been expecting.

"Something came up," he said when she asked him what had happened. "At the last minute."

And she thought how Ernests had been pushed beyond that last minute that was obviously so important for all these people who were now holding his life in their hands. She only hoped that the assistant knew about things that moved in and took over people's bodies.

"He would have known what to do, Maksis, wouldn't he?" she asked, sitting in Maksis' lounge room, still trying to come to terms with what she had been told. Wanting to hear that everything would be all right.

Maksis had nodded, rolling a cigarette around and around between his fingers. "Of course he would have, Nika. If they have said that it was a success, then it probably was."

She did not remember much from the day that Ernests had his operation. She had felt so pressed up against that wall that she could no longer breathe. She had walked in the grounds, without Ernests, and then she had sat in a grey-cold waiting room and turned the pages of magazines, without seeing anything. In the afternoon, the woman behind the little glass window had told her to go home as she would not be able to see Ernests that day.

The following day, she and Maksis sat together in the waiting room while Maksis smoked what seemed like one continuous cigarette. They both knew that there might not be a way through the wall – not even over the wall. She sat, thinking of all the things she and Ernests had talked about. She hoped that she had said everything that she had meant to say. She remembered another time when there had been things she should have said and did not say.

But he had survived the operation, and now this man, who was neither the head surgeon nor the assistant surgeon, was telling her that everything had been successful. She should not be worrying that it was the assistant surgeon and not the head surgeon who had operated.

Later, when she and Maksis were ushered quietly into the room with the steel beds and the white counterpanes and the three long rectangular windows, she saw only his bandaged head and his pale face against the white hospital pillow.

"I love you!" she whispered, forgetting about shaved heads and assistant surgeons, knowing that she would not be able to say anything more. She put her hand on his, on top of the white hospital blanket. She closed her eyes while Maksis stood to one side, in front of the long, narrow window.

Ernests moved his hand, trying to take hold of hers.

She opened her eyes and looked at him. "You'll be better soon." Was she hoping or was she trusting?

He nodded, ever so slightly. She sat down on the chair next the bed, and Maksis bent over the bed and said something to his cousin. Nina did not hear what he said. Ernests looked at Maksis and tried to smile.

Each day, she returned to the hospital and sat on the chair next to the bed. Sometimes Maksis was with her; a couple of times Elza was also there. Ernests became more awake, and he was able to sit up. When she reached for his hand, his fingers closed around hers; it felt so familiar, and she wondered if perhaps everything would be all right after all. But his eyes were strangely uncoordinated as though they had become strangers to each other, no longer wanting to work together. When she saw his eyes looking in different directions, unable to focus, she wondered if the assistant surgeon had merely opened up Ernests' head and then closed it again. Without doing anything. She tightened her lips, wanting to stop such thoughts from escaping. She had to believe that everything would be all right; she told him how wonderful it was that the operation was behind them. He told her that he was trying to cling on to life, not because of life itself, but because of his love for her.

When she talked about Andris and Grosīte and the Wictorssons, Ernests thought of ripples radiating out from one small incident, wrapping around so many people.

XXVI

My nights were always filled with dreams. Sometimes they were grey and black with sharp edges, and they forced me back to places where I did not want to be. I would lie in bed, unable to wake up, unable to move beyond or out of the dream and unaware that I was actually dreaming. I was held in some strange dimension where buildings and then blackened walls moved in upon me, and where bricks and stones fell around me, like a waterfall solidifying and then disappearing. In between everything there were confused images of faces and the sounds of hard voices and heavy boots. Then all the sounds and images joined together, becoming part of the one paralysing experience as everything converged upon me, pressing me down on to the bed, through the bed, through the floor and into the blackness of suffocation.

But there were also other dreams. Like those about my father.

I would meet him as if by accident, on a road or in a field. It would be summer or spring, and I would feel the freshness of the air, and sometimes I could actually smell the moist blackness of the earth. I would come upon him without warning, and I would find myself wondering where he had been, and why I had not seen him for so long. He would stretch out his arms towards me, and I would begin to run, shortening the distance between us, breaking loose from my hesitation. He would laugh, his bowler hat on the back of his head, and I would reflect on how well he looked. He never seemed surprised to see me. Always, it felt as though he had been expecting me.

I knew that I had so much to ask him, but I could never

remember exactly what. It was as though he had always been there, and we had already spoken about everything and further questions were irrelevant.

Then he was gone, and the dream swirled off into the grey mist of even deeper sleep, or else, I woke, trying to remember, trying to bring him back, still trying to keep him with me.

At other times, I was pulled at great speed into a place of infinite blackness, and I felt completely free; I was moving both away from and into the earth. Everything around me was twisted back upon itself, and there were no opposites, just a state of being. I knew that I was no longer in control, but I wondered if I had ever been in control. I had always been at the mercy of forces stronger than myself. But now the forces seemed at one with me, and I was part of the speed and the darkness and the feeling of complete and utter expansion.

XXVII

On a cold, white morning in February 1960, the town hall on Lidköping's town square burnt down. Ernests stood astride his bike with his camera in his hand. He was on the edge of the crowd of people watching as the flames licked around the timber building and soared towards the sky. It was morning, but the darkness had not yet let go. Or perhaps it was not darkness but smoke that was filling the town square and stinging people's eyes. The fire lit up the entire area, its brightness dancing across the faces of the people watching while the heat melted tired snowdrifts near the building. But it was the noise that captivated him most – the roaring sound of a fire out of control. He had heard the same sound many times before; it was nothing new. While the people around him gaped across an abyss they did not recognize and did not need to recognize, he thought of other fires where the destruction and the abyss had melded into one reality, and where no one stood and took photos. He thought how everyone then had been only looking for a way out, until each person enclosed in that *everyone* realized that there is no way out of an abyss, particularly when the bottom is rushing downwards, and no one can any longer see the top.

Those were his thoughts as he held his bike steady and looked at the flames and the people, and took photos. He also remembered sitting on the steps of the town hall shortly after he had arrived in Sweden. That was a long time ago, but everything was a long time ago, and he knew that he now had much more time behind him than he had in front of him. He wondered if they would rebuild the town hall, and he wondered if he would see it if they did.

Ernests did not see the town hall rebuilt. The area was still fenced off, and the workers were still measuring and hammering and moving long lengths of timber across the town square when he fell into a coma. It was November and the leaves on the trees had blown away or had fastened around tree trunks and under bushes and benches. Some of the leaves that had formed soft piles on the ground had been swept up by street-cleaners or had been raked into new piles by caretakers and house-owners and had then been gathered up and burnt. There was a smell of mustiness in the air from all the leaves. Mustiness and the cold smell of approaching winter.

For more than a year, he had been in and out of hospital. The operation that was supposed to have been a success had not been a success after all. For the first few months after he and Nikolina returned to Lidköping, he had been kept buoyant with medicine and visitors – visitors who brought flowers that Nina carefully put into vases. The colourful flowers looked at Ernests, urging him to get better quickly, until the collective smell only made him feel worse, and Nina removed the flowers from the vases and threw them away.

He had lost more weight. He had aged. The bandage had been removed long ago, and the markings on his head had became fainter, and his hair had tried to grow back. His sight had only slightly improved, even though his eyes had now agreed to work together. He moved out into the spring sunshine of 1959 and dared not think that he might actually be cured.

Andris fetched the bikes from the cellar and cycled with his father. They rode along the side of the river, out towards the lake, and they circled the town square, criss-crossing small back streets. Sometimes they entered the forest, which, with its dark, troll-shaped trees and crooked pathways, often reminded them of some of the darker fairy tales written by the Brothers Grimm.

Then Ernests became stronger and began to cycle on his own.

He visited Edvards and Augusts, and the three of them talked about the cyclical nature of life and about life after death and whether we simply returned to what we were before we were born. No one had an answer. Nina did not like him talking about death. She knew that the will to live could overcome almost anything, and she wondered where they would have both been now had they not had the will to live. But she also knew that death was unavoidable, and she wondered about the line between willing to live and willing to die. She knew that it was not a straight line; it wound around, like a river running across flat ground spewing hills.

Alise, who had lived next door to Aunt Auguste, had been interrogated in 1940. She later told Nina how she had only wanted to die, because then she would have been free. Nina had often wondered if it had just been questioning and beatings; she guessed that it was much worse. Women did not talk about it; they did not want to return to those cold bare rooms with naked lights hanging from ceilings. It was easier to pretend that it had never happened. If they were fortunate enough to be thrown out of the terrifying House on the Corner, they not only understood the similarity between death and freedom, they also understood what was meant by gratitude. Gratitude that they were still alive, that they were still in Latvia, and that they had not been sent to Siberia – or even worse. But Alise was not able to equate life and gratitude with all the other emotions that kept spinning around inside her. Three months later, she hanged herself in her own kitchen.

As Ernests became stronger, Nina clung to her belief that life was stronger than death. She read many books about cancer and tumours, but she could not find the answer she was hoping to find. 1959 turned into 1960, and their applications for Swedish citizenship were finally approved; they were no longer non-people.

Then, as the spring of 1960 hurtled towards summer, Ernests

began to slip downwards, falling slowly, anticipating the bottom but no longer spreading out his arms to stop his fall. At the hospital in Lidköping, they said that the medication was no longer working. He stayed at the hospital for several days, and then he was sent home. The pattern was repeated during the autumn. Sometimes it seemed as though he was improving, and everyone wondered if they could dare hope again. Then the fall would resume, and he would be back in hospital with people asking themselves what should be done next.

When he fell into a coma in November, he was taken to the hospital by ambulance. It had happened before. The other people in the house had become used to the ambulance stopping outside and the two ambulance men, with their stretcher, climbing the stairs quickly – their shoes making disturbing, blunt sounds on the stone steps – before returning more slowly, saying things like: Mind that corner! Careful there!

The people would stand behind their doors, ears against the locks, wondering how things were with the man on the top floor. This time.

This time, the men did not have to say anything because he would not have heard them. They were quiet coming down the stairs. They did not even talk with each other. They pushed the stretcher into the back of the ambulance, and one of them got in next to it. Nina, pulling on her coat as she came out of the door behind the stretcher, telling Andris, who was holding the door open, that she would soon be home, got into the back of the ambulance. Then it pulled away from the kerb. The people with windows at the front of the building looked out at the street from behind white lace curtains. The people with back windows quietly opened their doors, looking furtively up and down the stairwell, trying to catch hold of something, anything, that would reassure them of their own immortality.

The first snow came, and Ernests still lay unconscious in the bed with the white cotton blanket, in the hospital by the river. Nikolina would sit and hold his hand, wondering if he knew that she was there or whether he had already slipped too far away from her to find his way back. She would sit, listening to the sounds of wooden shoes on hard timber floors; doors opening and closing; voices but no words; beds being wheeled in the corridor. Sometimes she stood at the window, looking down on the grey river, the small summer boats no longer clinging to the banks, the silver rain beating patterns on its grey surface. When the snow came, she watched tiny white spots become larger in a frenzied dance that joined everything – the river and its bank and the red brick hospital – into her one and only reality.

Some days, she did not walk to the hospital, and then she would always feel guilty that she was not there. The hospital had the phone number to the family of one of Andris' school-friends, Lars-Åke, and she argued with herself that she needed to move away, in order to be more present.

It was on one of those days when she opened the door to Lars-Åke. He said that the hospital had phoned, but, when Andris rang from the telephone in the cellar, he was given no information; he was simply told to come to the hospital as soon as possible.

"Your father, he must have woken up," she said to Andris, pulling on her coat and boots.

Lars-Åke, standing just inside the door, watched while she tucked her hair under her close-fitting hat and picked up her black handbag. Then he followed them both down the stairs, leaving them at the front of the house, thinking only about people waking up from comas, hoping that it was possible.

It was snowing heavily, and cold, icy flakes rushed against their faces, joining together and covering everything in a frozen, white dust cover. They walked as quickly as they could, but the footpath had already disappeared under the persistent onslaught, and each footstep made an imprint which immediately disappeared behind them.

She thought how Ernests had been far away but had managed to come back to her. She was already thinking what she would say to him when she saw him again. After all the weeks of silence.

Andris did not believe that his father had woken up.

He said: "He may not have woken up, Mimīt."

He had not woken up, but had finally let go and slipped away.

The tears were not new tears; they stretched back into the past, and they swept together Ermonis, Jānis, her father, her baby daughter and Auguste. And now Ernests. She felt that she was standing on a small rock in the middle of the ocean. As the sea rose, the surface of the rock was becoming smaller and smaller and everyone was being washed away. Soon there would be no one left.

Had she said all the right things before he went away? Did she tell him, this time, how much she loved him?

XXVIII

When Andris and Nikolina entered Rozalija's room at the Old People's Home, Rozalija lifted her head from the pillow and said: "He's gone, hasn't he?"

She lay back on the pillow and did not say anything more. There was nothing more to say. Two weeks later, on Christmas Day, she died. In her own unemotional, undemonstrative way, she had always loved Ernests. He had become her responsibility after they fled. But too many people had died, and she did not want to live any longer.

After the funerals, the flowers, all the well-intentioned friends and the overwhelming realization of loss, Nina wrote in a small, unlined notebook: 'No one can give you peace; it is something that comes from within yourself, and it is always connected to integrity.'

Later, she sat for a long while and looked at what she had written, trying to remember where she had read the lines. She was sure that the wording was wrong, but it was the thought that mattered. She wondered if the thought had perhaps come from Emerson. She wanted to put a name next to the words, even if the quote was incorrect, because she knew that the words were important. She had always believed in self-reliance, but now she was beginning to understand what that actually meant. This was her challenge now. Now, when everything had been taken from her. Everything, that is, except Andris.

Life tried to return to its original path, but banks had fallen away, and boulders blocked the flow. The course had changed, yet from bends and high ground it was still possible to look back and see how it used to be. 1960 imperceptibly became 1961, and the Russians put a man into space. The Cold War continued with America and Soviet Russia moving cautiously around each other while calculating moves. The war in Vietnam was ongoing, and America was already beginning to increase the number of troops. Eventually, people would begin to protest against the war and against the killing. The protests and the killing and the images would become the background against which the rest of the world would continue to live.

Colours had burst into life after all the black and white of the war years, and different music blared from radios and television sets. Life was no longer only about survival, it was also about comfort and self-realization, with a new generation standing on the threshold, waiting eagerly to take charge. So many people were scrambling out of a cocoon, while some, who had only ever wanted just to survive, hesitated.

She did not hesitate though she occasionally wondered at all the new ideas. Her hair had turned completely white and she wore it as she had many years ago, pulled back from her face. She had her books and her music and her memories. She continued to live in the flat on the third floor with Andris, and she continued to work at the porcelain factory.

XXIX

It was the eighteenth of April 1964, a Saturday, and the telegram arrived in the afternoon. The young delivery boy wore glasses and a blue cap. I remember looking at him as I took the rectangular, pale-brown envelope with the little window, thinking that his hair, visible beneath his cap, was probably just a little too long. I quickly opened my handbag that was standing on the small chest of drawers in the hall and searched for a coin. He said that he had been there in the morning, but that there had been no one at home. I nodded. I had been visiting some friends. The boy, with the glasses and the long hair, tipped his cap in thanks and then ran back down all the flights of stairs. I listened to him as he moved further and further away, and then the front door banged closed, and I could not hear him any more.

I closed the door and, fetching a knife from the kitchen, I carried the telegram to the living room, which was also my bedroom. I sat down on my bed and opened the envelope. For a long while, I remained with the opened envelope in my hand. The afternoon light was filling the room, and there was a tired, almost depressed, feeling about everything. I looked at the clock on the dresser and saw that the hour hand had almost reached three.

I pulled the strip of paper out of the envelope: Please phone. Elza.

I thought how telegrams are always minimalist. I knew that something must have happened. Was she ill? Had something happened to someone? To Ilona? To Jānis? To Maksis? A sudden chill ran through me, finally settling in the dark-brown floorboards. I felt anxious, but I did not know why. As I was placing the paper back in its envelope, there was the noise of a key in the lock. Andris. He would phone Elza.

He phoned from the phone in the cellar, and, after he had gone, I wondered whether he had sufficient coins with him. I should have thought to ask him before he left. He was gone for a long while, and I expected that he had to wait to use the phone.

I stood at the window, looking down at the cement courtyard behind the flats, wondering if he really was waiting or if he had been talking all the time. The afternoon was already becoming older; shadows were beginning to stretch across the cement. Soon it would all be in shadow.

Eventually, there were familiar steps on the stairs, and the door opened. And closed. He came into the living room and put his arms around me. Yes, something had happened. I knew that now; he did not have to say anything.

He said, "It's Uncle Maksis, Mimīt."

I remember that I nodded. Somehow I had known, even before he told me.

Maksis had been sitting on the tram when he died. He had been in Norrtälje, but he was returning home to celebrate his birthday.

He had left the train at Ropsten on the Stockholm side of the water, and he had then gone down the grey stone steps to the tram. Perhaps he had had to wait for a few minutes, or perhaps the tram was already standing at the small platform on the Stockholm side of the bridge. He may have lit a cigarette while he was waiting for the conductor to punch his ticket, and then the tram probably slid, almost noiselessly, into life, and began to move across the bridge towards Lidingö.

I wondered whether he had been sitting near the window, looking out at the water, his cigarette between his fingers. The windows would have been closed – it was still cold – but he may have still been able to sense the smell of salt sea and seaweed in the air. The tram would have pulled into the little station at Torsvik, and some people would have alighted while others would have climbed on board.

The tram would have moved off again, a smell of sea and spring now caught in the two small carriages. I could see how the people on the tram were probably all wrapped in their own separate realities. Some may have been looking out of the windows; others were possibly reading newspapers. It was still morning; most people would have still been thinking about the day ahead of them.

Then he died, and all the separate realities would have immediately fused into one. Someone has died. I could see the person next to him pulling the cord to stop the tram, and I could see the person behind him lean over, asking him if he was all right. Then the conductor would have come running along the aisle, wondering what was happening and if there was anything he could do.

As the people on the tram were sucked out of individual worlds and were brought together into one immediate instant, they discovered that there were other people around them. Leaning forwards or looking backwards, they asked each other what had happened. As the tram stopped awkwardly between stations, with black, shiny cliff rocks on one side and jumbled spruce on the other, the driver would have left his seat and then pulled himself up into the second carriage, asking his conductor what had happened.

The conductor was probably pale, possibly even shaking, still processing that cry: Stop! Someone's died!

He would have looked worried. How did the man die? Why did he die on his tram? He may have told people to move back and to sit down, and he may have asked if there was a doctor on the tram.

I do not know if there was a doctor on the tram, but I now know that Maksis died of a heart attack. As with everything else in Maksis' life, it was sudden. It came out of nowhere. There was no warning. No long period of preparation. One moment he was living, looking out of the window of the tram and the next moment, he was dead.

The driver, knowing that there was nothing he could do, would have returned to his seat, and slowly the tram would have continued to the next station. Maksis' station.

While a tornado of emotions rushed through me, I thought that perhaps this was better than what happened to Ernests. At least Maksis did not have to suffer. He did not have to anticipate the end before it actually arrived.

I should have known by then that it is not possible to hold on to things or people. Not even Maksis, who had told me so long ago that he would always be there for me. Now he was also gone. I reached out across the table and held on to Andris' hands with both of mine.

Then I remembered that the heartache belonged to others as well as myself, and that was when I asked Andris about the funeral.

XXX

She would leave for work very early in the morning. In the winter, it was always dark when she switched on the little radio near her bed, the music wafting through the flat, filling all the corners, and she liked to think that the person with the earphones in the small insulated recording box knew all her favourites, and that was why he played them. Sometimes he played Tchaikovsky's Piano Concerto; sometimes he played Bach or Haydn; other times he played Beethoven; often he played Mozart.

She enjoyed this time in the morning, before work, but she rarely had time to listen to the whole piece. Regretfully, she would press the small button on the radio, and the instruments would abruptly stop sending their sounds across the airwaves. A strange silence would then descend upon the rooms as she stood in the hallway, pulling on her short, black zip-up boots and her heavy winter coat before opening the door. After it closed behind her, all that could be heard were her footsteps on the stairs, disappearing into the lower distance.

The brick buildings of the porcelain factory, spread out around the chimneys of the kiln building, were very close to the river, about two kilometres from where she lived. In the winter months, often battered by icy cold winds, holding her coat tightly around her as her feet manoeuvred slippery footpaths or deep drifts of snow, the walk always seemed so much longer. She would see other huddled, grey forms moving anonymously in the same direction. No one said anything. No one acknowledged anyone; it was as if everyone was completely isolated in small separate cocoons where there was no speech. Not until the heavy iron door of the factory closed behind them, and they stood stamping off the last of the sticky snow or the cold, wet sleet while they hung up coats with mittens pushed down into deep pockets and piled long knitted scarves and hats on to high shelves, did they notice that the other forms were people like themselves. Then they nodded greetings or, suddenly discovering speech, talked about all those things that people talk about early in the morning when they have just closed a door against the cold and the dark.

In the summer, the walk was filled with the smell of new vegetation and, sometimes, a light night rain still glistening on the grass. Then the sun was already lighting the sky, and the grey, shadowy, huddled forms of the winter had changed into people – people who nodded and exchanged the words that they had discovered somewhere between the darkness of the winter and the birthing of the summer. Life was much better in the summer. Life had always been much better in the summer.

Summer and then winter and then summer again. The seasons came and went. The years came and went; all the time, she was swept along in front of them.

Andris finished school and was gathered up into the Swedish military machine while his mother's thoughts revolved around memories of Ermonis and Jānis and Ernests, though she knew that there was no comparison, and she knew that her son would definitely be coming home again. When he finally hung up the uniform after ten months of compulsory service, she thankfully let go of some of the memories and drew a tentative line between the past and the present.

After Andris married, the line became thicker and darker, as she moved from the flat on Rådagatan, where she had lived for so many years, to a flat in a small house on Västerlundsgatan. Now, instead of the cement courtyard, she was able to look out on a garden with green lawns and flower beds, and, for a while, Andris and Diane lived in a flat upstairs.

She was no longer at the porcelain factory, and her time was her own. At first, when she left the alarm unset, knowing that she would be able to listen to the early morning music through to the very last note, there was a very slight feeling of anxiety as she caught a different of glimpse of time, now without any restraints. While, earlier, she had been but one of many small teeth in the complicated machinery of time, she now felt that she had suddenly snapped off from the wheel and that she had been flung out into something that was timeless. She felt a need to re-attach herself, but wondered how it would be possible. Then she remembered her family and friends and, in the cemetery on the edge of the town, Ernests and her mother.

In the early 1970s, Andris moved with his family to a small cottage fifteen kilometres outside of the town. The cottage was surrounded by crops of rye and yellow rape and red clover, while, on the edge of all the grey-green and yellow and red, small stands of forest sketched dark-green borders. These were the trees that had been permitted to remain when the farmers had moved in – so long ago – with their families, their ploughs and their animals. He asked his mother several times to move with them, but she shook her head, knowing that even if there was now no danger of her being swept away from time itself, she needed to retain her independence.

Instead, she moved to a flat on Östbygatan on the east side of the river. From her window on the second floor, she was able to look down on to a children's sandpit in the middle of undulating green lawns. There was no pear tree covered in springtime white, or peonies clumped beside rhubarb and the pungent-smelling bushes of blackcurrants, but neither was there an expanse of grey-white cement fitting tightly between identically shaped buildings. Beyond all the green, she could see other blocks of flats, all with three floors, and holding everything together was the sky. When the grandchildren visited, she would sit with them while they talked about things that were so far beyond the window that no one could see them. They would sit in the small living room with the African violets drawing a blue, pink, purple line along the window-sill, drinking pretend-coffee from special cups, and her thoughts would join with those of the children as they wandered through fairy-tale forests that were both the past and the future. Sometimes, she would watch while the children ran their fingers over things that, by then, contained only the past: photos, books and small mementos trying to hold on to different points in time. Sometimes, they all imagined how things might have been, or how they still might be.

    She had her music and her books and her memories. She even had her window, looking into the past and the future.

XXXI

The two weeks before the funeral are like waiting for a train to stop, waiting for the jolt that does not come. That moment of knowing – knowing that she is dead – goes on and on, without relief. After the funeral, it will be possible to mourn; at the moment, it is just a continuous knowing.

The children are upset, each in a different way, and their father understands without always being able to give them the comfort that they need. Everyone tries to make sense of that which was unexpected while grief fills the whole house, like water pouring into an over-full creek bed. The banks hold and the grief remains.

He knows that people relate to loss in different ways; he can appreciate one child's moodiness and another child's constant tears. He tries to understand the reality that is pushing down on each and every one of them and even on himself.

Why didn't she phone? Why was she all alone? Questions without answers. Answers with all the wrong questions.

XXXII

In the early summer of 1986, Nikolina takes the train to Stockholm to visit Elza and the children. She knows that the children grew up a long time ago, but she still thinks of them as children, perhaps because the years between herself and them remind her of the difference – a gap that must always remain the same. Neither of them married, and Ilona now lives with her mother in the flat on Bodalsvägen.

She enjoys the train trip. The train is comfortable, quiet and clean. She thinks of other trains she has travelled in, and she wonders at all the changes and how the changes happened quietly while she was elsewhere, probably doing other things. The conductor checks her ticket and hands it back to her. She returns it carefully to her handbag while he moves down the carriage, barely swaying with the steadiness of the train. She looks out of the window, watching fields and houses fly past. She is eighty, but she does not know where all the years went. She tries to imagine eighty years stacked up, one against the other, but the image is unwieldy, and her thoughts move off to wind around the memories of people she has known. And loved.

The train is pulling into Västerås. Several people are already standing up, collecting their bags, preparing to leave the train. She looks out of the window and sees people on the platform beyond the train: people who have just left the train and people who are about to board. The whistle sounds, and the train begins to move again, without any sound. She remembers that she was thinking about people she has loved, and she decides that life could have been much worse in spite of all that happened.

When she reaches Stockholm Central, Jānis is there to drive her to Lidingö, and she notices that he has not changed since she saw him last time. He has always looked like his father, but somewhat shorter, with a slighter build. He hugs his aunt and then lifts her small travelling bag into the boot of his car – an older Saab. She sits down in the passenger seat and makes herself comfortable. He indicates the seatbelt, but she shakes her head.

Compared with Lidköping, there is a deluge of traffic coming from all directions like an enormous kaleidoscope, and she soon feels dizzy, almost nauseous. Several buses drive past, and she is acutely aware of the noise and the fumes while, beyond the buses, she can see buildings and people and even more traffic. Lights turn from green to red, and, as Jānis suddenly brakes, a truck hurtles out from a side street.

With one eye on the traffic lights, Jānis puts his hand on her knee and tells her not to worry. She closes her eyes for a moment and holds firmly on to her black handbag.

When she opens her eyes again, they are in a calmer part of the city, and she can see water and the bridge that they will soon be crossing. She begins to relax. Jānis makes a left-hand turn and then a right. They stop at yet another set of traffic lights, and some pedestrians cross the road in front of them: an elderly man and a woman with three small children. For a moment, the two realities merge, without the people on the road knowing anything about the people in the car. She thinks how little we really know about each other, each of us a container filled with different experiences that make us who we are. The containers all look much the same on the outside, but it is the inside that matters, and it is difficult to see inside a closed container.

She thinks of the many different kinds of containers: those that dictated what she should do, where she should go, what she should think, and those that, like herself, were simply swept along by everything that happened. She reflects that the inside of most of these containers, – Russians, Latvians, Germans – were simply ordinary people who only wanted to live ordinary lives.

All of them decent people. Then she thinks of the discordant ideas that seeped into other containers, marking them with brown-red rust, setting them apart. She knows that it only ever takes a few people to cause chaos and uproar. She looks again at the people who have now crossed the road, and her thoughts circle around Dostoyevsky's Raskolnikov. She decides that life has shown her that most people are good, even if they may sometimes do good things for bad reasons or bad things for good reasons.

She is still thinking of containers and people and Dostoyevsky when the lights change to green, and they move off again. Very soon they are on the bridge, and Nina can see Lidingö spread out before her. A large ferry and some small boats cut through the water beyond the bridge; without turning her head, she is aware of the pattern of spires and buildings that make up Stockholm behind her. She relaxes her hold on her handbag.

Jānis carefully parks the car below the flat on Bodalsvägen, and Nina can see Elza at the kitchen window; she is waving. In the background, almost hidden by the curtain, Nina can see Ilona. They enter the building, and, with Jānis carrying her bag, they walk up the two short flights of steps to the flat itself. She thinks again of the containers, and then she thinks of shared experiences. Yes, she is quite certain, life could have been much worse.

XXXIII

In the late afternoon, I sit for a while in the living room and try to read, but the words will not remain still on the page. At length, I give up and doze in my chair. Now it is late, and I am feeling strangely tired and my ankles feel uncomfortably warm and swollen.

I walk to the kitchen. For a moment, I think about bathing my feet, but I know that I do not have the energy, and it does not really seem very important. I try to remember when I last ate, then my thoughts go in all directions, and I forget what it was that I was trying to remember.

There is some tea standing on the sink. I wonder how long it has been standing there; it already has that thin film of repulsiveness common to cold tea. I leave it standing on the sink, and I move into my bedroom. I draw the curtains and turn on the light, and then I sit in my chair by the bed. It is quiet, though I can occasionally hear people in the other flats walking around, moving chairs or talking. If I listen really well, I can even hear a television. It is nice to know that there are people around me. A toilet flushes somewhere in the building. Outside my door, I can hear someone running down the stairs. Probably a young person; there is a young couple living in the flat next to mine.

We are young, and then, suddenly, we are no longer young, and life begins to close the curtains on the stage. 'Wait,' we call out, 'we are not yet finished. There are so many things we still want to do, must do. Please wait!' But the curtain swings across, and the stage becomes dark. Do we wait for applause? Do we expect it?

I believe I was young once. A long time ago. I remember a little grey cottage and some people; the lines of the cottage are no longer completely clear, and some of the people have no faces. My father smiles at me. How thin he is! I had forgotten that he became so thin. I smile back and reach out to touch him, but suddenly he is gone, and my mother is standing there instead. She is almost young. Pretty? Beautiful? I look down at myself, and I see that I am a child with a white pinafore and no shoes.

People begin to move in and out of my vision. I catch sight of Auguste, and then I see my Aunt Paulina and Grandmother Kindahle. Aunt Paulina is dressed all in white. She always wore white: she and Uncle Peteris were Seventh Day Adventists. I find it strange that I should think of that now, after all these years.

And there is Jānis. He is only a boy, not much older than my eldest grandson. He waves, and I lift my hand to wave back, not sure if he actually is there or if everything is merely a dream. He moves off, beyond my line of vision. He is laughing. As he disappears, I can see that he removes his cap and runs his fingers through his hair.

I move in the chair. I hear voices outside the building. I take off my glasses for a moment, and I rub my eyes. I feel really very tired.

There is someone in the room. He is standing opposite me.

"Hello, Nika," he says gently. "It's been a long time."

I nod, amazed at how young Ermonis looks. But he never got any older, not like me. He must feel that I am an old, old woman.

"You're not old, Nika," he says as though he can read my thoughts. "You are no older than when we said goodbye. Do you still remember?"

Yes, I remember. I remember him leaving the house and walking down the street; I remember that I had wanted to run after him and that Mother had held me back. A surge of sadness threatens to engulf me. All those years! He is still sitting there opposite me. He smiles. I want to ask him so much, but it is too much of an effort. Where would I begin?

"I know that you never forgot me," he says softly.

I shake my head. How could I have ever forgotten him? He was the touchstone, the benchmark against which so many others failed, or almost failed. I wipe my eyes and replace my glasses.

I must have dozed because when I next look at the clock, an hour has slipped away into eternity. The room has not changed. I get up from the chair, feeling weak and very unsteady. I hold on to the edge of the bureau, trying to find some kind of balance. Then I think of the cold tea in the kitchen, and I begin to feel nauseous.

A wave of dizziness sweeps over me. Should I phone Andris? Should I phone someone? I drink some water from a glass on the bureau, and then I turn on the lamp above my bed. Slowly I walk to the door and turn off the ceiling light. The room takes on a softer, friendlier look. I lie on the bed, on top of the bedclothes, resting my head on the two soft pillows, pulling the extra blanket over me. It is pink and synthetic, and it is attempting to give me some sense of warmth and security. I should have enjoyed the feeling, but the dizziness is becoming stronger. I remove my glasses again and place them, with difficulty, on the bedside table.

Exhausted, I lean back on the pillows and watch as I run towards a tall window. The window is closed, and through the glass I can see that it is winter. I stand at the window, fascinated by white ice angels scattered all over its surface. They seem to be moving. Dancing.

Maksis comes up behind me and laughs. "So many angels, Nika!"

I turn and hug him. "Oh, Maksis! I have missed you so much!"

The image fades. I am alone in my room, and the window is dark again behind dark-coloured curtains. I feel a sudden wave of anxiety pass through me, knotting my stomach. My hands are cold. The dizziness is becoming worse.

"You'll be fine." The voice is familiar. Close by.

"Ernests!" I cry out, in spite of myself.

He is standing near the door, near the end of my bed, looking down on me.

"I really didn't want to leave you when I did, Nika" he says, removing his glasses and wiping them on his shirtsleeve before replacing them on his nose. "But I was swept away – all too quickly – and there was no way back." He pauses for a moment. "Life was not always easy for us."

My thoughts spin back a lifetime. No, things were not easy. Thinking of those last years when he had been so sick and damaged.

"If there had never been a war; if we had never had to flee; would things would have been different then?"

I nod. Yes, I am sure that things would have been different if Latvia had remained free. But would they have been better? I have no way of knowing. I push the blanket to one side. I try to reach over to the bureau for the glass of water, but it is too far. I fall back, exhausted, on the pillows.

Ernests moves silently from the door and walks over to the bureau. He picks up the glass and hands it to me. I feel the cold wetness of the outside of the glass as I raise it to my lips. The water touches my tongue, but I know that I will not be able to swallow any of it. I nod my thanks as he replaces the glass on the bureau.

I sink back on to the pillows, and he sits on the edge of the bed.

"You know," he says, "I always loved you, Nika."

Yes, I know that he did, in spite of all the things that tried to get in the way. I wonder about taking his hand, but I do not have the strength.

I am concerned about the dizziness and the weakness. Thinking about the very few things in life that are really important, I whisper, "And I loved you as well, Ernests. I still love you."

I am feeling quite strange, neither in the room nor out of it, neither in my body nor out of it. I must phone. I swing my feet down to the floor as the feeling, both light and heavy at the same time, sweeps through me yet again. Then I see Ernests stretch out his hand to me, and, with a final burst of energy, I take it.

XXXIV

The day of the funeral dawns bright, but cold. Behind the thin layer of cloud that is spreading a diffuse whiteness across the blue, there is still a feeling of sun – an indication that summer is hanging on with one hand, even as leaves are turning yellow and flowers are beginning to lose their colours.

The small stone chapel stands close by the entrance to the cemetery, guarding those sleeping beneath the neatly-tended rows of gravestones and the carefully-mowed lines of green grass. There are many birch trees – collections of yellow leaves dancing against slim white trunks – firs and pines, ash trees and elm trees, while, between all the neat rows of headstones, there are geometrically-cut hedges looking like squat, green rectangles, stretching out long arms from the grey paved path.

In the parking area, car doors slam; shoes crunch on grey-black stones; cellophane paper around lilies and white and red roses and dahlias rustle softly as flower arrangements are moved from hand to arm. On the grey-white paved stones, shoes echo differently, all the sounds mingling with subdued voices saying nothing and yet everything. At the same time. The sounds of a funeral.

The people, with their shoes and flowers and sorrow, are sucked in through the door of the chapel where the vicar stands solemnly at the front, near the coffin with the small wreath of red and white flowers. Someone is playing the organ. Someone coughs. There is a silence, then page-turning. 'From God, let me *not be parted...'* More music fills the space, pushing against thoughts and emotions. Then there is just the space.

Andris sits at the front of the chapel; there is nothing between him and the coffin. He is aware of words pushing into the space; words about life and death. He wonders if the words are supposed to join these two points, pulling them neatly together, creating a new life-death *point where there is no sorrow and no regret.*

The words begin to lose themselves in the repetitive petals of the dark-red dahlias in front of him; for a moment, he can see her standing beyond the coffin, smiling at him. He wants to reach out and pull her back into his own reality, but then he understands that there is an instant where both realities merge and become part of each other, and that the instant itself becomes a new reality.

The vicar opens his bible; he clears his throat, almost nervously, and begins to read. Andris hears the words dreadful *and* house *and* God, *but they hang there isolated and without any kind of meaning while he continues to grapple with what is and has been and what is no longer.*

Eventually, all the words and the prayers and the music come to an end, not suddenly, but like the small ripples left after a boat cuts through the water; ripples that continue to alter the surface even after the service finishes, and he finds himself outside the chapel. He watches the vicar closing the heavy door while he wonders about the music, which is no longer playing but which continues to move outwards, displacing his thoughts and his memories.

At the side of the chapel, he looks at the flowers arranged carefully near the small sign with her name: Nikolina Abolins, *and he thinks how strange it is that her name will always remain, while she herself is no more. He acknowledges friends and relatives and their words of condolence while his mind replaces* Abolins *with* Āboliņa, *and he thinks how the past and the present and the future are all irrevocably connected.*

People are beginning to drift away like the yellow leaves

blowing lazily across the gravel paths. They button their jackets and clutch handbags, murmuring final expressions of sorrow while wondering about all the other things that could or should be said.

The cloud has moved away, but the cold remains, sharply blue. He turns away from the flowers and the memories, and begins to walk towards the parking area, one hand clutching the car keys in his pocket, the other holding Diane's hand.

Life everywhere is life, life is in ourselves and not in the external. There will be people near me, and to be a human being among human beings, and remain one for ever, no matter what misfortunes befall, not to become depressed, and not to falter – this is what life is, herein lies its task.

Fyodor Dostoyevsky, in a letter to his brother on the 22nd December 1849

Acknowledgements

First and foremost, my thanks go to Andris, without whose unwavering belief in me, together with the memories and factual information he so willingly shared, the book would never have been written. At the same time, I am deeply indebted to Monica for her patient, observant reading of the manuscript, for her thoughtful criticism and for her consistent intellectual support. I would like to thank Ilona and Janis Kindal, as well as my children, for sharing their own memories and experiences, and Signe Eklund and Anne Swan for reading an early draft and for their subsequent comments and advice. Many thanks also go to Annette Abolins for her invaluable design assistance and to Ilze Mazvērsīte for painstakingly deciphering so many hand-written letters and documents.

www.ingramcontent.com/pod-product-compliance
Lightning Source LLC
Chambersburg PA
CBHW022025290426
44109CB00014B/759